"[McKeough's] advice is fresh, probing and fundamental.... The value of *Riding the Bull* is far, far above its cover price. Definitely a good buy."

QUILL & QUIRE

"Patrick McKeough is a canny Canadian tortoise who has quietly beaten any number of glamorous American investment hares. He applies one of the classic investment methods, tempered by a couple of decades or so of experience—the combination that invariably underlies outstanding investment letter performance."

PETER BRIMELOW,
SENIOR EDITOR, *FORBES* MAGAZINE

"[McKeough] provides a guide to setting up an appropriate, balanced portfolio, identifying types of stocks that offer big profit potential without substantial risk.... The advice in *Riding the Bull* is useful in any market cycle."

THE MONTREAL *GAZETTE*

RIDING THE BULL

How You Can Profit from
the 1990s' Stock Market Boom

PATRICK McKEOUGH

KEY PORTER·BOOKS

Canadian Cataloguing in Publication Data

McKeough, Patrick
  Riding the bull

Includes index.
ISBN 1-55013-522-8

1. Stock -exchange. 2. Investments. I. Title.

HG4551.M35 1993   332.64'2   C93-094233-7

Key Porter Books Limited
70 The Esplanade
Toronto, Ontario
Canada M5E 1R2

The publisher gratefully acknowledges the assistance of the Canada Council and the Ontario Arts Council.

Design: Annabelle Stanley
Printed and bound in Canada

94 95 96 97 6 5 4 3 2

CONTENTS

ACKNOWLEDGEMENTS

Many friends and colleagues played a part in producing this book. In particular, I want to thank my old friend John Sartz, manager of the Landmark Small Cap fund. John was kind enough to review the book on a trip to Florida when he might have preferred to forget about the stock market.

Above all, many thanks to my long-time associate, Bob Walkden. Bob has contributed many story ideas and portfolio analyses to *The Investment Reporter* over the years, starting long before I began writing it. Some of these have found their way into this book, in whole or part. Bob and I have disagreed on investment matters from time to time, but I find that the older I get, the smarter he gets.

PROLOGUE: TWO PREDICTIONS FOR THE DECADE

At the start of the 1980s, the publisher of *The Investment Reporter* asked me to come up with a theme for a new direct-mail advertising campaign. He wanted one that would sum up the investment prospects of the new decade.

I suggested "the opportunity of a generation".

Mind you, at *The Investment Reporter* we try to concentrate on investment quality. We try to downplay our stock-market predictions. In real life, the people who get rich in stocks are those who pick out a balanced selection of high-quality stocks. They gradually buy large quantities of these stocks, over a period of years or decades. They invest regularly, and wind up buying more shares when prices are low, and fewer when they're high. They try not to rely too heavily on predictions. Experience has taught them that predictions are the part of investment decision-making that's most likely to lead you astray.

That's a little different from what happens in fiction and in

1

investors' dreams. There, you get rich by buying at the bottom and selling at the top. The trouble is, as Bernard Baruch (one of history's all-
time great investors) once remarked, "This can't be done—except by
liars."

Still, when you make your living as a stock-market advisor, you can't
help but have an opinion on the stock market. My opinion at the time
was that the market offered "the opportunity of a generation". This, as it
happens, was at odds with what a lot of people were thinking. Browse
through the late-1970s and early-1980s magazine archives in your local
library and you'll see what I mean. *Business Week* ran a cover story titled
"The Death of Equities". It said the stock market was going out of style,
if not existence. *Newsweek* ran a lengthy and widely remarked upon and
oft-quoted cover story about inflation. The cover art was a picture of a
burning dollar bill. The implication—inflation was here to stay. Money
would soon be worthless, everything was going to hell, and so on.

Meanwhile, the developing world (and parts of the developed
world) seemed to be collapsing under the weight of heavy debt and
high oil prices. The Soviets had marched into Afghanistan, and who
knew where they'd go from there. Debt was high, and interest rates
were stratospheric.

Yet if you went browsing through companies' annual reports, it was
easy to be optimistic. All this bad news had already had its effect on the
stock market. From the late 1960s through the early 1980s, stock prices
had fluctuated as they always do, but had mainly gone sideways.
Meanwhile, despite the problems of the 1970s, the economy had made
a lot of progress. So, for a dozen or more years, stock-market value built
up while stock prices went nowhere. Stocks were extraordinarily cheap
at the start of the 1980s, compared to earnings potential, to dividends
and to asset values.

The economy wasn't exactly thriving, mind you. But it was essentially healthy. It was clear back then that the next really big move in
stock prices had to be upward. (You might say the market had turned
into a "long-base situation". This is a classic investment situation where
risk is low and profit potential is high. More on that further along.) So,
we went with "the opportunity of a generation" in our advertising.

Thousands of investors responded to it. They were soon glad they did. Stock prices soared in the 1980s. It turned out that *The Investment Reporter* provided its readers with some of the most profitable yet low-risk investment advice available anywhere.

What comes next? Once again I have an opinion that many people disagree with. I think we're now in an investment situation where the next big move will also be upward.

The reasons are different from those of the 1980s. Back then, stocks were cheap. Today, stocks are expensive by some measures. But when you consider today's low interest rates plus attractive future growth prospects, I'd say today's values in the stock market are about average, compared to the past 50 years. In the stock market, however, a price movement never gets to "average" and stays there. Instead, prices swing back and forth, from undervaluation to overvaluation, and back again. I think we're headed back to the ridiculously high stock-market valuations of the late 1960s.

When I called the 1980s stock market "the opportunity of a generation", I meant just that. I thought it would take a couple of decades, if not longer, before a similar opportunity came along. Then, in the second half of the 1980s, a funny thing happened. The whole world changed, starting with the collapse of the Berlin Wall. Because of the extraordinary changes that have taken place in the world in the past few years, underlying values in the 1990s stock market are going to improve much faster than they ever have before.

As people come to appreciate the changes that have taken place in the world, the stock market may run up to ridiculous levels, much as it did in the late 1960s. This, at any rate, is my opinion.

It seems to me that people disagree because they have gotten lost in the details, the minutiae of everyday events. They have failed, or refuse, to recognize the meaning of changes that have taken place and are taking place in the world. Until lately, remember, the world has been divided into a handful of rich countries that operated under some form of free enterprise, and a multitude of poor countries (in the former Soviet sphere, but also in South America and elsewhere) that relied on central planning. Now the poor countries are almost unanimously giving up on central planning and switching to some form of free enterprise. Many are even making an attempt at switching to political systems that you might loosely refer to as democracy.

People in these countries are just like us. When they copy our system, they will eventually wind up with similar results. It will take time, of course. But it's a situation that will feed on itself—a virtuous circle, you might say.

It's all too easy to underestimate the significance of it all. It's easy to overestimate the obstacles. You get a discouraging view from news reports of strikes, shortages, political disruption and so on in the newly liberalizing countries. Just remember that when a country overthrows a dictatorship, it has a lot of pent-up steam that needs to be blown off. It has many local and regional Erich Honecker's and Enver Hoxha's that need to be retired. In fact, one of the more encouraging aspects of this world-wide liberalization process is the remarkable absence of mass hangings. All the more reason to think this revolution will be different from revolutions of the past.

In any event, matters were just as grim in Germany and Japan after World War Two. Look what happened there.

When World War Two ended, lots of highly intelligent and well-informed people thought the Depression was sure to resume. After all, the armaments industry was headed for a slump, and this would throw lots of people out of work. Meanwhile, returning soldiers would flood the labour market and drive wages down. Government debt was high, higher than today, in relation to Gross National Product. Things were slow for a few years, of course. But then we got the post-war boom.

With all this in mind, here are two predictions for the remainder of the 1990s.

Prediction One: An extraordinary opportunity is now unfolding in stocks. It may turn out to be even better than the opportunity of the 1980s. You might even go so far as to call it "the opportunity of the century". Stock prices (some—not all) will rise even more for a time in this decade than they did in the 1980s.

An optimistic outlook? Only in part. Only for some of us.

Prediction Two: In the year 2000, many investors will look back with dismay at their 1990s investment results. They'll gaze at a chart of the soaring stock-market indexes of the 1990s, and ask themselves, "How the hell did I ever manage to lose money while that was going on?"

Like I said a little earlier, people who get rich as investors do it by picking out a portfolio of high-quality stocks, then buying more and more of them gradually, over a period of years or decades.

Many investors wind up with unsatisfactory investment results, however, even in the midst of a boom. That's because they spend their time searching for short cuts. All too many of these turn out to be dead ends. It happens all the more when stocks are soaring, because everything seems so easy. It will happen more than ever in the late 1990s, because things are changing much more quickly than ever before. The Scalding 1990s will turn out to be a good name for the decade, because so many people will wind up getting burnt.

Successful investing is a long-term, pitfall-riddled process—like child rearing, say, or building a career or a business. The stock market always offers us plenty of opportunities to make fools of ourselves. It will always leave open the possibility of making all-too-human and costly mistakes. They'll always seem harmless (or even a good idea) when we make them.

This book is about investing in stocks, but with a special attention to avoiding the sucker bets—the situations that invite you to use your toes for target practice.

THE BOOM OF THE 1990s

These days, when a friend asks, "Are you bullish or bearish?", I'm embarrassed to answer. When pressed, I have to admit I'm more bullish than anybody I know. I'm as bullish as I've ever been, in fact—as much as in the late 1970s and early 1980s, but for a new set of reasons.

Free Tables and Chairs
In the late 1970s and early 1980s, stocks were just plain cheap. Back then, you could find respectable companies that were trading for less than their net working capital. Without getting technical, that's like buying a profitable restaurant for the value of supplies and cash in the till, and getting the freezer, griddle, tables and chairs, customer goodwill and so on thrown in for nothing. Some stocks were so cheap that you could borrow to buy them and pay off the loan with the dividends.

These low prices were an historical oddity. They came about for lots of reasons. For one, unemployment soared in the 1970s because baby boomers and working wives flooded the job market. Then too, the market had to adjust to the idea that values of the world's currencies were no longer fixed in relation to each other. The major countries had set them afloat. It also had to adjust to the jump in the price of oil. For that matter, communist gains in the third world rattled 1970s investors. After all, many of them grew up as fascism swept Europe. Then too, North American finance and industry had reached a state of regulatory deadlock in the 1970s. Deregulation was desirable and inevitable, but painful.

All these factors held down stock prices. Nobody knew for sure how long the opportunity would last, of course. But most investors recognized that stocks wouldn't stay cheap forever. Sure enough, stocks have gone way up since then.

The Stock Market Suffers from Manic Depression

Today, stock prices are about average. Some people would quibble with that, of course. After all, p/e's (the ratio of share prices to per-share earnings) are up where they were in the 1960s. But 1960s p/e's were high at the top of the earnings cycle, when the "e" or earnings was high. Now we're lifting off the bottom of the earnings cycle, when the "e" is low. Let's put it this way: in the 1960s, the most highly regarded stocks traded at 40 to 60 times earnings, and earnings were at a peak. Today, earnings are near a low, and the most highly regarded stocks trade at 20 or 30 times earnings.

Stock prices are high compared to per-share book values (what the corporate books say assets are worth per share after you deduct liabilities). But book values help you find the floor. Now we're looking for the ceiling.

Remember, the market never really settles down into a plodding, predictable middle age. Instead it swings back and forth between manic-depressive extremes of under- and overvaluation. It always goes further, up or down, than most investors expect. Though today's prices are about average, the pendulum still has momentum. It is still swinging away from "too low". It will go on till it hits "too high".

Prospects for Growth

So stock prices are about average, and the pendulum is swinging toward higher valuations. This alone is reason for optimism. But just as important, today's prospects for world economic growth are superb. It's an understatement to say they're as favourable as at the end of World War Two.

The outcome of World War Two transformed (West) Germany and Japan from the nation-scale equivalent of common criminals, into law-abiding taxpayers—from biker gang to born-again Christian, you might say. This liability-into-asset transformation sparked a 20-year boom. It turned these former antagonists into our suppliers and customers. It allowed a broader division of labour, which made everybody more productive. Now a similar transformation is taking place, but on a grander scale.

It is of course happening in the former Soviet sphere. But it's also going on in China, Mexico and Latin America, in Indonesia and Pakistan—and in far more remote places than these. The much-talked-about "peace dividend" plays only a minor part.

Up till lately, the world has been divided into the handful of rich countries that practise some form of free enterprise, and the multitudes of poor countries that rely on central planning. Now the poor countries are almost unanimously giving up on central planning and switching to some form of free enterprise. The living-standards gap hints at the growth possibilities.

Better Than It Looks

All predictions (that is, all predictions that turn out to have any truth in them) lean heavily on theory, anecdotes and mere snippets of information. People who have been to the newly liberalizing countries come away with a more encouraging view than you get from news reports. Coverage of strikes, shortages and so on paints a depressing picture. But matters were every bit as grim in Germany after World War Two. Back then, a typical Sunday family outing might consist of a stroll of many miles from city to countryside, there to pick through the dirt in a thoroughly hand-harvested field, in hopes of chancing upon an overlooked potato.

You can't trust the official statistics from Eastern Europe. The governments that gather and publish them, after all, are trying to wring foreign aid and debt concessions from the West. Besides, the locals have a long history of hiding assets from the authorities. Open-air markets are thriving in Eastern Europe, dealing mainly in goods that have arrived unofficially. If GNP is indeed dropping in these countries, it's because they're shutting down antiquated, money-losing plants, where nobody accomplished much anyway.

The post-Cold War boom will aid some more than others. Heinz and Procter & Gamble are, for instance, gaining vast new markets for the soup and soap they produce so well. Readers Digest has started publishing Hungarian and Russian language editions. Readers makes most of its profit on mail-order sales, however. When the real boom starts, mail order may prove to be an especially profitable business in newly liberalized countries, because their merchandising networks are so undeveloped. All three of these companies (they trade on the New York Exchange) are apt to grow and prosper, with the customary setbacks and spurts, throughout the 1990s.

Comeback of the Dinosaurs

Looking a little further ahead, large gains may also go to, for instance, even Canada's dowdy and almost uniformly unloved commodity producers. Take newsprint makers, like Abitibi and CP Forest. Many investors today look on them as investment dinosaurs. After all, young people don't read newspapers anymore, the thinking goes.

But look at the world newsprint market. Communist newspapers used to run about four pages—just enough space to print speeches by party leaders. That will change as soon as business competition surfaces and the newspapers begin selling ads. It's the demand for ads, after all, that determines the thickness of a publication. In the 1990s, the four-page *Daily Workers* of the world will give way to homegrown versions of the *Sunday New York Times*, and that will balloon world demand for newsprint.

This is of course already happening in China. There, if you want to place an ad in a newspaper, you have to reserve the space months in advance.

Impoverished North American steel makers may even rise again. After all, worldwide prosperity will bring a rise in world steel demand.

Meanwhile the downfall of central planning will mean a drop in state-owned or subsidized competition.

The big U.S. automakers have been buying plants in the newly liberalizing countries. Their manufacturing and sales expertise is bound to mean a rise in world car sales, and steel demand.

In this decade, some of today's investment dinosaurs—General Motors, even—may turn back for a time into growth stocks, as they were 50 or 100 years ago.

Waiting for the Boom

The post-Cold War boom may have already begun to affect the stock market. Maybe that's why the U.S. and Canadian stock markets held up so well in the early 1990s recession.

The big gains, though, will really begin only after liberalizing countries make their currencies "convertible". That simply means they have to give their money some sort of backing (or convince the market that they stand ready to buy it if it falls below a fixed level). They could do this by building up reserves of hard currencies, like the dollar, mark or yen, or by establishing lines of credit with international financial institutions. That way, their money will have some value in foreign-exchange markets.

When these currencies become convertible, trade will flourish and underground economic activity will come out in the open.

How long will it take before all these wonderful things begin to happen? The only precedent we have is the end of World War Two, and the post-war boom that followed.

Stocks went up when the end of World War Two came in sight (just as they went up following the opening of the Berlin Wall). After that, stocks went absolutely nowhere between 1946 and 1949. Prices put on a series of false starts in those three years, of course. But they made no lasting progress. Then, matters unexpectedly began to gel. In 1949 the market started to soar. By 1969 the Dow-Jones Industrials rose six-fold, from 160 to 1,000.

My best guess is that the stock-market boom of the 1990s will begin in earnest around October 1994. That's in accord with the "four-year rule". A terrific buying opportunity usually turns up about midway through the presidential term. That's when the incumbent president begins to do what he can to spur the economy and arrange for rising prosperity around election day. Democrats may think President Clinton will be above all that. If he wants us to look back on 1992 as his "first" (rather than "only") presidential term, that's what he'll do.

Should you wait till October 1994, then plunge in the market? Certainly not. Far better to buy gradually, over a period of years. But chances are high that the second half of this decade will prove even more rewarding to investors than the first. This time, the reasons are different. Stocks aren't cheap as they were 10 years ago. As I say, they're priced about average. This buying opportunity comes out of a speed-up in economic growth that we face in this decade—an unprecedented era of wealth creation around the globe.

When you find your optimism is wilting under news of IBM's latest layoff, or the federal budget deficit, or the hole in the ozone layer, try to remind yourself of the following. You used to be able to divide the world up into two parts: the rich countries in North America, Western Europe, Japan, South Korea, Taiwan, Hong Kong, and a few other areas around the globe that practise something resembling free enterprise; and the poor countries that let central planners make economic decisions.

Starting in 1989, a liberalization process began to take hold around the world. One of its key aims is to get rid of central planning, and replace it with something resembling free enterprise. The most widely recognized example of this process is in Eastern Europe. There, tens of millions of highly educated and ambitious people are beginning to have an opportunity to put their efforts to productive use. But the same transformation is taking place in the Caribbean, Mexico, South America, southeast Asia, China and Africa.

Economists say that Germany, Japan and the U.S. have acted as "locomotives of world economic growth" in the years since World War Two. They'll continue to do so in the 1990s. But they'll be joined by a fleet of tugboats that will spur world economic growth the way the opening of the American west did a century ago.

OVERCOME THOSE DEPRESSION HEEBIE-JEEBIES

ome investors and economists disagree with the view you read in the previous chapter. As far as they're concerned, the 1980s was a replay of the roaring 1920s, so they assume the 1990s will usher in a 1930s-style depression. Stocks lost 90% of their value between 1929 and 1932, and these die-hard pessimists think something like that will happen in this decade. They are a small and dwindling minority, of course, but they are hard to ignore.

It's impossible to rule out a depression. For practical and logical purposes, you can't prove a negative. But it may ease your concern to remember that 20 years ago, long before the 1980s North American debt buildup, talk of a 1930s-style depression was as common as it is today.

Back then, depression talk centred on the need to correct the excesses of the 1960s. The economy had rebounded from the 1970 recession. But economic growth was weak by post-war standards. Yet inflation was above average. The stock market never regained its 1960s vigour. The Dow-Jones Industrial Index seemed permanently stalled below 1,000, a level it first reached in 1966.

A 1972 book, *The Kondratieff Wave*, popularized the ideas of Nikolai Kondratieff, a Moscow economist who worked on five-year plans in the 1920s. Kondratieff studied commodity prices and other data going back to the 1700s. He detected what he felt was a recurring pattern: a 50-year up-and-down cycle of boom and bust. He said it included a number of well-defined stages related to war and peace, and economic and social trends.

For instance, early Kondratieff enthusiasts felt the 1960s and early 1970s had a lot in common with the pre-Depression 1920s. Illegal drugs were common in both eras. The 1920s had alcohol (banned by Prohibition) and the 1960s had LSD and marijuana. Consumer credit was common to both, though charge cards made credit easier to use in the 1960s. The Vietnam War corresponded with World War One. (Some Kondratieff enthusiasts feared the widely predicted swine flu epidemic of 1976 would correspond with the worldwide 1918-1919 influenza epidemic that killed millions. Swine flu fizzled. This turns out to have been only one in a series of Kondratieff-inspired false alarms.)

Depression talk got more common as the 1970s progressed. In October 1979, the 50th anniversary of the October 1929 stock-market crash, virtually all business publications ran stories about the Kondratieff Wave and the likelihood of a 1980s depression. A front-page *Wall Street Journal* article said economists and business people rated the chances of such a depression as "at most one in five". It quoted a steel company executive who said "an orderly depression" was developing because of "several decades of inflation and unwise credit expansion". And all this before the 1980s debt buildup!

Back in 1980, after all, U.S. debt, public and private, was only around 1.7 times as great as U.S. Gross National Product—$1.70 in debt for each $1 of output. That was up from 1952's low of 1.4 to 1. The ratio has since risen to as high as 2.4 times. That reading is a high since 1932, when the ratio hit 2.7 to one. For Kondratieff enthusiasts, the similarity between the total debt-to-GNP ratio in 1932 and 1990 is the final omen.

But maybe a society's tolerable burden of debt inevitably ratchets upward. After all, as we get richer, more people are able to save some money. Many of these cash-rich savers want a fixed return on their savings. What's more, debt growth was inevitable in the 1980s. That's when most baby-boomers hit their mortgage-borrowing prime.

In any event, society as a whole should be able to handle a higher level of debt today than 60 years ago. After all, we have more practice with it. Besides, it's not the high debt that causes all the trouble. It's the rapid unravelling of debt that disrupts things.

Kondratieff enthusiasts have to massage and shoehorn today's statistics to make them compare to those of the 1930s. The slowing inflation we've had since 1980, for instance, is not the same as the deflation— falling prices—of the 1920s and 1930s. Total U.S. money supply actually shrank in the 1930s depression. So did government spending. Now Kondratieff enthusiasts talk about "veritable" declines in these figures— growth of less than the rate of inflation. But most debtors owe fixed amounts, not adjusted for inflation. So they can live with veritable drops in the money supply and government spending. After all, even today's low inflation continues to whittle down the burden of their debt.

Besides, debt is just one part of the economic-social-political picture. Lots of other things have changed since the 1930s. Kondratieff enthusiasts think the 50-year cycle has biological roots. If so, it got started long before money or debt existed. So each cycle should play out differently, depending on current conditions. One big difference between the 1930s and today is that now we have a more flexible monetary system. It's based on central bank credit, rather than gold. Perhaps a Kondratieff downswing did begin back in the 1970s. Today's more flexible monetary system would have buffered it and spread it out. If so, we are about due for it to end. That's more in line with the work of economist Joseph Schumpeter. He brought Kondratieff to the West's attention in his 1939 work, *Business Cycles*. Schumpeter said slack economic activity at the low of the 50-year cycle opens the way for what he called "waves of creative destruction". That's when "bursts" and "swarms" of technological changes sweep aside mature industries. They spur great entrepreneurial activity, and bring vibrant economic growth.

Schumpeter's favourite example was James Watt's 1765 improvements to the Newcomen steam engine. The Watt version made possible the power looms, machine tools and railways of what came to be called the Industrial Revolution. No doubt Schumpeter would see a similarity in the invention of the lowly desktop computer, which these days seems about as revolutionary as a refrigerated water cooler. Today's low-priced computing power (not to mention communications satellites and fibre optics) gives us vastly more return on human effort than we got even five years ago.

Kondratieff died in a 1930s concentration camp, and his work was banned in the Soviet Union until Gorbachev's liberalization began in the 1980s. Since then, Kondratieff has undergone a rediscovery in Russia, but with an upbeat, Schumpeterian tint. Some Kondratieff enthusiasts in Russia think the West may be nearing the end of a 1930s replay, rather than setting out on one. They note that since 1970, economic growth in the West has been only half as fast as in the preceding 25 years. They think microelectronics, biotechnology and the downfall of communism will soon spark a wave of creative destruction that will outdo the post-war boom.

Suppose they're wrong. Suppose we go into a 1930s-style depression. In that case, prices of virtually all stocks, commodities (including gold) and real estate will drop. Short-term interest rates would fall, as central banks pump money into the system. Long-term rates might rise, however, as investors dumped bonds over fears of a rebound in future inflation. You'd mainly want to own T-bills, to preserve your buying power. After all, some extraordinary bargains would appear when the market finally hit bottom. North America's biggest stock-market rise occurred in the middle of the Depression, after all. The Dow Jones Industrials rose nearly five-fold between 1932 and 1937.

Owning nothing but T-bills would indeed protect you from a replay of the 1930s, just as living in a mine shaft would protect you from plane crashes. Anything's possible. But, then again, maybe the supposed omens of a 1930s-style depression are the financial counterpart of Elvis sightings.

Your best bet is a balanced portfolio of stocks, and an assortment of federally guaranteed fixed-return investments, with maturities staggered between 90 days and five years. If you have 10 or more years to retirement, my advice is to put half to two-thirds of your money in stocks. It will pay to be optimistic in this decade, and it will be worthwhile to sit through temporary setbacks.

If you find yourself dwelling morbidly on similarities between today and the 1930s, consider how some other important factors have changed.

How Things Have Changed

In the early 1930s...	*In the early 1990s...*
• fascism on the rise	• communism retreating
• money-supply shrinkage	• money growth slows but keeps growing
• husband alone works	• both spouses work
• rising trade barriers	• falling trade barriers
• stagnant technology	• rapid technological advances
• uninsured bank failures	• government insurance on bank deposits
• uninsured incomes	• unemployment insurance
• cuts in government spending	• rising government spending
• accelerating deflation	• slowing but persistent inflation
• weak consumer sector (leaves economy volatile)	• strong consumer sector (makes economy more stable)
• gold-exchange standard (economic rigidity)	• fiat money (inflation and economic flexibility)

Common-sense comparisons, to be sure. Is there any better kind?

PROFIT BEATS PREDICTIONS

Here's a system for picking stocks and profiting from them that concentrates on investment quality and tries to avoid relying on predictions. It limits your risk and involves little commission expense. It has worked well for *Investment Reporter* subscribers over the past half century.

• Invest gradually. That way you buy more shares when prices are low and fewer when they are high.

• Invest in shares of well-established companies. Choose those that are part of the core of the economy and can build a repeat business. These are the best bets for your retirement stake. They have a big advantage over companies that depend for profit on, say, finding a successor every few years to the Teenage Mutant Ninja Turtles.

• Buy stocks you might want to hold on to indefinitely. That way you minimize transaction costs and taxes. What's more, stocks like these often prosper most over a period of years or decades.

• After you buy these stocks, keep an open mind on them. If bad news surfaces and you find yourself hoping the bad news will go away, sell right away.

• For that matter, when you change your opinion on a stock for any reason and decide to sell, sell right away. Don't wait for a rebound.

• When looking at annual reports, pay closest attention to the financial statements and their footnotes. Pay less attention to the words (especially in the president's letter to shareholders). Pay least attention of all to the pictures and their captions.

• Be sceptical of predictions. That includes your own predictions, as well as those you get from the company itself, or outsiders. Predictions are worth considering, because they give you a perspective on the facts. But predictions are the weak link in the investment process.

• Invest mainly in stocks that pay dividends. This is a simple way to eliminate most of the market's worst investments. For a while you may miss out on a few high-growth opportunities, of course, but on the whole, sticking with dividend payers gives the odds a tilt in your favour.

• Pay as much attention to asset values as to earnings. Asset values are less liable to be misrepresented than earnings. In fact, asset values are often understated. They are more stable than earnings, and they are apt to hold up better in a business setback. You'll need to distinguish between book values and the current value of assets—more on that later.

• Consider sales per share as well as earnings per share. You might call sales the raw material of earnings. If a money-losing company is selling for, say, 25% of its annual sales, it may be a buy (though only for aggressive investors). If it is selling at, say, 10 or 20 times its sales, it probably isn't a buy.

• Diversify your holdings across the five main investment sectors—finance, utilities, manufacturing, resources and the consumer sector. (More on this and other portfolio management techniques in the next chapter.) This will give you a range of holdings that respond differently to different economic conditions. That way you'll own some stocks with stable businesses, and others whose profits vary with the business cycle. This system won't help you figure out when to buy and sell. You'll mainly want to sell when your investment objectives change, and that's largely a function of your age and income.

The strength of this system is that it doesn't attempt the near-impossible task of outsmarting other investors consistently. That's what you'd have to do if you wanted to buy at the bottom and sell at the top. Instead, it aims to profit by tapping into the natural growth that well-established companies enjoy over long periods. Over the years, most of the successful investors I've met have told me they practise a system much like this one.

Why You Should Stress Dividends

If you are in the top income-tax bracket, you may be inclined to invest mainly in stocks that don't pay dividends. Presumably you get higher capital gains when a company reinvests its income instead of paying it out in dividends. However, most legitimate, prosperous corporations start paying dividends as soon as they can. If you look back at all the market's great success stories, you'll find that many have something in common. They started paying dividends early on, and gradually increased the rate. The yield (the dividend divided by the stock price) may have stayed low for decades. But the actual dividend kept going up.

Why You Should Stress Established Companies

Investors can make huge profits when they own stocks in a little company that breaks into the ranks of big companies. The trouble is that investors have an all-too-human tendency to overestimate the chance that this will happen. Scores of clichés and famous quotes about "ground-floor opportunities" and "better mousetraps" lure us into that overestimation. The unfortunate fact is that it takes more than a better mousetrap to make a business succeed, much less climb to the top.

You also need to perfect the mousetrap's design, market it to consumers who may be blind to its advantages, produce it at acceptable cost, and defend it against lower-cost competitors. It can be done, of course. But it's harder than it looks, and beyond the capabilities of most stock promoters. Most new businesses go broke within five years. When a better mousetrap is involved, it simply passes into the hands of the creditors.

Investors also underestimate, on the whole, the advantage of an entrenched position in an industry. People are creatures of habit. They keep buying the old mousetrap long after they should have switched.

Mind you, you need to watch for signs that old, entrenched companies are slipping. You also need to diversify. You should include a small company or two in your investments. But it pays to invest mainly in established, profitable companies that are entrenched in their industries and have proven themselves by surviving the past few recessions.

Why You Should Buy Gradually

Everybody wants to buy at the low and sell at the high. But as Bernard Baruch remarked, nobody manages to do so. This is as true for institutional investment managers as it is for individuals. The Peter Lynch's and John Templeton's (two of the world's best all-time mutual-fund managers) made their clients rich by knowing what to buy, not when.

A New York mutual fund research company, Weisenberger Investment Companies Service, sent a questionnaire a while back to managers of 1,000 stock-market mutual funds. It received 220 replies. Then, based on their 5-year and 10-year results, Weisenberger plucked out 46 top performers and 52 poor performers from these 220.

Among the 46 top fund managers, 29% try to stay fully invested in the stock market at all times. You might say they abstain from market timing. Only 7% of the top performers routinely raise or lower their funds' cash holdings, in tune with their views on the market.

The poor performers lean in the opposite direction: only 19% stay fully invested; 27% regularly adjust their cash.

It's hard not to have an opinion on which way stock prices are likely to go if you spend all day studying the market. But most successful investors recognize that market timing is the weak link in your investing decisions. This is a fact that takes years, if not decades, for most investors to learn. Meanwhile, unfortunately, some who have yet to learn it are managing mutual funds.

Profit from the Flywheel Principle

Let's put it this way. Many investors think of successful investing as a process that requires a crystal ball, or at least a computer. They think you need to be able to detect shifts in business and economic conditions, uncover overlooked trends and so on. Far better to look for the business equivalent of the lowly flywheel, a device that has been around since prehistoric times.

The flywheel is a heavy disc—a potter's wheel is a good example. It sits on a pivot, and keeps spinning with only an occasional flick of the potter's wrist. Most successful investments are a lot like that. They keep spinning out a profit (or, at least, cash income) despite fluctuations in the economy, the comings and goings of employees, or changing fashions in the industry they serve.

Things can still go wrong, of course. The chief executive can take on Campeau-esque pretensions, or bet too heavily on an economic forecast that errs. Or, the organization can become sluggish, like a flywheel that wears its pivot down and starts rubbing against the table it sits on. But in most well-established, well-managed companies, this flywheel principle works as it is supposed to. It sets momentum to work in your favour.

You can enhance your results by studying companies and the economy, and by diversifying and balancing your portfolio. It also pays to minimize brokerage commissions you pay, by limiting your trading. But if you make money in the long run, the flywheel principle deserves most of the credit.

Remember too that entrenched companies are more likely to survive unexpected setbacks and challenges. After all, they've done so in the past. Nineteenth-century philosopher Friedrich Nietzsche may have been thinking about his investments when he remarked, "What doesn't kill us makes us strong."

A company comes out ahead in several ways when it survives a money-losing period. It doesn't matter if it's a recession, an industry-wide setback, or a situation unique to the company itself. Difficulties like these are a great teacher. They spur managers to come up with more efficient ways of doing things.

Recessions bring an added advantage to the survivors. They reduce the competition, by clearing the field of weak companies. The survivors get to buy assets cheap. They can take advantage of market openings that occur when competing firms go under. Companies that have survived for a decade or two, living through and learning from the recessions that went with them, are better bets than newcomers.

The funny thing is that academics have overlooked the advantages of entrenched companies over newcomers. But that may be changing. A couple of years ago, the up-and-coming Sante Fe Institute, of Sante Fe, New Mexico, discovered something that it calls the "law of increasing returns": the idea that once things get rolling, they can feed on themselves up to a point.

This contrasts with the conventional academic view of business, which focuses on diminishing returns: the idea that beyond a certain point, each additional sale involves greater costs, so profits have to fall.

This discovery grew out of research on an up-to-date model for the global economy. The Institute's researchers might have stumbled upon the discovery sooner (and at lower cost) by reading our *Investment Reporter* and seeing how we assign Marpep Quality Ratings, and how we decide on additions to and deletions from our "Key Stocks".

Bigness carries other benefits too. Big companies develop systems to spot and deal with trouble long before it gets out of hand. They can afford the pay and benefits that attract top-calibre workers.

For instance, an academic might suppose that Torstar, one of our *Investment Reporter*'s "Key Stocks", would have long ago run into diminishing returns in publishing *The Toronto Star*. But Torstar constantly improves the product and its service. For instance, it has computerized and simplified its home-delivery management. This makes it easy for customers to order a temporary halt in delivery, rather than cancelling the paper altogether. It makes it easy for customers to call and ask about billing, ads and so on. When you make things effort-free for the customer, you build customer loyalty. But you need a certain critical mass and degree of organization to do so. That size and degree of organization breed training and management systems that can thrive in fields with only a vague resemblance to your original business.

As one minor example, Torstar spent $17 million a while ago to buy half of Hebdo Mag Inc., the leading Canadian publisher of photo-classified magazines. Thrown-together versions of these publications (which consist of photos of merchandise for sale) appear already on many newsstands. Chances are that photo-classifieds have great growth potential, and a nation-wide market.

You might say Torstar is carrying out a process that I'd call "McDonaldsization". McDonalds took the lowly hamburger stand and turned it into a major international industry. Torstar may wind up doing the same with photo-classifieds.

Mind you, bigness alone can cost you money if it makes you over-estimate your ability to prosper in an unfamiliar market. BCE Inc. (owner of Bell Canada) lost money when it first started diversifying away from the telephone business. Legislation blocked it from building on its communications strengths, so it plunged into real estate and high technology.

BCE might have done much better if it had aimed to take advantage of its assets. It has wires and fibre optics strung across the country. It has an active account—an existing business relationship—with virtually every family and business in areas where it operates. It may one day get a chance to make much more productive use of those assets. Cable TV comes to mind. New data-compression software lets operators send cable-TV signals through wiring that was originally installed for tele-phone use only. For that matter, the company might also offer fire and burglar alarms, temperature and air-quality sensors, home-maintenance scheduling (your phone could unlock the door for a repairman and monitor which rooms he enters while on the premises).

I'm delving into imaginative finance here, of course. Whether BCE will ever get a crack at these areas is a political question. But meanwhile, BCE pays an above-average dividend, and it's an example of a big, well-managed, deeply entrenched company that seems apt to keep up with the market in the long run.

Beware Earmarks of Low Quality

Part of the trick of making money in the long run is simply to avoid getting involved in investments of low quality. You can often spot low-quality investments by the effort put into promoting their stock. We could heat our offices with the paper that comes in each day's mail from little companies we never heard of that want us to recommend their shares. Most are worth less than the space their materials will soon take up in the landfill. A few seem like honest attempts at founding a business. Others seem to aim mostly at selling shares to investors, presumably to enrich insiders. They range from simple bad deals to out-and-out scams.

If you feel tempted to invest in the shares of unestablished companies, here are a few of the many earmarks you should watch out for.

• Excess attention to the industry the company is in or plans to be in, coupled with a lack of detail on the company itself. Remember you're buying the company, not the industry.

• Grandiose descriptions of a company's place in its industry. (One recent mailing from a company with $20 million in sales described itself as "a leader in the $55 billion food industry".)

• Lumping an unknown company in with established, recognized companies. You might call this the counterfeiters' trick; counterfeiters often try to pass a phony bill by including it in with a number of real ones.

• Excess attention to growth in sales, while drawing attention away from offsetting factors such as growth in shares outstanding, or a string of losses. Pushing sales higher is easy, if you are willing to sell at a loss. Making money on those sales is the hard part.

• Excess attention to the float (the number of shares in the hands of the public). This matters more to promoters than to investors. A small float makes it easier for the promoter to balloon the price of the stock. But reality has a way of bursting those balloons.

• Reliance on glowing predictions by unnamed "analysts" on the prospects of the company and its industry. Often these analysts work for the company's public-relations firm, or for brokerage firms that are as low down as the company itself.

Small but legitimate companies may resort to any of these tactics when they need to raise funds. But if you spot one or more of them in promotional literature from a small company, you should at least be extra careful before you invest. Better yet, invest elsewhere.

CHOOSING YOUR INVESTMENT PORTFOLIO

I's a common misconception among investors that all investment losses are due to inadequate research. If you only look deeply enough, they assume, you'll spot the potential problem before the market does. Or, you'll be in a better position to evaluate the problem and assess the damage. But investment research is one area where you do run into diminishing returns. After all, knowing the location of every railway tie in the CP rail system won't tell you how much traffic CP will move on those rails. Even if you know that, you still won't know if CP's interest costs will rise or fall. You won't know if its corporate strategy is mistaken or on the mark. You don't know the price it will get for its forest products or its oil. Above all, it won't tell you when to buy or sell the shares, much less decide if you should.

More knowledge is generally better than less, of course. But even a company's top officers sometimes buy at the top and sell at the bottom.

No researcher will ever know the company as well as they do. In fact, you would need infinite knowledge of the company, the market and the economy to avoid all mistakes.

Far better to recognize that you will make investment mistakes. But if you aim at building a portfolio of high-quality investments, and if you balance them among the five main economic sectors, mistakes won't hurt you. In fact, the costs of your mistakes will pale beside the profits you earn in investments that work out as you hoped.

A Portfolio Protects You

In short, everybody makes investment mistakes. Some of your favourite stocks are bound to go sour. You deal with this fact of investment life by buying a portfolio of stocks. To build a portfolio that's right for you, you have to pay close attention to three things: investment quality, balance and diversification.

Investment quality is the most straightforward of the three. Basically, it comes down to buying shares in companies that have been in business for a number of years give every indication of remaining in business for a number of years if not indefinitely and seem likely to make money and pay dividends in most of those years.

However, investment quality always involves a judgement call, and nobody's judgement is perfect. You have to diversify to overcome the limits to human judgement. You need to spread your stock-market money around, with respect to four key factors:

• Economic sector.

• Geography. You wouldn't want all your stocks to be based in California, nor in Ontario.

• Market favourites and stocks that are out of favour (market leaders and market laggards, in other words).

• The MRI, or Marpep Risk Index (more on that near the end of this chapter).

Strike an Economic Balance

The most basic part of portfolio diversification is to spread your funds out among the five main sectors of the economy. These are finance, utilities, manufacturing, resources and the consumer sector. Not all stocks fit neatly in any of these categories. Many companies are involved in more than one economic sector. However, the five-sectors approach is way better than simply buying a grab-bag of stocks.

Generally speaking (very generally speaking), the two most volatile economic sectors are manufacturing and resources. The two least volatile are finance and utilities. The consumer sector falls somewhere in between. You'll find lots of exceptions to these general rules, as you will to any investment rule. In the U.S., lots of finance-sector savings and loan stocks were extremely volatile in the 1980s, for instance. So were many junior Canadian trusts. Now, in the 1990s, the top Canadian and U.S. financial companies are profiting from the bankruptcies of their lower-quality competitors.

If you invest for income, you may decide to exclude resources and manufacturing. Instead you may choose to concentrate on stocks in the more stable sectors—consumer, financial and utility stocks.

Firms in the resource and manufacturing sector are cyclical. Their profits soar in a boom, and they plunge (or turn into losses) in a recession. So they are more likely to raise and lower their dividends erratically.

The Lure of Low P/E's

Some investors think they can safely forget about investment quality and diversification if they simply choose stocks with low p/e's—that is, a low ratio of share prices to per-share earnings. The general rule on p/e's is that lower is better.

This ratio has gone through a broad popularization in the past decade or two. It has become a staple of the stock-price listings. Inevitably, though, some nuances got lost along the way. You need these nuances to help you apply the general, low-p/e-is-better rule. Like many investment rules, this one comes with many exceptions.

For instance, a low p/e in resource or manufacturing stocks can signal danger rather than a bargain. Remember, the "e" or earnings of a cyclical company is highly volatile. A cyclical's earnings can jump by several hundred per cent or more (often much more) in an economic expansion; these companies can earn pennies one year and dollars the next. Their profit can plummet by 50% to 100%, or turn into a loss, when the economic boom turns to bust. In the late 1980s, just before the recession hit, many cyclical stocks were trading at p/e's of 10.0 or less. Some traded at p/e's as low as 5.0. This was true in the resources (forestry, mining and oil) sector, and in manufacturing. Investors recognized the volatility of earnings in these sectors and priced the shares accordingly.

Note too that the "e" is a creature of current accounting practices, but these are always under scrutiny. Accounting changes can lead to one-time write-offs that aim to correct misleading impressions of earlier years. But these one-time write-offs may also taint an investor's view of the future. A perfect example occurred in 1991, when oil and gas stocks had to record heavy write-offs to reflect the low current prices of oil and gas. Earnings snapped back the following year. That same year, many companies had to take one-time write-offs for their future health benefits to retirees, rather than pay them out of each year's earnings as they did till then.

Portfolio Basics Help You Deal with Risk

Dealing with risk is one of the most important but challenging tasks an investor faces. Yet all too many investors neglect it or overlook it entirely. That may be partly because investment risk is different from the risks of dice, cards and other forms of gambling. These all operate according to the laws of probability, with their neat formulae, reliable ratios and precise odds. Investment risk is generally more subjective. That's especially true these days, with the move toward freer trade and the global economy, along with the speed-up in technological and social change.

Investment risk is also a lot more irregular than gambling risk. For years at a time, in fact, you can sometimes flout all the standard investment caveats and escape unscathed. You can even make money at it. This is why so many investors treat investment risk and the problems it can cause as unfortunate accidents that luckily only encroach on the lives of others.

Another reason why so many investors neglect risk is the stress that investment literature—brokerage literature especially—puts on capital growth and appreciation. Investors come to think that the only way to profit is to take on a great deal of risk. But by relying more on dividends and less on capital gains, you can cut your risk and add to your net profit.

Some investors feel they can ignore risk when the investment outlook is favourable. But the investment outlook can change without warning. Besides, some stocks will always go against the trend. We have lots of reason to be highly optimistic on the outlook for the next few years, and perhaps longer—till the end of the century, say. However, periods of major change always multiply the costs of taking on unrecognized risk.

Investment Quality Goes Beyond Price

You can cut or control your risk in a variety of ways. But the crucial variable is investment quality. This is one of those terms that gets more than its share of misuse. I'm using it to mean dominant and enduring, in contrast to faddish or fanciful.

Investment quality is a characteristic of a company. It's independent of the price of the company's shares. A high-quality stock can get too high to be an attractive buy, of course, but it's still a high-quality stock. It's probably worth holding on to in most cases, even if it gets overpriced and you think it's vulnerable to, say, a 10% drop. After all, you'll never sell at the very high, nor buy back at the exact low. Even if your high-quality stock does go down after you sell, it may turn around and shoot back up before you get around to buying it back. Even if it does go down after you sell, and you buy it back before it resumes its rise, you'll have to pay buying and selling commissions. What's more, you may have to pay tax on your profit.

A low-quality stock may improve the value it offers by falling in price, on the other hand. But it is still low quality. It is still likely to suffer far more than a high-quality stock in a business or market setback.

High-Quality Companies

Of all the characteristics of high-quality companies, the most visible and obvious is size. The biggest companies in an industry have advantages over their smaller competitors. They have many employees, share-holders, suppliers and customers. This means governments at all levels will take a keen interest in their well-being. A big but troubled company can often secure the bailout, loan guarantee or whatever it needs to stay in business—Chrysler is the all-time best example of that. The small company may simply go broke. Or, it may get taken over for a pittance by the big company.

Corporate and institutional investors also monitor and support large companies more closely than smaller ones. They act as an early warning system for individual investors. When big companies are headed for trouble, alarms go off sooner than they do for smaller companies.

But more to the point, companies ordinarily get to be big only by doing the right things and attracting the right people. This develops a momentum all its own. The right things get to be corporate habits. The right people find they have a career path at big, high-quality companies that encourages them to stay put.

Big companies have the resources to take on big projects and tackle big markets. They have extensive facilities—manufacturing, distributing, customer service and so on—that let them build long-term relationships with customers. Then too, they gain from managerial depth; when one executive quits or gets sick, another can step in to take his or her place.

The lower you set your investment-quality requirements, the more of these advantages you give up. Investors do that because of the lure of the big payoff. No matter how remote the chances of securing it, the big payoff has always had a disproportionately powerful impact on the human psyche.

Mind you, low-quality stocks can and often do perform better than high-quality stocks over short or even lengthy periods. But low-quality investments are far more likely to go sour. When they do, they do so suddenly and unpredictably, inflicting a far more serious loss than stocks of high quality.

The quick test of a portfolio's investment quality is: how long would a prudent investor dare to ignore it? You shouldn't ignore any portfolio for any significant period. But if you had to leave your portfolio untouched for a number of years, you'd probably want to own the highest-quality stocks you could find.

Aggressive and Defensive Investments, Risk and Volatility

A while ago I had a look at the portfolio of a young friend of mine who has set out on his investing career with a highly defensive approach: he is stressing capital preservation at the expense of growth. He is concentrating on stocks from our *Investment Reporter*'s two top-quality ratings. Most of his high-quality choices also happen to offer high-dividend yields.

This differs from the portfolios of many young investors. They are more likely to lean toward aggressive investments: those that stress growth over capital preservation.

The difference between aggressive and defensive investments is mainly one of emphasis. High-quality stocks, whether they are aggressive or defensive, have a lot in common. Low-quality stocks are all aggressive, though their owners aren't always aware of it.

Many investors mistakenly believe volatility is the prime difference between aggressive and defensive investments. That's because they confuse volatility and risk. The two are different, though they do have a way of turning up in the same places. Aggressive investments do tend to be more volatile than defensive investments, of course, and riskier as well. But volatility is a characteristic of the market for a stock. Risk is a characteristic of the company that issued the stock.

If risk means anything in investing, after all, it means the possibility of losing money. That only happens when you sell, or when a company you own shares in goes broke and the shares become worthless. Volatility simply means price volatility—the price of your investment changes a great deal, and in short spurts. It's the opposite of price stability. From time to time, high-quality stocks become more volatile than usual. This can happen because of fast-changing regulatory or business developments, say. Several telecommunications companies on our *Investment Reporter*'s "Key Stocks"—BCE and Motorola, for instance—have been highly volatile since the early 1990s, due to changes in their industry. But because of their investment quality—substantial assets, solid business base, a record of earnings and dividends and so on—these two still expose you to relatively low risk of substantial long-term loss.

A promotional stock that is intrinsically almost worthless, on the other hand, can display low volatility for long periods. That happens, for instance, when the promoter is in control of the market. Share prices may move up gradually as brokers place the stock with unsuspecting investors who believe they are buying an attractive long-term investment. Despite the lack of volatility, a stock like this still exposes you to great risk. It can plummet with little warning.

You recall the case of Hawk Resources. In 1986 and 1987, Hawk rose ever so smoothly from $4 to $8 as its promoter, Guy LaMarche, touted the stock in Europe. Hawk didn't show much volatility—it just went up. Then, at the March 1987 Prospectors and Developers Convention in Toronto, an embittered former colleague of Mr. LaMarche shot him to death. Hawk collapsed to below $2 the following week. By the end of 1988, it had worked its way down to $0.11 a share and has never recovered. If Hawk ever had any value, another promoter would have got it moving again by now. This, then, is a case of low volatility and high risk.

Lots of factors can raise or lower a stock's volatility. Few would surprise you. The type of business a company is in, and the degree of stability in that business, have a big impact on its volatility. Companies in the manufacturing and resource sectors of the economy generally show above-average volatility; companies in the utility and financial sectors show below-average volatility; and the consumer sector is about average. A variety of factors can lessen a stock's volatility, on the other hand. These include a record of earnings and dividends, prominence within an industry, a substantial asset base and so on.

The shares of a company in the midst of an operational or financial restructuring are almost certain to be more volatile than those of a company that is in a settled phase of operation. This is true regardless of economic sector.

High overhead, heavy debt and changes in the market can also expand a stock's volatility. So can a major expansion program. Thin trading shares are generally more volatile than liquid, active traders; it takes a smaller buy or sell order to move their share prices.

Aggressive investing exposes you to greater risk than conservative investing. So, if you invest aggressively, you should plan to monitor your selections carefully, regardless of their current degree of volatility. When risk is high, after all, matters can deteriorate quickly. You need to pay close attention if you hope to figure out when to sell profitably, or to cut your losses.

But remember, lack of volatility differs from lack of risk. Some investors buy a portfolio of stable stocks, then gradually lose interest and stop staying well-informed about them. But even the most respectable stocks can lose ground gradually, over a period of years, even when other stocks are rising. Their drop can accelerate when prices generally go down, or when their problems come to light.

Ordinarily, stocks get volatile for one key reason: nobody knows what they are really worth. Nobody knows how things will turn out for them, but investors do recognize that the range of possible outcomes varies widely.

One measure of risk is the low point of that range of possible outcomes. BCE could drop back to $40 or even as low as $30, if everything went wrong for it—if Unitel and other competitors made huge inroads in its long-distance phone business, and if the CRTC decided not to give the company local rate increases, and if manufacturing subsidiary Northern Telecom fell behind its competitors. A greater loss seems hard to imagine, however. More likely, BCE will rise to $60, if not $80, by, say, the end of the decade, while paying a high and rising dividend.

A $0.50 stock might seem to offer better odds. It could go to several dollars a share much faster than BCE can get to $80. But the risk is that it will go to zero, something that's rather less likely in BCE's case. In fact, if that $0.50 stock is still $0.50 a year from now, you might say it's less volatile than BCE.

Deciding How Much Cash to Hold

All investors should hold a balanced portfolio that includes stocks, cash (that is, cash equivalents—T-bills, savings accounts or money-market funds) and fixed-return investments, such as bonds or term deposits.

My standing recommendation on the fixed-return portion of your portfolio is to stagger the terms between one and five years. That is, divide these funds up more or less equally so that you have one-fifth in each of one-, two-, three-, four- and five-year terms. At the end of each year, your five-year bond, term deposit or GIC will have "aged" down to a four-year term, the four-year down to a three- and so on. Your one-year fixed-return security will have matured, so you can reinvest the money in a new five-year term. (Staggering your maturities is an old idea, but recently I've seen it referred to as "laddering".)

A commissioned salesperson whose income can dry up overnight might want to hold as much as half of his or her assets in cash. So might actors, real-estate agents or developers, or anybody else whose earnings come in spurts. On the other hand, if you and your spouse both have secure government jobs, and have disability insurance, your income is far more certain. So you can afford to put less in cash and fixed-return investments, and more in stocks—if you wish. In any case, you'll want to arrange your finances so that you always have cash when you need it, and circumstances will never force you to sell. Circumstances that force a sale often seem to come when prices are at a low.

By splitting your funds up among stocks, cash and fixed-return investments, you dampen your portfolio's volatility. But you need some volatility in your portfolio to maintain your interest in it. You must avoid the risk of becoming complacent.

Bonds Are More Efficient Than Stocks

Lots of brokers and advisors disagree completely with my buy-staggered terms advice on the fixed-return portion of your portfolio. Instead they advise their clients to trade bonds. Nothing to it—buy when prices are low and sell when they're high. The trouble is that when they try to call the bond market, they almost always eventually get it wrong.

According to the efficient-market theory, it's impossible to outperform the stock market over a long period of time. That's because of market efficiency, the theory goes—a stock's price at any time reflects all known news having any impact on it. Yet some investors and advisors do manage to beat the market; they limit their losses in bad years, while still cashing in handily in good ones. (Needless to say, I'm glad to find that our *Investment Reporter*'s name turns up often on surveys, in the *Hulbert Financial Digest* and elsewhere, of advisors whose recommendations do in fact beat the market.)

The efficient-market theory fails to account for the fact that many investors lack patience and an eye for hidden value. Lots of investors, particularly institutions, pay too much attention to quarterly earnings reports. They pay far too little attention to assets, business solidity and other factors that are much harder to fudge.

Then too, you can beat the market just by sticking with top-quality investments—well-established, reasonably well-financed companies.

The funny thing is that the efficient-market theory seems to work better in the government-bond market. It's easier to go wrong with interest-rate predictions than with stock-market predictions, at least. Robert Beckwitt, a portfolio manager at Fidelity Investments in Boston, recently studied the consensus interest-rate forecast of a twice-yearly survey of economists that has appeared in the *Wall Street Journal* since 1981. He compared two ways of following these predictions: doing what they advised and doing just the opposite. If you did as the economists said, more or less—bought 30-year Treasury bonds when the forecasts said rates would fall, and bought 90-day T-bills the rest of the time—you earned an average annual return of 8.8%. (The average return from simply holding T-bills during the period was 7.5%.) If you followed the economists' advice in reverse—buying bonds when they forecast rising interest rates, and buying T-bills when they said rates would fall—you earned 13.7%.

This doesn't prove the efficient-market theory, by any means. But it does suggest that bonds trade in a more efficient market than stocks. That's understandable. Bond quality is uniform, and there are no hidden values. When you buy or sell bonds, you are simply betting on interest-rate trends. Nobody consistently wins those bets.

Bonds are a way to earn predictable income. If you want capital gains, buy stocks. Forget about trading in bonds, because to succeed there you have to outguess too many other investors.

Simplicity: An Overlooked Portfolio Virtue

Most investment guides and advisors stress the benefits of balance and diversification in an investment portfolio. All too many overlook the virtue of simplicity: that is, reaching your investment goals by the most direct route.

If you disregard the need for simplicity, you're liable to wind up reaching for solutions to investment problems. This is a little like reaching for yield—choosing the highest yield, even if it brings hidden risk. Reaching for solutions is even riskier, however, because it can carry you even farther afield.

Here are some of the consequences of disregarding simplicity in your investments:

• Overdiversification. Too many stocks are as grave a portfolio error as too few. Somewhere between 5 and 20 is about right for most of us. Allow the total to run much higher than that, and you may wind up with a portfolio crammed full of neglected investments—so many that you can't even name or remember them all. Inevitably this leaves you with overrepresentation in some areas, and underrepresentation in others. It also leads you to fritter away priceless time for which you can surely find much better uses.

• Overtrading. You might call this a form of overdiversification, but it's sequential, rather than concurrent.

• Buying glamour stocks and conversation pieces. A boom comes along every few years, in biotechnology stocks, computer stocks, gold stocks or whatever, and we all feel an urge to get in on it. When you give in to that urge, you trade a simple goal for one that is complex and almost impossible to achieve. That simple, achievable goal is earning a worthwhile return on your investments. You do that by tapping into the growth that takes place naturally, over time, in high-quality companies that operate near the core of the economy. Instead, you hope for a windfall, a rather more complex and pitfall-riddled occurrence.

To profit from a boom, you need in most cases to give up security and take on extra risk. Do that often enough and it is bound to backfire on you.

• Focusing on trends, and disregarding finances. A while ago, for instance, a salesperson from a security dealer—the penny-stock brokers, formerly known as broker-dealers—called to tout me on a penny stock that trades over the counter in Toronto. He assured me it would be a big winner, because it had bought 20% of a burglar-alarm distributor. I asked him to mail more information. He sent a single sheet of paper that was mostly pictures. It said nothing about the burglar-alarm maker's sales or earnings. It merely explained that crime is going up because of alienation, drug addicts and "state-supported persons" who have too much spare time. So, everybody needs a burglar alarm.

You need to weigh the impact of long-term social and economic trends on your investments, of course. But the best way to profit or protect yourself from loss is the simple way: invest in established, profitable companies, because they are the ones most likely to profit from trends like these. (Incidentally, this is one more example of why it pays to avoid security dealers and invest only through conventional, exchange-member brokers.)

• Loading up on hybrid investments and innovations. If you could only buy one security, your best choice might be a convertible, retractible, floating-rate participating preferred, or some other investment innovation that combines every feature you could ever want in a single package. But you can secure those same features by buying a variety of securities, each with its own special advantages.

This goes doubly for tax shelters. Each one is different, but most are designed so that the insiders can't lose, and the outsiders need extraordinary luck, plus tax deductions, just to break even. Investment hybrids and innovations with a short life span, such as stock options, are generally even worse. The vast majority of non-professionals lose money in options, as do many of the professionals.

Mind you, a tax-shelter partnership, convertible or some other hybrid or innovation may be right for you at times. You might even want to buy a stock option or futures contract a few times in a decade. While resisting the urge to trade, you might still vary the amount of funds you keep in reserve, depending on whether you think stocks are cheap or expensive. But you still need to think of simplicity as a portfolio virtue. Most of the time, it means you're better off with most of your money in good ol' stocks, bonds and cash.

• Reaching for security. Many investment innovations lure you in with promises of security and guarantees against loss. In investing, as in life generally, it's impossible to hedge against every possibility. Nor can you insure yourself against every risk. Look at it this way: it's only in dire circumstances that you need the promises and guarantees. But that's when they are likely to fall short, or disappear entirely.

That's especially true of preferred shares. When a company turns into trouble, preferred holders supposedly get paid off in full before common shareholders get anything. In practice, it rarely seems to work that way any more. More often, the company reorganizes, and the preferred holders give up almost as much as the common holders.

Simplicity Is Key

Sometimes the key to your financial health is to balance your income and outgo, by simplifying your lifestyle. Failing to do so can lead to reckless and costly investment decisions. Take the case of Mr. A, an investor who ran into predictable trouble a few years after he retired. Throughout his working years, he held a nicely balanced and diversified portfolio of stocks, bonds and mortgages. It produced an appropriate (for him) mix of income, safety and appreciation.

Mr. A spent the final decade of his career as a trade consultant. He travelled around the world first class, and ate and stayed at the finest places, always at his clients' expense. He hoped to maintain that lifestyle in retirement. After he retired, he bought a Florida condo to live in each winter, and held on to his Toronto home for use in the summer. This added more than he expected to his monthly housing outlays.

Soon, as you can guess, his income fell below his outgo. So, rather than cut back on his spending, he made the common investment mistake of reaching for yield—investing in high-risk second mortgages at the height of the 1980s Toronto real-estate boom. When one of his second mortgages went into default, he panicked over the loss of capital and income. This led him to make a second mistake. In reaching for a solution, he sold all his stocks and replaced them with bonds and first mortgages.

His investment income has been declining steadily ever since, as his holdings mature and he reinvests at lower and lower rates. At the same time, he has lost the inflation hedge he had in his common-stock portfolio. The irony of it is that if he had stuck with his original portfolio, the one he owned when he was still working—which was balanced, diversified and relatively straightforward—he'd be far ahead financially from where he is today. He'd still be able to afford the luxuries he is now forgoing.

Mix Leaders and Laggards

Many investors instinctively recognize the need to diversify—to invest in a variety of companies and industries, with some representation in all five main industry sectors: finance, utilities, manufacturing, resources and the consumer sector. Less widely recognized is the need to invest in a mix of market leaders and market laggards. In other words, you should also balance your portfolio between what we might call "hot stocks" and "dogs". All too often, the former go sour all at once. On the other hand, owning too many of the latter can leave you with a weak-performing portfolio for long periods.

We're All Biased

Some investors are naturally inclined to invest mainly in stocks that are out of favour, whose share prices have been going down for some time. Ordinarily these offer better asset value than market favourites. The trouble is that stocks like these may be out of favour for a good reason. They may stay out of favour a long time, even indefinitely. After all, some stocks go out of favour and never return. If you concentrate on out-of-favour stocks or market laggards and you find you have to do some selling during a market lull, chances are you'll do so at a loss.

Other investors lean toward market favourites—stocks that have gone up lately, usually but not always with the help of rising earnings. Market favourites offer better prospects than market laggards do for additional short-term gains, simply because they have momentum working on their side. The trouble here is that stocks like these are always ripe for a correction—a sudden though possibly temporary drop of 10% to 25% or more. This may of course go deeper and last for years.

Your best bet is to diversify between leaders and laggards, just as you do on other criteria.

How to Invest for a Happy Retirement

There's no such thing as an ideal retirement portfolio. But some portfolios meet the requirements of retired investors much better than others. As they enter retirement, most investors assume, with undeniable logic, that the absence of work-related expenses will greatly reduce their overall outlays. However, they often overlook the extra costs of filling up all that newfound leisure time—with hobbies, travel and so on.

Then too, you have to consider taxes and inflation. Neither of these is apt to disappear soon. Both take a toll on your investment income. In short, you should count on spending as much in retirement as you spent when you were working.

Safety Takes on New Importance

For the retiree, investment safety assumes new importance. With a little care, however, that extra measure of safety is easy to achieve. You'll want to adhere to these five simple rules.

First, and most obviously, you should limit your use of margin loans to matters of convenience—to smooth out cash flows, facilitate budgeting, and possibly take advantage of opportunities such as stock-purchase rights. But margin loans should never exceed 15% of your total portfolio value.

Second, you'll want to increase your emphasis on income-producing investments. When you buy stocks, you'll mainly choose those with above-average dividend yields, or with the potential for rapid rises in dividends—mature growth stocks, for instance.

Third, you'll insist more than ever on quality in your investments. You'll want to see a record of earnings, dividends and so on in every stock you hold. Now more than ever, it's important to have as little as possible to do with so-called "concept" stocks that have a business plan but no business.

Fourth, your overall portfolio stance should shift toward defensive investments and away from the aggressive kind. That means you'll invest more in finance, utility and consumer goods-and-services holdings, and less in manufacturing and resources.

Fifth, in the interest-bearing part of your portfolio, you'll want to stick mainly to maturities of five years or less. This limits the harm you'd suffer in periods of rapidly rising inflation and the higher interest rates they bring. What's more, you should stagger your maturities over the next five years, so you have funds coming up regularly for reinvestment. If rates seem high or low, you may of course want to skew your maturities somewhat. But you should avoid the urge to bet heavily—by loading up on long-term bonds when you think rates will drop, or in cash equivalents when you think rates will rise.

Finally, adhere religiously to portfolio fundamentals. Set investment goals and priorities, and pursue them through a balanced and diversified portfolio. After all, an unbalanced and undiversified portfolio of even the highest-quality investments can lead to disappointment.

How to Spot Risk in Your Portfolio

When we analyse investment portfolios in *The Investment Reporter*, we use our Marpep Risk Index, or MRI, as a warning indicator. It helps spot excessive portfolio risk.

A stock's MRI is the ratio of its p/e to its yield (in percentage points). The p/e is the share price divided by per-share profit; the yield is the dividend divided by the share price.

The stereotypical "good buy" is an established stock in a healthy industry, trading at around 10 times earnings, and paying out half its earnings in dividends: For example, a $10 stock with earnings of $1 a share and a $0.50 dividend. The p/e ratio (the share price divided by per-share earnings) is $10/$1, or 10.0. The yield (the dividend divided by the stock price) is $0.50/$10, or 5.0%. Divide the p/e by the dividend yield and you get an MRI of 2.0.

If the price doubles to $20 but the earnings and dividend stay the same, you have a p/e of 20 and a yield of 2.5%—for a far less appealing MRI of 8.0 (20 divided by 2.5).

Note, though, that MRIs are a tool for portfolio analysis, not individual stock analysis. Stocks with MRIs far above the "good buy" 2.0 level may still be attractive long-term buys. But if all your stocks have MRIs above 2.0, you are vulnerable in a market setback.

Use MRIs, P/E's and Other Ratios to Achieve Portfolio Balance

Many investors start out by going to extremes in their choice of investments. This happens because they narrow the range of information they use to form investment opinions.

Take corporate earnings and p/e ratios (the ratio of a stock's price to its per-share earnings), for instance. The p/e ratio is just one of many such ratios. But it is generally the first ratio that investors learn to use. Some investors take it too seriously. They develop a taste for, say, stocks with p/e's below 10. In other words, they shop for investments with an eye only for low p/e's. They overlook other kinds of information—such as the source and pattern of a company's earnings, and its prospects for earnings growth. This can lead you into all kinds of investment pitfalls.

For instance, you may load up on shares of cyclical companies when their earnings are at a peak. Investors generally recognize that earnings of cyclical companies go through wide fluctuations with each rise and fall in the economy, so they pay less for cyclical earnings when the economy appears vulnerable. A low p/e on a cyclical may mean its earnings are headed for a setback. When a cyclical stock's earnings fall, its dividend is likely to follow.

A Better Rule for Cyclicals

In fact, a better rule for cyclical stocks is to buy them when earnings are depressed and p/e's are high. If you do that, however, you need to stick with top-quality issues.

Some income-seeking investors stress dividends rather than earnings, and dividend yields (dividends divided by share prices) rather than p/e's. They reason that earnings are an accountant's estimate, whereas dividends are cash money. Here too, they're taking too narrow a view of things.

All too often, an overly high yield, like a low p/e, signals danger rather than a bargain. If you're going to shop purely on the basis of dividend yield, it's especially important to stick with high-quality issues, such as the top banks and utilities. Even then, prices may begin to fall—pushing the yield up and the p/e down—long before problems come out in the open.

Let's put it this way: You should balance your portfolio among the five main sectors of the economy, and stick with quality. But you should also balance your portfolio between high-MRI stocks and low-MRI stocks. This ensures you own some stocks that are in favour with investors (they usually have high MRIs), and some that are out of favour (which generally leads to a low MRI). That way the market can change favourites and you'll still profit.

HOW TO PRICE STOCKS

W hen investors try to decide if stocks are cheap or expensive, they usually single out five key measures. Four of these are reasonably straightforward; the fifth lends itself to a variety of interpretations.

The straightforward four are p/e ratios (the ratio of share prices to per-share earnings), p/s ratios (the ratio of share prices to per-share sales), dividend yield (dividends divided by share prices) and the p/b ratio—the ratio of share prices to per-share book value (what company books say assets are worth per share after you deduct liabilities). Less widely followed, but gaining attention fast, is the p/cf ratio—the ratio of share prices to per-share cash flow.

All five of these measures have value. But all five suffer from serious drawbacks, and each one can mislead you.

The Old, Reliable P/E

Many investors spend a lot of time searching for the perfect stock-market indicator or ratio: the one that tells you infallibly what and when to buy, and when to take your profits. Such investor aids do exist, of course. The trouble is that they routinely stop working right after you uncover them. Often, in fact, those that worked best in the past will reverse course as soon as you begin using them to choose invest-ments. They'll choose losers instead of winners. Certainly this has been true of the lower-is-better rule that many investors follow when it comes to p/e ratios.

The p/e has undergone a broad popularization in the past decade or two. It's now the most widely used and widely available measure of investment worth. In fact, the stock tables in many U.S. and Canadian newspapers—*The Wall Street Journal, The Financial Post*, the Saturday *Globe and Mail* and others—list p/e's along with stock quotes. Many investors have come to see the high p/e ratios of the summer of 1987 as a sure-fire tip-off of the stock-market crash that was coming that fall. This view can mislead you, as I hope to show a little further along.

The Low P/E Minefield

Some investors restrict their investments to stocks with low p/e's— below 10.0, say. The idea here is that a low p/e assures you of more profit for each dollar you invest. Unfortunately, newspaper p/e ratio tables, and even some company press releases, take a naïve and unquestioning view of profits. They may overlook dilution (the drop in per-share earnings that can occur in a company when it has convert-ibles, stock options or warrants outstanding).

Some companies and newspapers are casual in their handling of extraordinary, non-recurring items in a company's earnings. These extraordinary items can bloat earnings one year, but lead to a miserable year-over-year comparison when things return to normal. Rogers Communications, for one, makes money on asset sales some years, but generally loses money on operations.

When this happens, the true, stripped-down p/e ratio—the one you get based on earnings from operations, and excluding extraordinary gains—may be much higher than the one listed in the newspapers. That's why it pays to look at both the diluted and undiluted earnings figures, and at earnings before and after extraordinary items, and at the long-term earnings pattern, before making an investment decision. The company's reports may also tell you to be on guard for temporary earn-ings bulges or shrinkages.

When you look at p/e's, you have to keep reminding yourself that a company's accounting and management policies give it plenty of room for stage-managing its earnings reports. The managers have leeway to speed up or defer maintenance and other expenses; they can treat some outlays as long-term capital investments when they really ought to be written off immediately, like this year's cleaning bills.

Many times, a low p/e signals danger rather than a bargain. The p/e may be low because knowledgeable investors are dumping or shunning the stock, because of hidden problems that are on the verge of becoming apparent.

This is often the case with highly cyclical companies, such as steels in the manufacturing sector, or forest and metal companies in the resource sector. Their record turns the low-p/e's-are-best rule upside-down. The best time to buy these stocks is when their earnings are depressed and their p/e's are astronomical—as they have been recently, and as they were back in the last recession, in 1982. The riskiest time to buy stocks like these is at the tail end of a boom—in the late 1980s, say—when earnings are at a peak and p/e's are low.

How to Tell a High P/E Ratio from a Low One

On average, the 500 companies in the Standard & Poor's 500 Index traded at 13.5 times their per-share earnings from 1950 through 1989. Those 39 years give you a reasonable long-term average. They include times of unusually high p/e's (the 1960s and parts of the 1980s), and times of unusually low p/e's (parts of both the 1970s and 1980s).

This long-term guideline worried many investors in the early 1990s. Earnings plunged due to the recession, yet stock prices moved sideways or up. This led to much higher p/e ratios. The p/e ratio on the Standard & Poor's 500 rose from under 15 in January 1991, to more than 26 in the spring of 1992, as the recession undercut corporate earnings. This recession was particularly hard on resource stocks, however, and they play a bigger role in Canada than in the U.S. So the p/e on the Toronto Exchange 300 shot up to more than 150.0 by early 1993.

Since then, p/e ratios have come down. What's more, interest rates have come down too. My guess is that p/e's will soon hit bottom, then generally rise on average in the 1990s, because of two factors. One is low interest rates. The other is the spreading realization that many high-quality companies can indeed profit much more under worldwide economic liberalization than they could back in, say, the 1980s.

Mind you, I'm not kidding when I call this decade the Scalding 1990s. The fast changes taking place around the world will be much harder on ill-prepared companies, just as they are on ill-educated workers. We can expect to see a two-tier market develop in p/e's, just as in the late 1960s and early 1970s. Matters may reach a point where no price seems too high for shares in successful companies, but nobody wants to buy those that are less successful.

Sometimes It Pays to Pay a High P/E

When an experienced investor warms to the subject, he or she can rattle off scores of rules (and exceptions to those rules) about what p/e ratio would be high, low or about right in a given situation. It depends on all sorts of variables. These include the quality and durability of earnings, returns on competing investments, the sector, the industry and the company outlook, growth rates and so on. To profit most from any of these rules, you need to apply them subtly. You need to recognize that they give you clues, not answers. You need to recognize that an opposite approach can also work and make money for you, if you temper it with other rules that apply to other matters.

You should be willing to pay a higher p/e for companies that manage to report regular earnings gains when the economy is buoyant, but that also manage to make some money in years when the economy is weak. This, in fact, is an earmark of a high-quality company. It makes increasing amounts of money when times are good, but stays at least marginally profitable (or avoids eye-catching losses) when recession strikes.

You should also expect to pay a higher p/e for companies that have strong balance sheets—that is, little debt, plus adequate cash on hand. (Of course, many of these are the same companies that manage to report regular earnings gains when the economy is buoyant, but that also manage to make some money in years when the economy is weak.)

You should also be willing to pay a higher p/e for an established company when its earnings are depressed by a weak economy. A good example here is Southam, publisher of a number of Canada's top newspapers. Another is Alcan, which has a commanding position in world aluminum production. Alcan's earnings are depressed because aluminum prices are weak, due in part to the dumping of aluminum inventories by companies in the former Soviet sphere. This dumping can't go on forever.

Few companies are worth much more than 20 to 25 times what you might call their normal earnings. These are the earnings you get in the middle of an economic cycle—in between the depths of a recession and the peaks of a boom. The trick is to figure out what is normal, and what is out of the ordinary. You should only pay a p/e of 20 or higher on boom-time earnings if you believe a stock has extraordinary potential.

How to Compare P/E to Potential

When assessing the p/e that a growth stock deserves, here's one time-tested rule to keep in mind: the p/e or multiple of earnings that you pay should equal or fall below the long-term profit growth potential, in percentage points. In other words, you should only pay 25.0 times the latest 12 months' earnings if you expect per-share earnings to grow by 25% or more yearly for the foreseeable future.

The best rule on p/e ratios is to follow the lead of experienced, successful investors. They build healthy, diversified portfolios, and wind up owning stocks with a variety of p/e's—just as they choose stocks from a variety of investment sectors, geographical areas and so on.

The P/S Ratio

The p/s is the ratio you get when you compare a stock's price to its sales per share (you get sales per share by dividing total sales by the number of shares outstanding). A low figure means stocks are cheap in relation to sales. That's a crucial measure; after all, you might look on sales as the raw material of profits.

The p/s ratio is far more stable than the p/e, because sales are much more stable than earnings.

P/s's can tell you a great deal about individual companies. That's because management has far less control over sales figures than it has over earnings or dividends. Managers can't fiddle with and manipulate sales figures as easily as earnings. (In fact, fiddling with sales figures verges on fraud.) If a low-profit or no-profit company has high sales per share in relation to share prices, it may have more potential that you'd notice from looking at its earnings reports. It may be able to restore or boost profits quickly, simply by getting costs under control.

The p/s ratio can also help you cull your list of high p/e stocks. A company selling at 25 times its earnings may be worth a look. But a company selling at 25 times its per-share sales is almost always way overpriced, regardless of what its promoters say.

Three Drawbacks of P/S's

The p/s ratio has its uses, but it also has drawbacks. Here are three of these drawbacks to keep in mind when looking at p/s ratios:

• The p/s ratio ignores leverage. A company's capital comes from a variety of sources. A $10 stock that has $200 in sales per share has a low p/s ratio of 0.05. But it may never turn those sales into per-share profits if it has a high debt, because interest payments will eat up the operating income.

• P/s ratios vary widely, depending on the industry. Service companies and those that operate rich mines and oilfields can be attractive despite a high p/s. That's because they can sometimes bring many of those sales dollars to the bottom line—turn them into profits, in other words. Wholesalers and distributors usually have a low p/s; they have huge sales per share, but they always earn a low profit on those sales.

• When companies are on the verge of bankruptcy, they always have low p/s's. That's because their sales hold up better than their share prices—sales may merely slump while share prices plunge. The p/s ratio, remember, is just one more tool to spot value or a lack of value.

Kenneth Fisher, a California money manager and *Forbes* columnist, has studied p/s's. He recommends that you buy stocks with per-share price-to-sales ratios of 0.75 or less, and never buy any with a ratio greater than 3.0. That still gives you plenty of stocks to choose from, and makes a lot of sense to me.

Use the P/S Ratio to Measure Risk

The p/s ratio is a financial measure that deserves more attention than it gets. Like our Marpep Risk Index (see previous chapter), it's especially helpful in spotting excess risk in your portfolio. In fact, you can apply the Marpep Risk Index rule to the p/s ratio. If all your stocks have a p/s above 2.0 (in other words, if all your stocks trade at more than twice their per-share sales), you leave yourself vulnerable to deep losses at any time, but especially in a market setback.

You can make wider use of the p/s than that, of course. But the more you use it, the more judgement you have to apply. You should never buy a stock purely because of a low p/s ratio. After all, it's much easier for a company to make a sale if it is willing to lose money on that sale. But companies can't go on losing money indefinitely.

From March 1965 through April 1989, Standard & Poor's 500 stocks traded at an average of 68% of their sales per share, according to one 1991 study. In spring, 1993, they were trading at 92% of their average sales per share—a p/s of 0.92. Stocks in the Toronto Exchange 300 Composite had a median p/s of 1.06 at that time. That's high, but it can get higher, and sales will keep on growing.

Use the P/B to Find Value

Book value is the value that a company's books show for its assets, minus all its liabilities, divided by the number of shares outstanding.

From 1950 to 1988, U.S. stocks traded at an average of 1.68 times "book". In mid-1993, stocks in the Standard & Poor's 500 Index were around 2.7 times book. This partly reflects the many corporate restructurings of the 1980s. These often involve write-offs of the value of non-productive assets. These one-time events reduce the value of assets that appears on a company's books. As a result, book value becomes more honest, even understated. As time goes on it becomes more likely to fall below the true value of assets.

Then too, few sets of corporate books take into account the rise in value of a company's real estate and other assets that has taken place since acquisition. While the ratio of share price to book has gone up, the ratio of share prices to net asset value may have changed much less.

Deciding What's Expensive

On a p/b basis stocks in the Standard & Poor's 500 Index were more expensive than Canadian stocks in mid-1993. Stocks in the TSE 300 traded at one and a half times book. The difference comes partly from the fact that more Canadian than U.S. stocks are in cyclical industries, particularly in the resources business. The resources business is still somewhat depressed, due to the lingering after-effects of the recession. When you compare U.S. and Canadian firms industry by industry, the difference in this price-to-book ratio is wide in some, narrow in others.

This, however, is really beside the point. After all, book value tells you something about dollar values—historical asset values—that appear on a company's books. Thanks to inflation, the value of all sorts of assets has risen above the value at which they appear on company books. A low ratio of share prices to book value is a useful (though by no means conclusive) indicator of value. But when you try to read something into a high ratio of share prices to book value, you are trying to turn this modestly useful value indicator into a market-timing indicator. You are using it to decide when stocks are "too high". That's a use for which it is not particularly well-suited.

Book Value Helps You Find the Floor, Not the Ceiling

A low ratio of share prices to book value works best as a crude guide to investment bargains. When a stock trades much below book value, you have to assume that the values on its books are too high, or its share price is too low. Often, the share price turns out to have been too low.

A high ratio of share prices to book value merely tells you that you need to look further before you buy. If a stock's price is high in relation to book value, and high in relation to per-share earnings and per-share sales, then you can assume risk is high too.

The situation is different when the share price seems high only in relation to book value, but appears reasonable in relation to per-share earnings and per-share sales (and, for that matter, to the dividend). Then you have to call on other investor rules of thumb to decide if a stock is a buy or a sell.

When you read a company's annual report and weigh book value, keep these points in mind:

• Book value makes a better floor than ceiling. Book says little about how high a stock can go. But when shares of respected companies fall much below book value, they attract swarms of value-minded investors.

• Corporate books often put an unduly low value on some types of assets—land, mineral discoveries, patents, trademarks and brand names. That's because the books value these assets according to what they were worth when the company acquired them, minus depreciation and other write-offs.

• Inventory values can evaporate quickly. A company's books are supposed to value its inventories at the lower of cost or net realizable value—what they'd fetch in a quick sale. However, net realizable values of some kinds of inventories (clothes, books and recorded music, and electronic goods) are hard to estimate. They can drop quickly due to changes in fashion or technology.

• When companies are losing money, they can languish far below book value for years at a time. Meanwhile, book value shrinks with each new loss.

Keep Book Value and Asset Value Separate

Book value and asset value are two different ways of measuring the same thing. Confusing one with the other is sure to mislead you.

Book value reflects the asset values that appear on the corporate books, minus all liabilities, divided by the number of shares outstanding. Book value has a way of ratchetting downward. When asset values fall or business slumps, companies generally deflate book values by writing off part of the value that appears on the books. When asset values rise, on the other hand, book value stays the same. This creates what I'd call hidden assets: corporate assets that are worth more (sometimes far more) than the value they carry on the company's balance sheet.

When investors talk about "asset value", they usually mean "net asset value" or "net appraised value" (you see both these terms referred to as n.a.v.). This figure reflects somebody's guess of what a company's assets might be worth at current prices, rather than at the prices that appear on the books.

Book and n.a.v. can both tell you something. But book relies less on guesswork than n.a.v. does, and its tendency to ratchet downward gives it a conservative bent. You should look at both figures when both are available. But pay more attention to book value, because it is less apt to mislead you.

Asset Value Versus Earnings Estimates

Remember, guesswork plays a big role in predictions of any sort. But that's especially true of earnings estimates, regardless of whether they come from a broker or advisor, or the company itself. When you calculate an earnings estimate, you're not merely saying something about corporate income compared to outgo. You're also predicting which way the economy will move in the period of the estimate. Your estimate reflects an expectation of whether interest rates will rise or fall, and if business activity will speed up or slow. For that matter, you're also predicting how management will choose to report earnings.

Asset values are easier to estimate than earnings. When you estimate asset values, you are talking about today's situation—the market value of assets—rather than events that will take place over the next year or longer. Surprises do come along from time to time, of course. But accounting firms generally insist that their public client companies publish balance sheets that show accurate debt information. When book values overstate the value of assets, the accountants will eventually insist that the company reduce the value that appears on the books. But when the value of assets climbs above book values, those book values remain as they were.

The funny thing is that many investors buy and sell stocks with each subtle shift in the earnings outlook. But they routinely overlook asset values.

It pays to try to do the reverse. Pay more attention to asset values, and less to earnings predictions and short-term earnings fluctuations. After all, earnings are what happened or will happen in a single 3-month to 12-month period. Assets are what the company has acquired in the years or decades since it went into business. If nothing else, assets are harder to fake.

Dividend Yield

Dividend yields (share prices divided by dividends) go back even further than p/e ratios. Many newspapers include them in the stock tables, along with stock prices and dividends.

Between 1950 and 1989, stocks in Standard & Poor's 500 traded at an average of 24.3 times dividends, for a dividend yield of 4.12%. Dividend yields now are well below average—in fact, they are close to or below the low end of their 3% to 6% range of the past few decades. But you can't look at dividend yields in isolation. After all, stocks and the dividends they pay compete against all other forms of investment. Dividend yields are low right now, but so are interest rates. In fact, dividend yields are on the low side right now in relation to T-bill yields but they do not tell you much about the market. They do tell you something about individual companies, however. One thing to keep in mind at all times is that high yields, like low p/e's, may signal danger rather than a bargain.

P/CF Ratios Can Tell You More Than P/E's

A p/e ratio is simply a tool for understanding and choosing investments. But you can say the same thing about the "e" or earnings figure that makes up the bottom half of a p/e. It's an accounting firm's calculation of how much profit a company made in a given period. It's always a matter of opinion, and that opinion keeps changing. That's why companies so often restate their earnings.

Sometimes, cash flow is a more telling measure of corporate health than earnings. The simple description of cash flow is what earnings would be if we didn't have to allow for depreciation and the gradual write-off of non-tangible assets. The idea is that cash flow measures the cash flowing into a company's treasury, taking into account only those deductions that involve cash outlays, and ignoring mere bookkeeping entries like depreciation and depletion.

Mind you, those "mere bookkeeping entries" are there for a very good reason: to reflect the fact that machines and buildings depreciate or wear out and have to be replaced, and that mineral properties get depleted and ultimately quit producing.

Still, in the long run, cash flow per share seems to correlate better with stock prices than either earnings or dividends. One of the oldest and most successful U.S. advisors is Value Line. A crucial part of its system is that a company's stock price generally hovers around a fixed multiple of per-share cash flow. The multiple differs from company to company. (Draw it on a chart and you have "the value line".) This helps you decide if a particular stock is expensive or cheap in relation to current cash flow. It's little help in predicting future prices, however, unless you can predict future cash flows.

Cash flow (and the p/cf ratio—share prices divided by per-share cash flow) can help make sense of oil and gas producers and real-estate issues. In oil and gas, non-cash deductions for depletion often exceed the cost of finding more oil and gas. In real estate, the customary corporate-profit calculation overlooks capital gains from rising property values. Capital gains used to make up a big part of real-estate company profits, and no doubt will again one day. For both kinds of companies, cash flow tells you more than earnings.

Some investors, especially in the U.S., have greater faith in net free cash flow. This is cash flow minus outlays for dividends and capital spending. It tells you how much cash a company can use to raise dividends or invest.

All these figures help investors understand what they're getting into. There are other versions of cash flow; some institutional investors look at up to 14 measures of cash flow. Some of these may only apply to a handful of companies.

"Cash Flow" Can Mislead

The more obscure and little-used a cash flow measure is, the greater the risk that it will paint a false picture of a company's finances. In fact, you need to beware of stock market analyses based on quaint measures of cash flow.

Take "operating cash flow". Coca Cola Beverages—the Canadian Coke bottler, a subsidiary of Coca Cola U.S.—for a number of years used to list operating cash flow per share on the bottom line of its income statements, in the spot where you traditionally find earnings per share. The company pointed out, without elaboration, that operating cash flow is "defined as operating income plus depreciation".

Operating cash flow is a measure of how much profit a company would make if it didn't have to pay interest, income taxes or preferred dividends, nor deduct depreciation. Back in the 1980s, corporate finance types used to use this figure to determine how much debt a potential takeover could service, if it were refinanced as much as possible with borrowed money. They didn't worry about income taxes, because the debt load was sure to leave the company unprofitable, and tax-free. They also disregarded depreciation. This was just an accounting concept, they felt. Besides, they planned to sell out before anything broke down. You wouldn't say they were disregarding interest costs, however. After all, the point of the calculation was to see how much interest expense the company could carry.

Cash Flow and Wishful Thinking

In the Coca Cola Beverages case, operating cash flow was wishful thinking—like the profit a pig farmer would make if his pigs could fly and he didn't need to truck them to market. Coca Cola Beverages had debt on which it had to pay interest. It had earnings on which it had to pay income taxes. This turned the concept of cash flow upside-down. After all, cash flow is supposed to disregard mere bookkeeping entries, not unavoidable outlays like taxes and interest. The company might as well have offered a cash-flow figure that disregarded its labour costs, or the cost of winter heat.

This practice may have instilled unrealistic expectations in the minds of investors. When the stock was still trading at around $8 a share, the company reported earnings of $0.17 a share for the nine months up to Sept. 21, 1991, down from $0.21 a year earlier. It reported operating cash flow of $2.20 a share, up from $2.16.

Oddly enough, the strength of the Coke brand name was enough to make many investors overlook this quirk in the company's income reports. I mentioned it one time to a money manager I know. He said, "Yeah, they do have kind of a funny way of reporting, don't they?", then changed the subject. I repeatedly advised selling the stock in *The Investment Reporter*, and it ultimately dropped 75%.

Stock Prices Due to Rise

If you take a mechanical view of stocks today, early in 1993, you can talk yourself into a highly pessimistic outlook. To do that, you have to ignore a great many facts. Earnings are down, but headed upward. Dividends are low—but so are interest rates. Big companies are getting rid of workers—but not because nobody wants their products. They are getting rid of workers because modern technology and methods have raised productivity, so they can produce more with fewer hands. Ultimately, rising productivity creates wealth.

Today's most pessimistic observers ignore all this. They say stocks got way too high in the 1980s, and are again too high, so they have to get super-cheap, as they did a couple of times in the last two decades (1982 and 1974).

In view of the changes taking place in the world, however, a replay of 1974 or 1982 is, quite simply, too much to ask.

After all, stock prices don't get super-cheap because investors are periodically struck by some lemming-like urge to sell at historically low prices. Stocks get super-cheap when the investing public analyses the investing outlook and decides that conditions are bad, and will get much worse. That analysis gets distorted at times. But, ultimately, it has some connection to reality.

In 1974, investors sold at historically low prices because oil prices, gold prices, inflation and interest rates were soaring. They sold because of Soviet and Chinese diplomatic and military gains in Asia and Africa. They sold because the Watergate affair undermined world confidence in the U.S. government.

In 1982, investors sold at historically low prices because of double-digit inflation, unemployment and interest rates, coupled with soaring oil prices.

Today, we have the lingering after-effects of the recession, and a relatively high level of debt. However, we also have low interest rates, and much less unemployment than in the last recession. Mind you, current and potential armed conflicts are regular features on the evening news. But you need to put them in some sort of perspective. Try to consider how much more serious they would have been in the heyday of the

Cold War. Think of the effect they might have had on business planning, for instance. Regional conflicts were vastly more serious back in the days when the world was divided up into two armed camps. Now they are a sideshow—a fistfight at a wedding.

No single market-timing indicator—or group of indicators—can say for sure when stocks are too high. For that, you have to rely on your judgement. My judgement tells me that stocks will be a lot higher a few years from now, if not a lot sooner.

6

THE ONE-PAGE SUMMARY

I f you're unsure of what you've got, you're likely to be even less sure about what you need. You can go to work at correcting both these failings by drawing up a one-page summary of your investments. Many investors find that when they need or want an inventory of the securities they own, they have to go on a safari of sorts. This involves rummaging through drawers, closets, safe-deposit boxes and so on—often for hours. If not for the need to calculate income taxes each year, in fact, some investors might never review their holdings. (It's particularly easy to neglect your RRSP, or IRA or Keogh plan holdings. After all, you only pay taxes on the money when you take it out.)

This lack of attention deprives your investments of the value you can bring to them by simply staying alert. If you have forgotten you own shares of a company, you are less apt to pay attention to or follow up on news tidbits that could have an impact on its future.

A one-page summary of your finances is an easy way to deal with this all-too-human deficiency. Here are some reasons why it pays to do so.

• Seeing at a glance what you've got illuminates the strengths and weaknesses in your financial situation. This puts you in a better position to set priorities. You'll find yourself thinking about a proper home for new funds that you have coming up for investment.

• The summary helps you keep on top of your record-keeping. It reminds you of important dates such as term-deposit or bond maturities, or the change or expiration of conversion privileges.

• The summary is a constant reminder of the savings that may be available from tax planning, estate or insurance matters.

• The summary is of course a great help to your executor or representative should you die or become incapacitated. Remember, without a summary it might take you a half day to round up your documents and figure out what you own. Imagine how much longer the job would take in the hands of somebody who's not familiar with what you may only jokingly refer to as your filing system.

How to Get Started

Your one-page summary should show assets and liabilities, assets first. You'll need six columns, though not all items will have an entry in each column. The six columns are quantity (face value, number of shares or whatever), description, cost, current value, percentage of total portfolio value, and annual income (in the case of a liability, annual cost or payments).

Start by dividing your assets into three broad categories.

First, list assets that you are unlikely to sell under normal circumstances, and that do not ordinarily produce income. Most important of these are your principal residence and cottage. Here you'd also include your car, furniture, collectibles, art and jewellery.

In listing values for these items, be conservative. We all have a way of overestimating the value of our heirlooms and personal treasures. That's especially true of antiques, collectibles, art and jewellery. You might want to do a little shopping, and figure out what it would cost to replace them. Then, cut that figure by 50% or more. That's an optimistic guess of what they'd bring in a quick sale.

Second, list what you might refer to as contingent assets. These assets do or can produce income, but in most cases you'll never sell them. They include the cash equivalent or cash surrender value of corporate or institutional pensions, annuities and life-insurance policies.

Third, list your working assets. These are assets you hold mainly for their ability to produce income or capital gains. Here you include businesses, mortgages, income-producing real estate, interest-paying securities, preferreds, then common stocks—more or less in that order.

After assets, summarize your liabilities, personal as well as business and investment. This serves as a constant reminder to shuffle liabilities so as to minimize your interest expense, and write off as much interest expense as possible as an investment or business outlay.

Keep It Simple

You should be able to list all assets and liabilities individually. If not, you may want to customize your one-page summary, to keep it short. For instance, you can group your fixed-return investments. Include notes on interest rates and on the nearest maturity.

Likewise, you should be able to fit all your stock-market holdings on a single page (though you may need to go to foolscap size). If you group stocks to save space—by industry group, say, or by Marpep Quality Rating—be sure to keep a detailed portfolio summary close at hand.

Married couples should have a joint one-page summary, unless they are contemplating divorce or separation.

A one-page summary makes planning much easier. But you need to review it regularly, to profit from it. Once-a-year review is an absolute minimum. Quarterly may do for conservative investors, but monthly is probably best for most of us. Unless you're using a computer, draw your summary up in pencil, because a need to recopy may lead you to postpone and perhaps drop the entire project. Remember, it's consistency rather than neatness that counts. Finally, your one-page summary should say where you keep detailed records—tax returns, share certificates, deeds, transaction slips and so on. This will spur you to gather them up and keep them in a few logical and safe places. If you successfully resist that spur, as so many of us do, then your one-pager will simplify your executor's task when he or she goes hunting for these vital documents.

INVESTMENT RULES
OF THUMB

nvestment rules of thumb are cheap, plentiful and sometimes even helpful. But almost all of them will steer your investing in the wrong direction from time to time. Still, understanding something about these rules of thumb can give you an edge over other investors.

Many investors spend a lot of time searching for the perfect stock-market indicator or ratio—the one that tells you infallibly what and when to buy, and when to take your profits. Such investor aids do exist, of course. The trouble is, as I have said before, they routinely stop working right after you uncover them. Often, in fact, those that worked best in the past will reverse course as soon as you begin using them to choose investments.

That's because all stock-market indicators and ratios have a narrow focus. They include no more than a handful of investment statistics, often just one or two. But the stock market responds to an extraordinary variety of influences, close at hand and from around the world. Its focus changes unpredictably. Whenever that happens, proven indicators can quit working, and start throwing off misleading signals. That's why you should never base investment decisions on any single rule of thumb.

Rather than search for all-encompassing indicators, you're better off acquiring and learning to apply a collection of rules of thumb. These will help you learn how a variety of factors can influence the market. Then, when the market focus shifts back to these factors, you'll have some idea of what to expect.

The Mother of All Investor Rules

I have to acknowledge a debt to a rule I've repeated and profited from many times over the decades: the four-year rule. It goes like this: a highly attractive buying opportunity almost always occurs in the stock market in the year of the U.S. mid-term election, in the middle of the four-year presidential term.

This rule prepared those who followed it for the attractive opportunities that stocks offered in 1990, 1986, 1982, 1978, 1974, 1970, and so on.

You Can't Beat These Odds

Stocks went up in each case. But when I say buying opportunity, I mean a time when the odds are in your favour. Using this loose definition, the rule has worked in every year since 1934. Stocks either went sideways or up (mostly up) for a year or two starting sometime in the second half of the mid-term U.S. election year, in each of those years.

This seems due to the fact that the U.S. president and other U.S. office-holders have a stake in keeping the electorate in high spirits as election day nears. Happy voters favour the incumbent. What's more, voter interest runs high in presidential election years, so upsets are more likely. This gives all incumbents the incentive to arrange matters so that the unpleasantness that comes out of Washington, D.C., in every four-year presidential term—tax increases, troublesome new regulation, painful deregulation or whatever—gets loaded into the first two years of the term. This leaves more pleasant matters, tax cuts in particular, for the second two years.

Avoid This Bad Bet

By early 1993, however, some investors were misreading the four-year rule. They transformed it into the mistaken idea that stocks always go down in the first two years of the presidential term, as surely as they always go up in the second two years. This is, quite simply, a bad bet. Stocks have gone up, if only a little, during the first half of many presidential terms. In some cases they have gone through a modest setback, then a sharp rise.

Much, of course, depends on what President Clinton does in the early part of his term, particularly in view of the fact that his party controls the House and Senate. He could do a lot of damage, or a lot of good. Early signs are mixed. The funny thing is that while many investors distrust Democrats, Democrats often preside over bull markets, more so than Republicans. But even if the U.S. market merely levelled out in 1993, the Canadian market could still rise. After all, our market has lagged badly behind the U.S. market for the past several years.

Note that the four-year rule has its most direct effect on U.S. stocks. Our Canadian market won't always go up or down with the U.S. market, nor go as far or fast as the U.S. market. But the Canadian market hardly ever goes counter to the U.S. market for long.

Your Stocks and the Plurality Rule

One crucial indicator that offers a favourable reading right now is what you might call the plurality rule: when you go through Toronto and New York Exchange listings, bargains seem more plentiful than outright sells. In fact, a number of new issues from the mid-1980s have matured and now seem downright attractive, for investors who can accept some risk.

In the late 1980s, we kicked a number of stocks off our *Investment Reporter*'s list of Key Stocks, and had few "best buys" to offer in our "Investment Planning Guide" each month. Now the reverse is true. We've begun adding stocks to our Keys for the first time since the mid-1980s.

That doesn't mean stocks will soar anytime soon. It does mean that prospects are looking up, and attractive investment situations are more plentiful now than at any time in the past seven years. To me, this is a strong clue that now is a better time to buy than sell.

1993: The Coin-Flipper's Fallacy

In early 1993, a friend confided to me, "You may be right to be optimistic on 1993, but I've got my doubts. Do you know that the market goes down 60% of the time in years ending with '3'?"

My friend has been taken in by the coin-flipper's fallacy: the idea that the pattern in a series of coin flips has an effect, one way or the other, on the next flip in the series. Most victims of the coin-flipper's fallacy take what you might call a contrarian approach. They say to themselves, "Heads can't possibly come up again. So I'll bet on tails." But the logic is flawed. Each new flip offers the same 50-50 odds. My friend is taking the opposite view—betting the percentages, you might say. Since the coin came up heads 60% of the time in the past, he figures that means the probability of heads is 60%, not the customary 50%.

Generally speaking, the market goes up around two-thirds of the time. (When it falls, it does so twice as fast as it rose.) So the shoddy market performance of years ending in "3" is particularly out of character. The best explanation for it is the commonplace statistician's rule that "random events are apt to occur in bunches".

Your best bet is to disregard statistical market lore like this, unless you can see some common-sense explanation for it, as there is for the four-year rule. These bunches of random events often break down under a closer look. For instance, when the market went down in 6 of the past 10 years ending in "3", it lost a total of 75.6%. In the 4 years of the 10 when it went up, it gained a total of 117.8%.

An Investor's Four Costliest Words

Investor rules of thumb are simply an attempt at making some sense out of the market, of profiting from experience. In contrast, it's often been said that the four costliest words in investments are, "This time it's different."

This is a valuable warning, but it lends itself to misapplication.

You have to recognize that technology, law and politics change all the time. On the other hand, arithmetic and human nature never change.

So, "This time it's different" is apt to cost you money if you say it to yourself to overcome your common-sense qualms about buying a stock that exposes you to obvious risk. For example, when a stock quintuples and attracts a lot of favourable brokerage and press attention, your human nature makes you want to believe it can make a fortune for you too. But if it's trading at, say, 50 times its latest per-share earnings, and if it is involved in a fast-changing business where it can't hold on to a competitive edge, then arithmetic works against it. Few companies grow fast enough, long enough, to justify that high a price.

Rules of Thumb and Economic Laws

Investor rules of thumb shade into and borrow from economic laws. One of the best of these is Gresham's Law: "Bad money drives good money out of circulation." The last time it applied here was in the 1960s, when Canada and the U.S. took the silver out of their coinage. People stepped up their hoarding of silver dimes and quarters, while spending base-metal coins and paper money.

Some laws are a help if you keep in mind that they only narrow the range of outcomes. Take, for instance, the grandly named Law of Round Numbers. It lends itself to misleading simplification; basically, it says that prices (of a stock, a commodity, a currency, or a stock-market index, or the ratio of two commodities, or two currencies) act funny when they approach a big, round number with two or more zeros in it. When a price or price ratio hits one of these, it will often speed up...or slow down...or, it will reverse course entirely.

For instance, gold peaked at $200 an ounce in 1974, then bottomed at $100 in mid-1976; there are many other, less prominent examples. The best example of them all came when the Dow Jones Industrial Index first hit 1,000, in 1966. It immediately turned and plunged to 750 later that year. It got back to 1,000 in 1969...then immediately turned and plunged to 650 a year later. It took till 1973 to get to 1,000 again, and it immediately sped up and shot through that by-now magic number...only to suddenly run out of steam, and plunge the following year to 570.

The Dow ran into and briefly past 1,000 three times in 1976, then went back down to 750 in 1978. Back to 1,000 three times between late 1980 and mid-1981, then down to 780 in mid-1982...then back up and through 1,000 late that year.

After that, the 16-year-old Dow 1,000 ceiling turned into a Dow 1,000 floor. The Dow stayed above 1,000 for the rest of 1982, then set off at the start of 1983 on a breath-taking four-month, 25% rise. In 1986, the index stalled three times at 1,900...then suddenly regained its footing and shot up through 2,000 with barely a moment's hesitation.

Early in this decade, you often heard predictions that the Dow would stall below 3,000, just as it stalled below 1,000—and maybe for just as long. It didn't work that way, as we know. Chances are you'll hear the same thing as the index nears 4,000.

The Kitchen-Sink Rule

When they have bad news to report, managers of a top-quality company prefer to release it all at once, to avoid any suggestion that they have misled their investors. They apply what you might call the "kitchen-sink rule"—that is, they write off everything except the proverbial kitchen sink, to clear the corporate books of unpleasant surprises (and make future earnings that much higher). Lesser managers prefer to dole the bad news out little by little, hoping on the one hand that investors will overlook it...and on the other hand that a miracle will occur, and bring good news to overwhelm the bad. (When miracles occur under those circumstances, they usually make things worse.) Mind you, even the best managers prefer to release bad news when it is least likely to be noticed—at times like the first quarter of 1991, for instance, when news of business setbacks was all too common.

When a company loses money two years running, take note of the kitchen-sink rule. Are the company's managers doling the bad news out a little at a time (and exposing their lack of management quality)? If so, the situation may be more serious than it seems.

Mind you, money-losing periods running two or more years have become much more common following the 1990 recession than in the past. That's partly because of the length of the economic expansion that came before it. But you should still take a sceptical view of companies that report two or more years of losses. Above all, avoid loading up your portfolio with companies like these, because the two years of losses may be just the start.

Newton's Rule Gets Misconstrued

Many investors handicap themselves by misconstruing Newton's laws of motion. They believe "what goes up must come down"—so they put off investing in top-quality stocks in hopes that their prices will come down to bargain levels. Even sillier is the notion that what goes down must go up again.

In fact, Newton's first law says a body in motion will stay in motion until acted upon by an outside force. You might look on this as the key to successful investing. High-quality investments (such as our *Investment Reporter*'s Key Stocks) are "in motion"—working toward the goal of expanding their business and profit. Outside forces slow or interfere with their progress from time to time. But only rarely do outside forces stop or reverse their progress altogether.

More Rules: the 7 P's

Around the office, we refer offhandedly to our *Investment Reporter* approach to seeking stock-market profit as "that old-time religion". You could sum it up in a variety of ways. Consider, for instance, these seven words, each beginning with the letter "p":

• Plan. Begin your investing career with a plan. Size up your sources of income and where you spend it, and try to bring the two together within some long-range blueprint that leaves room for regular savings.

• Priorities. You need to determine which of your outlays are least and most important, and rank those in between. You'll need to allocate cash to living expenses, mortgage payments, providing for emergencies, child care and education, insurance and so on. You'll need to decide how much of your savings to earmark for retirement, vacations, new cars and so on.

• Preparation lets you execute your plan and its priorities. You should start with a one-page summary of your assets and liabilities. Then, organize a system of record-keeping that gives you ready access to facts on your financial condition, but isn't so demanding that you often let it get behind or, worse, let it lapse altogether. You'll also need to make contact and open accounts with banks, brokers, insurance agents and so on.

• Portfolio. Many investors start to think about their investment portfolio only after haphazardly acquiring a collection of stocks and other investments. Far better to begin thinking about what should be in your portfolio long before you have the money to buy it.

Decide early on what your objectives ought to be—what mix of appreciation, income and safety is right for you. Then, choose securities that have the appropriate investment characteristics and, as a group, provide balance and diversification.

• Prudence is crucial at all times. The trouble with most financial transactions is that you can carry them out without taking cash from your pocket. Instead you merely scribble your signature on a piece of paper or, easier still, say, "Okay, do that," over the telephone. When your transactions take on this ethereal quality, risk soars.

Before entering into any financial transaction, consider what you stand to lose. What will happen to your financial plan if things go wrong—how will you have to alter your priorities? Some of today's unhappiest real-estate investors started out as real-estate speculators a few years ago. They said to themselves, "I put 5% down on this condo, the price goes up 10% and I triple my money." Few considered whether rents were high enough to pay the mortgage in the event that condo prices merely went sideways. Fewer still considered the idea that condo prices might fall, as they generally have since the late 1980s.

• Patience is necessary, because investing's biggest profits come only in the long term, and because patience helps you avoid acting on impulse. Successful investing is a lifelong endeavour that calls for composure in the face of temptation, frustration and failure.

• Perspective helps you avoid getting carried away by enthusiasm on the one hand, or despair on the other. You want to look on each of your investments as part of the financial whole. If your plan determines your investments—rather than vice versa—then you'll have little reason to worry unduly or depend too strongly on any single one of them.

The Rule on Setting a Limit

When they place an order with a broker, many investors like to put a limit on prices they will accept or pay. You can overdo it, of course. Put too strict a limit on prices you'll pay and you'll wind up filtering the winners out of your portfolio; you'll only buy the stocks that go down, never those that go up.

But suppose you want to buy a stock that is quoted at $19 7/8 bid, $20 ask—last trade at $20—and the TSE 300 and Dow-Jones Industrial indexes are rising. It may be best in that case to bid $20, or even tell your broker to buy "at the market". If prices have gone down in the past hour, on the other hand, try putting in a bid at $19 7/8. If you still haven't got a "fill" a few hours later, you can always raise your price to $20.

A minor difference, to be sure. But if you could get your stock cheaper, why not try? Besides, put in a market order and you might be surprised at how often you pay $20 1/8, or more.

If you're going to use market orders at all, you should always attach some sort of limit to them, especially if you are buying a thin trader. When a stock is $19 7/8 bid, $20 offered, for example, you might tell your broker to buy the stock for you at the market, but with a limit of, say, $20 1/2. After all, sometimes a passing factor such as a news report can spur a great deal of temporary interest in a stock. When that happens, a number of orders to buy at the market can hit the floor at once, and overwhelm the available supply of stock. In that case the price can run up to, say, $23 before traders take advantage of the situation and sell (or sell short). If you put in a market order with no limit in a situation like that, it's entirely possible to pay $23, then watch your stock drop back to $20 (or less) in minutes.

Beware the Tailor-Made Rule

After making up their minds on which way the stock market is headed, many advisors try to dream up rules of thumb and indicators that support their view. These rules and indicators may focus on matters that the market and investors choose to ignore. This often happened after the 1987 stock-market crash. Again and again, pessimists—the bears—

came up with reasons to expect a 1930s-style stock-market collapse and depression. The market has so far refused to accommodate them.

Many of these rules and indicators centred on high p/e ratios. They disregarded the fact that p/e's always go up in a recession. Others centred on soaring mutual-fund sales, another statistic that is easy to misconstrue. It's true that in the past, mutual-fund sales soared just when the stock market was peaking. This time around, however, mutual-fund sales were likely to soar and stay high for some years. After all, the baby boomers have now reached an age when people start buying mutual funds.

The market offered much better bargains in 1982 than in 1992, of course. Throughout the early 1990s, some advisors told investors to stay out of stocks until they once again offered the opportunities that were available 10 years earlier. But seeking perfection is rarely a workable strategy, in investing or in life generally. That's exactly what you are doing when you stay out of the market until it offers the bargains of the century, like those of 1982.

Stocks are far from giveaway levels right now, early in 1993, but they are far more reasonably priced today than they were, say, at their heights in the 1960s. And today's market opportunities have something in common with those of the late 1950s and early 1960s. There are even some statistical similarities.

The Dow went up 239.5% in the 1950s, and suffered only two down years in that decade. It went up 228.3% in the 1980s, another decade during which it had only two down years. The Dow traded at more than twice its book value at the end of the 1950s, and again at the end of the 1980s. P/e ratios were high at the end of the 1950s, and again at the end of the 1980s. Dividend yields were low at 3.05% at the end of the 1950s, and have been low in the past couple of years as well. You could take this to suggest that the 1990s could turn out like the 1960s.

Stocks soared in the 1960s (up till 1968), as investors who were born before the Depression swarmed into the market. U.S. stocks were soaring at the start of the 1990s as the baby boomers swarmed into the market. Today's mutual-fund sales boom is due more to sheer numbers of baby boomers than to excess enthusiasm for stocks. Mind you, in the 1990s we have more reason to get enthusiastic than we did in the 1960s. Back then, we had Camelot and moon landings; today we have peace among the great powers, plus worldwide economic liberalization, and these are far more compelling reasons to buy.

Your best strategy is to buy stocks gradually during your working years, and sell in retirement. If you hold out for a 6% Dow yield, you may have to wait till the year 2001.

High-Water Marks as Guidelines

The early 1990s was a time in the investment cycle when experienced Canadian investors looked for what you might call high-water marks. These are indications of how high share prices or corporate earnings might go when the economic tide washes back in again, as it inevitably will.

Here's a crude example: Toronto Sun shares hit a $27 peak in 1989; now, in mid-1993, they trade for less than their book value of $15.14. Eventually the Toronto economy will recover, and Toronto Sun is apt to gain. It has a good chance of one day getting back to that $27 peak.

In short, to get an idea of how high a stock may go in the next boom, take a look at how high it got in the last one. But keep in mind that you should only use this approach with high-quality companies.

Sometimes, after all, high-water marks are due to hot air rather than an economic high tide. When value is low to begin with, a stock's price and value may get far out of whack, so that it reaches heights it will never regain. For instance, a stock with assets that are worth a dime will sometimes—mostly with the aid of skilled promotion—shoot up from, say, $1 to $5 a share. When it gets back down to $1, it will look like a buy to some investors, because it's 80% off its peak. Yet it is selling at 10 times asset value.

A stock's all-time high only tells you part of the story. You need to consider why it went as high as it did, what has changed since then, and if it can profit as well again when the economic high tide rolls back in.

The Rule on Privatizations

Many new stock issues come out favourably priced, compared to shares already in public hands. After all, who would buy a new issue if it cost more than existing issues? But a privatization is a special kind of new issue. A privatization occurs when a government sells shares in a company it owns to the public. Politicians are in charge, and they have nothing to lose and a great deal to gain by selling cheap. When governments privatize, they have an incentive to send the company out into the world with as low a price and as few drawbacks as possible.

We all tend to be generous when doling out found money, after all; that's human nature. But governments have far more direct reason to sell at a low price. Why risk offending potential voters? But in many cases, privatizations sell out in their initial offering, then go into a mild slump. This is because privatizations attract first-time investors, who expect to get rich much too quickly.

Privatized companies generally offer attractive odds. But the government that sells them to you stops short of offering you a guaranteed profit, least of all if you're in a hurry. Some privatized stock issues do go sour, partly because of timing: the politicians decide to sell at what they see as a good time for buyers, and this turns out to be a good time for sellers. After all, politicians' timing is rarely any better than that of the average investor or part-time stock-price chartist. (The government's timing is often worse, in fact, thanks to the many legislative and regulatory committees that have a say.) This points up what you might call the general rule on investment risk: risk is highest when everything looks terrific.

Then too, the kind of companies that have been available for privatizing are those most likely to suffer in a recession, such as Petro-Canada and Air Canada. Both are in cyclical industries that suffer from over-capacity.

Privatizations give you a chance to buy assets at a discount. That's an aid to profitable investing, but no substitute for sound portfolio planning.

Asset Plays and Investment Goals

Every privatized stock issue is different from the others, but all have something in common. Generally they have appeal as "asset plays". These are stocks that give you an opportunity to buy assets cheap. But cheap assets are cheap for a reason—such as lack of profit, industry over-capacity, poor management, or all three of these and others besides.

The value of an asset play comes out of the fact that it may be worth more, broken up and sold in pieces, than it is worth as an operating entity. Mind you, if asset value deteriorates or was overstated to begin with, you can still lose money.

Privatization adds a level of protection to an asset play. Asset values are rarely overstated in a privatization. In fact, they are often under-stated. That's because politicians like to get all the obvious problem assets off the balance sheet before selling to the public. If deterioration occurs, the government may step in to change the law, provide tax breaks or do whatever else it needs to preserve investor/voter goodwill.

These advantages are impressive, but they add up to something less than a guarantee. You also need to remember that it often takes patience to profit from investing in any asset play because privatized companies are in turmoil, due to the switch in ownership and the ori-entation that goes with it. As always, you need to diversify among the five industry sectors, and strive for portfolio balance.

The Baruch Rule on European Holidays

Bernard Baruch, one of the greatest speculators of all time (he made money and held on to it), had a system of sorts: whenever he found his stocks wandering aimlessly in spite of good news, he would sell every-thing he owned and go to Europe for a few months. This usually paid off, since the market malaise he sensed frequently led to a broad decline.

The Household-Name Rule

The best corporate expansion lets a company make fuller or more prof-itable use of its existing assets, employees or operations. An example is the much-derided move by the major Canadian banks into the invest-ment brokerage business, in the midst of the 1980s market boom.

Their timing—they bought just months before the 1987 stock-price crash—turns out to have been less than ideal. But most banks recognized that they had to buy when it became legal to do so, and when the brokerage firm they wanted to buy was available. One rule of thumb that applies to take-overs and to business generally is that those who wait for perfect timing rarely accomplish much.

The worst expansion aims at building an empire rather than making a profit. A textbook example was real-estate operator Robert Campeau's late 1980s move into retailing, through his high-priced take-over of Federated Department Stores and Allied Stores. This ballooned Campeau Corp.'s assets from $2.3 billion in 1985 to $14.3 billion in 1989—and pushed the company into bankruptcy a year later. A more extreme example appeared a little later in the case of the late Robert Maxwell, where hubris led to fraud.

This brings to mind a long-time caveat favoured by experienced, successful investors: beware the fast-growing company headed by anybody whose name suddenly becomes a household word. Today, most 1980s-seasoned investors would agree that instant celebrity spurs business leaders to tempt fate. Unfortunately, all too many investors will have forgotten that lesson by the time the next take-over boom begins.

The Rule on Spin-offs

Stock-brokerage analysts coined the word synergy back in the 1960s, to describe what they saw as near-magical gains that came about when companies got involved in a broad range of unrelated activities by taking over other companies. The idea was that the right fit between buyer and buyee would lead to a situation described mathematically as 2 + 2 = 5. It turns out, however, that many supposedly 2 + 2 take-overs wind up equalling three or less. Yet the word synergy has found a permanent place in investment jargon. That is, it seems to resurface whenever there is any doubt about the benefits of a proposed take-over.

The reverse process—divesting or getting rid of failed or unsuitable acquisitions—is apt to be more common than take-overs these next few years. One way to divest is through the spin-off: setting up the unwanted division as a separate company, then giving its shares to your own shareholders, as a special dividend. This process will produce its share of profit for investors. But profits won't come immediately. Investors who receive these special dividends often dump the shares soon after, and depress prices far below realistic levels.

The best way to profit from spin-offs is often to buy them at those depressed prices, three to six months after they begin trading on their own.

Indicators, Ratios and Tells

Some of the best investment indicators are merely anecdotal, like "tells" in a poker game—"I knew Homer had an unbeatable hand, the way he kept rubbing his eyes as if he couldn't believe it!"

In the summer of 1987, for instance, a stretch version of a Volvo would occasionally park (illegally) on York Street in Toronto's finance district. (It may have been the creation of AHA Automotive, the auto customizer that was a hot new issue in the mid-1980s; by mid-1987, AHA was already plunging and headed for bankruptcy.) Even back then, the car seemed ominous. Only at the tail end of an epic boom would any Torontonian buy a $35,000 Volvo and spend $40,000 to add 18 inches of leg room to the back seat.

On two occasions that same summer, I found a wad of brightly coloured Canadian banknotes blowing along York St. No great treasure—maybe $15 to $20 in each case—but certainly worth the effort of bending over to scoop it up off the sidewalk. This, too, could only have happened in the summer of '87. Nowadays, if you see what looks like folding money blowing along the sidewalk, you should look for the hidden camera.

A special sort of tell sometimes appears when the market is hitting a peak or a trough. At times like these, oddball predictions gain much more attention than they ordinarily would, because they match the public mood. Take the summer of 1987, for instance, prior to the stock-market crash that occurred in October of that year. The market's peak that summer coincided almost to the day with the so-called harmonic convergence of August 16, 1987.

José Argüelles, author of *The Mayan Factor: Path Beyond Technology*, predicted in lectures leading up to August 16 that the day of the harmonic convergence would be "A turning point of a magnitude exceeding anything we've ever known." He claimed to have interpreted ancient Mayan and Aztec prophecies that foretold a rare conjunction of planets and other galactic forces that would spur "a new awakening, a kind of planetary renaissance...or else, extinction." All this gained surprising attention in the months leading up to the big day, to the point that the *Wall Street Journal* ran a front-page story on the subject on June 23.

Believers gathered before dawn on August 16, at Stonehenge and other spots around the globe where ancient peoples performed religious rituals, to usher in the new age. Nothing much happened. But as it turns out, the harmonic convergence coincided with the peak in the 1980s bull market. The October stock-market crash followed little more than two months later. The truly amazing point here is that virtually nobody seems to have commented on the coincidence.

It would be easy to dismiss both the harmonic convergence and the stock-market crash as mass hysteria, if they occurred together. But a market peak is quite another matter. As the Wall Street saying goes, no bell rings when prices reach what will prove to be their high.

There may be cycles in human behaviour that we're unaware of. Maybe the human scepticism cycle hit a low in the summer of 1987 that coincided with the market peak; maybe that same cycle low put the metaphysically oriented in a buying mood as well.

I plan to keep an eye out for this sort of tell in the future. After all, predictions of harmonic convergence-style events get more common all the time, as we near the end of the second millennium.

The Friday-Monday Fake-out Rule

Ever notice how the market sometimes drops suddenly toward the end of trading on Friday, and leaves investors wondering why...then just as inexplicably finds its footing again early on Monday, and goes on to regain all of Friday's losses? The common explanation for this phenomenon is professional trading.

The pros are willing to hold shares overnight during the week, if they feel the market's outlook is encouraging. But they prefer to sell out (flatten their positions, as they say) for the weekend. Their nerves simply can't take holding shares through two days of closed markets. In a sense, then, the Friday-loss, Monday-gain pattern means the pros are optimistic on the market outlook.

A Friday-gain, Monday-loss pattern could mean just the reverse. It may mean the pros were selling short all week, but that they bought—covered their short sales—on Friday afternoons. That would make prices rise. Prices would fall again on Monday morning when the pros re-entered their short sales.

Some skittish investors overlook this interpretation, however. When stock prices drop on Friday afternoon, they worry about it all weekend, then sell on Monday morning.

More experienced investors will at least wait to see what happens Monday morning. If prices rise, they take heart: the pros are optimistic! Unfortunately, the sentiments of the pros are as weak a guide to the market outlook as any other short-term indicator.

Your best bet, as always, is to emphasize long-term fundamental appeal, and seek a balanced portfolio. That will give you the confidence you need to sit comfortably through Friday-afternoon market setbacks.

The Key-Man Rule

Investors closely associate some stocks, for better or worse, with a key man. He may be the founder, the president, or merely the promoter. In these cases, it pays to remember that the sudden departure of a key man can have predictable effects on a stock's price.

The sudden death of a key man—whether by violence, accident, a heart attack or whatever—can help the price of the stock if investors feel the key man is hurting the company. Charles Bluhdorn built Gulf + Western in the 1960s through a series of mergers and take-overs. Had he died suddenly back in the 1960s, Gulf + Western shares would undoubtedly have plunged. But Mr. Bluhdorn continued these tactics in the 1970s and early 1980s, when investors had lost their taste for them. In February 1983, following Mr. Bluhdorn's unexpected death, shares of Gulf + Western Industries spurted upward from $17 to $25—

a 50% gain in one month. Only then did Gulf + Western shares exceed the $21 high they hit back in 1969.

Founders, high-profile company presidents and so on often hang around longer than investors like. They may, from an outside investor's point of view, run the company according to their personal preference, rather than on a sound business basis. Their deaths may spur hopes of a more efficient and profitable use of the company's assets. One U.S. study of the stock-market impact of the sudden death of 53 such executives found that share prices rose an average of 3.5% between the time the founder died and the publication of his obituary several days later in the *Wall Street Journal*.

The Dumbbell Indicator

As I said a little earlier in this chapter, bells never ring when the market hits a peak or a trough. However, you can always look back at market turning points and find strikingly dumb actions that stand out as signalling a change in trend. One example that comes to mind is the financing that Dome Petroleum arranged for itself at the peak of the 1981 oil boom.

Just before Dome entered a profit and stock-market nosedive that took it to the brink of bankruptcy, its bankers agreed to lend it hundreds of millions of dollars at one eighth of a percentage point more than their cost of funds. Dome was paying less to borrow than most governments!

Another of these dumbbell indicators came in 1982, just as the market was setting off on the record-breaking rise of the 1980s. A well-known market guru announced on network TV that, first, the market was sure to fall 50% within a year and, second, his judgement had matured to a point where he would never again make a major forecasting error. (Stocks soared; the guru's popularity plunged.)

And of course, all Torontonians know somebody who bought a house at an outrageously high price, near the peak of one of the city's recurring real estate booms, on the theory that this was his or her last chance to buy at an affordable price. Mind you, these tells (to borrow a poker-player's term) are always more apparent in retrospect. What they have in common is a degree of certainty that borders on hubris.

Seasoned investors often feel certain about which way the market or various economic indicators will move. But they avoid the temptation to act as if they can foresee the future. No matter how sure you feel, sometimes you'll be wrong.

The Theory of Contrary Opinion

The dumbbell indicator is really just a narrow version of the theory of contrary opinion. This theory says you should wait till popular sentiment on the market reaches an extreme, then do the opposite. When everybody is optimistic, sell; when everybody is pessimistic, buy. The difficulty is in spotting those extremes. One way is to survey the published views of stock-market newsletters. But neither optimism nor pessimism ever reaches 100%—especially now that this information is so widely available. In fact, many stock-market newsletters change their views on the market these days whenever they discover they are in the majority.

Recent academic studies on contrary-opinion investing cast doubt on its value. False buy and sell signals are common. The market ping-pongs back and forth between extremes of optimism and pessimism. This is just one more example of an investment indicator that helps, but only if you use it along with everything else you know.

The Spot-the-Sucker Rule

Before you buy any investment, it pays to apply the spot-the-sucker test to it. This test started out as a poker-player's tactic. It works like this. When you sit down to play poker, look around and try to figure out who the sucker is—the player who is hopelessly outclassed by the other players, and consequently is feeding the pot, as poker players say. The sucker's losses make it easy for the more highly skilled players to win.

If you can't spot the sucker, then quit playing. After all, if you can't spot the sucker, chances are it's you.

In legitimate investments, growth in the company and in the economy takes the place of the sucker. This growth is the source of your profit, if any. Where else would it come from?

In options, futures, penny mines and other high-risk speculations, growth offers little if any advantage—certainly not enough to make up for the profits that brokers, promoters and floor traders take out of the pot. The sucker is the options, futures or penny-mines trader who loses. To make a profit, you need to outsmart him, and by a wide enough margin to offset the broker-promoter-floor trader costs.

Mind you, you can get lucky in just about anything, for short periods. But in the long run, most investors lose money in options, futures, penny mines and other high-risk speculations, because these are all set up to make outsiders into suckers.

The Rule of Thirds

Deep down, many inexperienced investors (and some not so inexperienced) harbour a belief that there really are some investors and investment advisors who never make a mistake—who never buy a stock that's headed for a slump, nor sell one that's about to soar.

The truth, of course, is that some of any advisor's recommendations are bound to go sour. In hindsight, these failures (like market successes) are always glaringly, even painfully obvious. Matters are somewhat less clear when you look to the future, however. Both positive and negative factors are always abundant. An advisor has to use his or her judgement to sort and weigh them, and decide if the market price already reflects them all. Nobody has perfect judgement. If anybody did, they'd very quickly acquire all the money in the world.

In fact, most experienced, successful investors will tell you that perhaps only a third of their investments are outright winners in the long term, over the course of several market cycles. Another third are mediocre performers. As many as one third are disappointments, if not outright losers.

Your goal, remember, is not to avoid all risk and all loss, because that can't be done. Instead, what you want is to come out ahead in the long run. That's relatively easy to do, if you stick mainly to high-quality investments, diversify and give your portfolio's inevitable winners the time they need to pay off.

The Rule on the U.S. Presidency

Many investors instinctively root for the Republican party, especially after the market's big rise in the 1980s, under President Reagan. Some assume the Clinton presidency is sure to usher in a period of much weaker stock-price gains. These fears seem groundless, to judge from a recent study by Purdue University professor Keith Smith. He dug through Standard & Poor's 500 records from 1921 through 1992, to judge how the market performed under Republican and Democratic presidents. He found that the market went up in 51 of those 71 years—71.8% of them— and fell during the other 20. The average annual gain was 13%.

A Republican was president in 39 of the years since 1921. The market went up in 28 of the 39 Republican years—71.8% of them. A Democrat was president in the remaining 32 years. The market went up in 23 of the 32 Democratic years—71.9% of them. In other words, the market goes up around 71.8% of the time, regardless of the president's political affiliation.

The average gain under a Republican president was 11.6%. The average gain under a Democrat was 14.1%, 2.5 percentage points better. The market is a volatile institution, however, so much so that this 2.5 point difference is not statistically significant.

Republicans were in office from 1921 through 1932, and the market's average annual gain in those years was just 7.8%. (That includes the rise of the 1920s, and the 1929-through-1932 collapse.) The Democrats took over under Roosevelt in 1933; through the end of Truman's term in 1952, the market rose 15.3% yearly, twice as fast as in the preceding Republican years. In the (Republican) Eisenhower years, 1953 through 1960, the gain sped up to 16.9% a year. In the (Democratic) Kennedy-Johnson years, 1961 through 1968, the market's rise slowed, to only 11.9% yearly.

Under Republicans Nixon and Ford, 1969 through 1976, the market rose only 6.1% annually. Then Democrat Carter got in, and the yearly gain in his 1977-through-1980 term rose to 12.6%. In the Republican Reagan-Bush era, however, the average annual gain went on to 15.9%.

The Republicans seem to reign during the more memorable market setbacks—1987, 1974, 1929. This, needless to say, brings down their average. You could argue, on the other hand, that inflation has been worse under Democrats than Republicans. In any event, differences between the two parties are rather less distinct than you'd expect, from listening to the speeches. Then too, their policies are also constantly in flux. The 1988 Democratic nominee, Walter Mondale, would have felt at home in our NDP; Clinton could pass for a Mulroney Progressive Conservative.

In short, there is no rule.

TECHNICAL ANALYSIS

When I was still in high school, I got a part-time job digging up investment information and making stock-price charts for a technical analyst. I kept it up for seven years. After finishing university, I worked as a technical analyst for several years, for an investment newsletter publisher and later for a stock broker, before becoming *Investment Reporter* editor.

Like most investors, I started out believing that there are investment indicators that give reliable, straightforward buy and sell signals—along the lines of "take chicken out of oven when internal temperature reaches 190 degrees". In fact, most indicators give muddled signals, or are out-and-out meaningless, most of the time. You have to use your judgement to make any sense of them. This is the built-in weakness of technical analysis. It tries to make a science of investment indicators, and it just doesn't work. Mind you, it works from time to time, often for long periods. But depend on technical analysis exclusively and it is sure to let you down, most likely at a time when you need it most.

Fundamentally oriented investment analysts are fond of pointing out that you rarely meet a rich technician (that is, an analyst who uses technical analysis to choose investments). But technical analysis—using stock-price charts and other indicators—can help you understand the fundamentals and can help you spot flaws in arguments based on fundamentals. It can be a help in making investment decisions, but only so long as you manage not to take it too seriously.

Before computers came along, technical analysts mostly drew up charts of stock prices, and looked for trends and patterns that provided a clue to where prices would move in the future. Today, the term technical analysis includes any form of stock-market analysis that disregards company fundamentals—earnings, sales, dividends and so on—and instead looks to an analysis of stock-market transactions for clues to where prices will go.

Technical analysis has great appeal to investors because it seems to offer fixed buying and selling rules that can make a lot of money for them in a short time. The fundamental approach in contrast seems full of contradictions and dreary minutiae. What's more, technical analysts can usually gather all the data they could possibly need. Their charts can go back 100 years, yet be up-to-date on trading that took place this morning.

Fundamental data is by contrast always months behind. It can never be complete because you never know what competitors or the government will do next.

Many technical analysts are purists. They choose to disregard all that tiresome fundamental data about company operations, earnings, dividends and so on. Instead they take it as an article of faith that everything an investor needs to know is "in the charts". Technical purists go through winning and losing streaks, of course. Joseph Granville is a good example of this sort of technician.

He stayed bullish all through the disastrous market slide of 1973-1974. From then till 1982 or so, his market calls were unbeatable. (Not infallible—just unbeatable.) But when stocks started to rise in 1982, Granville dismissed the move as a temporary rally. He stayed essentially bearish for years, though he went through at least one wildly bullish phase, just prior to the October 1987 stock-market crash. In fact, *Barron's* magazine quotes Granville as saying, on August 21, 1987, "Where do we go from here? Straight up."

Mistakes like those take a toll on your results. The *Hulbert Financial Digest* calculates that following the advice in the *Granville Market Letter* would have cost you 93% of your money in the 12 years starting in 1980; the *Digest* ranks Granville dead last in those 12 years among all newsletters it follows. But Granville went back on a hot streak following the 1987 crash.

In fact, for the four and a half years to June 1992, Hulbert ranks Granville's letter as number two on all the advisory services it follows. It shows Granville as having a 256.2% gain in a period when the Dow Industrials rose 96.8%, and the Standard & Poor's 500 rose 92.4%. But Granville's record started to deteriorate once again in March 1992, when he issued a clear and unequivocal sell signal. The stock market went more or less sideways for six months, then resumed its rise.

Technical analysts tend to give clear and unequivocal buy and sell signals, but successful investing is a more careful, gradual business.

Promoters Can Paint the Charts

If you invest in penny stocks, futures or any volatile or speculative investment, it pays to recognize that promoters and floor traders can at times use their own trading to ring the bells that make technical analysts salivate.

Suppose a promoter's stock is at $0.89. An influential chartist says that if the stock gets through $1, it will go to, say, $1.25. The promoter can turn this into a self-fulfilling prophecy. All he has to do is buy enough shares (directly or through associates) to get the stock up to $1.01. When it gets to that price, the chartist and his followers may start to buy. The promoter may be able to sell all the shares he bought, and more besides. Promoters refer to this as painting the charts, and it's one deep drawback of technical analysis.

This is a particularly common risk for part-time futures traders who routinely leave stop-loss orders with their brokers. Professional, full-time commodity traders take advantage of those stop-loss orders when they go "gunning for stops" (see page 169).

The Long-Base Phenomenon

The best way to profit from technical analysis is to combine it with fundamental analysis. One of the simplest and most profitable ways of doing that is to look for stocks that are just starting to come out of a "long base".

Markets get in ruts, just like investors. For instance, the market price of a stock may largely move sideways (though with wide fluctuations) for many years, while change (in the company, or in the market it serves) greatly improves its value. Eventually those improvements have a dramatic impact on share prices. You'll often hear investors refer to this as the long-base effect.

Many investors, chartists and technical analysts especially, gravitate toward conspiracy theories. They use them to explain the long-base phenomenon. For instance, some believe company insiders routinely hold back important news, sometimes for years, while they buy a company's shares at low prices. Then, after they've bought all the cheap stock that's apt to come on the market—after they've shaken out all the weak holders, as conspiracy theorists like to refer to it—the insiders let the news out. Then the stock rises up out of its "base of accumulation" (this is the sideways pattern the stock formed while insiders withheld the good news, and gradually bought or accumulated the stock cheap).

No doubt this happens from time to time, for short periods, on a small scale, but it's an unlikely explanation for the behaviour of a stock like Bell Canada Enterprises (now BCE Inc.) for example.

Bell stayed in the $14 to $22 range (adjusted for stock splits) from the late 1950s through the early 1980s. Then, starting in August 1982, it rose from $17 to $34 in 17 months; later it went on to $45.

Bell stayed in that range for so long because many investors simply fell in a rut. They got used to the idea of selling Bell in the low-$20s and buying it back $5 to $8 cheaper, so they quit examining Bell for changes that would carry it up out of that base.

Meanwhile, however, mail service was deteriorating, but business had growing amounts of information to transport. Technological changes (such as personal computers and modems and, later, fax machines) made it possible to send information over the phone. The long-distance telephone turned for many uses into a reasonably priced alternative to the mails.

To top it off, Bell reorganized in a way that separated its regulated and non-regulated activities. This got it out from under the control of the regulators and gave it greater scope for growth in its profit.

This gives you an idea of the long-base effect. Experienced investors have seen it many times over the years. A stock gets stuck in a trading range for several years, perhaps much longer. Traders fall into a habit of buying near the bottom of the range and selling near the top; impatient investors mark the stock down as a dog, and quit following it. Then, often for no obvious reason, the stock rises up out of its long base. It rises as resolutely as it earlier went sideways.

In an ideal market, we might buy only when prices were ready to rise up out of the base. In reality, this is almost impossible. All we can do is recognize what's going on: the stock has been stuck in a trading range for several years, but its value has meanwhile risen.

Here are some important points to keep in mind when rooting out these long-base stocks:

• Keep price breakouts in perspective. Sometimes a long-base stock reaches an all-time high just a fraction above the highest prices it reached in the past. It may keep going up. Or, it may turn and go back down into the base, especially if the market as a whole enters a sinking spell. Here, as always, it pays to buy gradually.

• Look for improvements in value while prices go sideways. These can come from company gains, improving industry conditions, or both.

• The long-base effect is just a tool. No way of picking investments is foolproof. However, knowing how long bases work helps you spot stocks with high reward potential and limited risk.

• Often the public perception of a stock changes after it rises up out of its long base. Up till the late 1970s, investors thought of Bell Canada as "Ma Bell"—a dullard utility. By the early 1980s, however, after Bell's share price had doubled, analysts and journalists began referring to Bell as "the telecommunications-based conglomerate".

• Not all long-term trading ranges turn out to be long bases. A sideways trend in the price of the stock may mirror the trend in the stock's real value. (In fact, sometimes a stock's price goes sideways while its true value goes down.) For that matter, there's nothing to stop a 10-year trading range from going on for 10 more years. Buying long-base stocks while they are still in the base calls for a great deal of patience.

Two Ways to Profit from a Long Base

Patient investors can profit by buying a stock only after it rises up out of a long base. But by then, some of the gains have already occurred. Or, you can buy while the stock is still in its trading range, if you think it is ready to rise up out of it. The second approach pays a bigger percentage return—though the return may take longer to arrive than you care to wait.

Stocks that have stayed in a trading range for a number of years often make several false starts before rising up out of it. You have to choose the approach that's best for you. But buy gradually, with the long term in mind, and you'll raise your chances of making money.

One key to successful investing, after all, is to match your investments to your investing temperament. If you buy stocks that are inappropriate for you, you're apt to feel tempted to sell them at all the wrong moments. For instance, wringing the maximum profit out of long-base stocks calls for a lot of patience.

Keep in mind that the high end of a long base, or long-term trading range, can hold a stock back for years, even as it makes fundamental progress. In fact, it may seem at times that a stock in a long-base pattern is trying to goad you into selling. It's as if it wants to rid itself of all the impatient shareholders and would-be free riders, before finally breaking out and rewarding the stalwarts.

Use the Pendulum Rule

One technical analyst's rule of thumb that's worth knowing about is the pendulum or round-trip rule. It goes like this: when a stock hits a new high, then falls sharply, then rises sharply and gets above the old peak, it should get as far above the peak as it fell below it. Say, for instance, that an $8 stock rises by $5, to $13, then drops by $2, to $11. When it starts to rise, you might expect it to get back up to the peak of $13. If it breaks through that $13 peak, it should continue on up to $15, according to the pendulum rule.

It works much the same in reverse. Suppose a stock starts out at $15 and gradually falls to $5. Then it shoots up to $7, but its rise quickly falters, and it still looks expensive on fundamental grounds. In that case, it's apt to head back down to $5. If it breaks below $5, the pendulum rule suggests it could go on down to $3.

Like a lot of chart-readers' rules, this one is highly unreliable. At best, it gives you a basis for making what you might refer to loosely as an informed guess. This, if nothing else, is better than no guess at all.

The Four-Strikes Rule

Another chart-reader's rule that can be helpful is the four-strikes rule: when the price of a stock (or a market index, or a commodity) hits a given high or low four times, chances are it will eventually break through that level. That's why "triple tops" (when a price hits a high level three times, but fails to rise through it and instead goes off on a major drop) and "triple bottoms" (when a stock bounces off a given low three times, then launches a major rise) are common. But "quadruple tops" and "quadruple bottoms" are rare.

A stock may touch the level a fourth time, then dawdle for months before rising or falling through it. Like any trader's or chart-reader's rule, this one works best when you combine it with the fundamentals.

MUTUAL-FUND INVESTING

Stock-market investing on the one hand, and mutual-fund investing on the other, used to be a little like sheep and cattle raising in the Old West—you did one or the other, but never both. These days, though, more and more investors seem to own stocks and funds. That's apt to work better than investing in funds alone; familiarity with stocks can help you make the most of mutual funds. But you need to understand the limitations and drawbacks of investing in funds.

Recently, for instance, a friend told me he's thinking of selling all his stocks and putting the money into "the top mutual funds". He says that if he'd done that years ago, he'd have made an extra percentage point or two every year, and he'd have had more time for golf.

The trouble is that fund leadership changes from year to year, just as in the stock market. Predicting next year's leader is as hard in funds as it is in stocks.

Then too, many funds with superb 10- or 20- or 30-year records made most of their gains in their early years, when they had less money to manage. (When fund management companies launch a new fund, by the way, they sometimes feed it easy profits—from their share of hot new issues, for instance. This builds the so-called "incubator" fund's growth record, and makes it easier to sell. If the strategy backfires—if the fund buys too many new issues that go sour—the fund manager may simply merge the new fund with another fund.)

Peter Lynch, author of *One Up on Wall Street*, had an average annual gain including reinvested dividends of 28% annually over 10 years when he quit managing the Magellan Fund in 1991. He started out in 1981 with less than $100 million, and he made his biggest gains in the first few years of the 1980s bull market. That spurred new sales of Magellan. When he quit, he was managing $13 billion.

As the fund grew, its performance became more and more average, more and more like the markets in which it invested. It "regressed toward the mean", as a statistician would put it. Mr. Lynch still beat most of the star fund managers of the early 1980s, however. Many lost all their early gains, and more besides. But in any event, Mr. Lynch no longer manages any funds that are open to the public.

John Templeton is the world's best-known and most successful mutual-fund manager. He got started just before World War Two, when he simply bought all stocks traded on the New York Stock Exchange at less than $1. Many of these buys went broke, of course. But many others were fine companies that had been beaten down unduly by panic selling.

If you invested $10,000 with Templeton in 1954, when he launched his Templeton Growth Fund, and reinvested everything since (presumably paying taxes out of pocket), you'd have holdings worth $2 million by 1992. That's the fund world's top performance over that period.

However, Templeton has raised its fees, which will cut into performance. More important, Mr. Templeton is 80. He remains in charge at the Templeton funds, but he has sold his mutual-fund management company.

Mutual Funds and Darwin

On average, money managers underperform the market by 1.3 percentage points a year, according to a recent study published by the

Brookings Institution. (If you weight those results by the amount of money in the funds, the average yearly underperformance doubles to 2.6 percentage points. In other words, the bigger funds do worse.) But you'd never guess it from looking at the records of today's funds. That's because there's a Darwinian process at work—today's funds are the survivors. Poor-performing funds never die. Instead, they get taken over by healthy funds. When two funds merge, they go by the better performer's record. In fact, it's possible for a superb 20-year record to be made up of a series of individual heydays by predecessor funds, each of which lost money for most of its investors.

Superb performance over a shorter period—several years, say—usually means the fund manager gambled and won. Specialized funds are in business to do just that, presumably because they can do a better job than individuals can do on their own. The Fidelity Group's Select Biotechnology Portfolio was the top North American fund in 1990, with a 44.4% gain. In 1991, it had a 99.1% gain. In the first half of 1992, the fund's value fell 20.2%.

Investors who got in at the start of 1990 more than doubled their money. However, most got in a little later—the fund had assets of $70 million at the start of 1990, and $1.1 billion by the end of 1991.

Mackenzie Financial's Industrial Growth Fund was one of the top performers among Canadian mutual funds in the late 1980s. In the early 1990s, its performance put it within the bottom 10% of all Canadian funds.

Mackenzie fell behind other funds because it stressed resource stocks. It concentrated on the biggest and highest-quality issues, mind you—Alcan, Inco and Noranda are some of its biggest holdings. But resource stocks have lagged behind the rest of the market, and this has undermined its performance.

Mackenzie's resource favourites have begun to stage a comeback. But you can't be sure Mackenzie will stick with them long enough to profit. After all, mutual funds do change their investing strategy from time to time, just like individuals. After a long period of soggy performance, both kinds of investors are liable to make an abrupt change at just the wrong moment.

Whether you buy stocks, funds or both, your best bet is to invest in a balanced, diversified portfolio, with some money in each of the five main economic sectors. If you hold Industrial Growth, treat it for now as part of the resource component of your portfolio. But you'll have to monitor its holdings. That way you'll know if the fund makes big changes in its portfolio, which will have an indirect effect on yours.

Generally speaking, you should look for funds that equal or beat the average fund consistently, but not spectacularly. No one can beat the market spectacularly every year without taking a great deal of risk. Eventually, taking risks catches up with you.

Keys to Mutual-Fund Profit

Here are some key points to keep in mind if you decide to devote part of your portfolio to mutual funds.

• Disregard extraordinary short-term performance. If a mutual fund's value shoots up 50% in a year when the market as a whole rose 5%, it may mean the fund manager stumbled on some extraordinary opportunity that escaped the notice of the rest of the industry. Similar opportunities will be hard to find. This may lead the top-performing fund manager to take extraordinary risks, if he hasn't done so already. Risks like that eventually backfire. Unlike the fund's early investors, new buyers won't have that initial 50% profit as a cushion. Then too, extraordinary short-term performance leads to a second problem (see below).

• Avoid funds that have undergone a huge expansion of their assets. Many mutual-fund investors swarm to the top performers. If the manager of a $25 million fund earns 50% for his investors one year in, say, biotech or junior oil and gas stocks, he may find he has $300 million to invest the following year. By then, the top-performing stock group that gave him the 50% yield may be at a peak. He'll still have to put most of the $300 million in it—he'll have to buy at the top, on other words. If stocks in the hot group go into a swoon and drag down the value of the fund, investors who flocked to it may leave just as quickly. This forces the manager to sell at the bottom.

• Keep an eye out for unannounced changes in your funds' investing strategy. As the market rises, after all, investor expectations rise along with it. Pressure for investment performance becomes ever more intense. Today's top funds are out-performing the market by using much the same tactics as the top performers or so-called "gunslingers" did, back in what used to be called the "go-go era" of the 1960s. These investment tactics mostly qualify as mistakes when ordinary investors indulge in them. Eventually, they always backfire.

They include concentrating rather than diversifying your investments. Another tactic is to buy lots of new issues. Another is to buy thinly traded stocks in large enough quantities to push up their price and create a paper profit.

Another is to buy mineral-exploration stocks (or what investors used to call penny-mining stocks, back when they traded for pennies instead of dollars). You compound the error if you focus on the promoter's stock-selling abilities, rather than on the company's geological prospects. You may wind up investing in remote and exotic locations far from the eyes of busybody skeptics, where anything may seem possible.

All this increases the risk, no matter how smart the fund manager. Even if your fund manager can spot the right time to sell, finding a buyer for mutual-fund sized lots of low-quality investments may prove impossible.

AUTOMATIC DIVIDEND REINVESTMENT PLANS

ardeners have a saying: "The best time to plant a tree is 20 years ago. The next best time is right now." You can say the same thing about automatic dividend reinvestment plans (sometimes referred to as DRIPs), particularly those that provide a cash investment option. Participating in these plans can make a big improvement in your long-term investment returns. They have two big advantages: they reduce your brokerage commissions, and they provide a framework for systematic saving and investment. You might think of automatic dividend reinvestment as "a bank account that works".

The time-honoured route to amassing capital (whether to retire, go into business or save for your children's education) is to make regular deposits in a bank account. This puts compound interest to work in your favour. After a decade or two, even insignificant-by-themselves deposits start to add up to real money.

The outcome of this kind of savings program depends on several factors: interest rates in the bank account, the rate of inflation, and your tax situation (after all, you have to pay taxes on your interest income). On the whole, this approach paid off nicely in the 1980s, because interest rates stayed above inflation. It's much less profitable nowadays, however, because interest rates are so much lower. (Long-term interest rates are still above inflation, but they are below the average return on stocks of 10% or so per year.) It will prove even less rewarding if inflation revives and jumps up above interest rates. In that case you'll be better off with another approach.

This is to select a small group of high-quality stocks and buy additional shares in them on a regular basis. The drawback to the second approach is a lack of flexibility. The minimum commission at most brokerage firms is now $50 or more. So if you invest, say, $500 at a time, you immediately lose 10% of your capital. You sidestep these problems with stocks that offer an automatic dividend reinvestment plan with optional cash investment. Brokerage commissions, if any, are negligible.

Recent market prices (generally the average of the past 5 or 10 trading days) determine how much you pay for the stock; there is no bid-asked spread. You can invest any amount you wish, within plan limits. The plan will credit you with fractional shares. In short, this "bank account that works" has most of the advantages of making steady deposits in a bank account. It will almost certainly provide you with a higher long-term return.

Stocks are riskier than bank deposits, of course. But choose your stocks wisely and they'll give you a hedge against inflation, which may pose a greater danger later on in the 1990s than it did in the 1980s. One drawback in this sort of portfolio is a shortage of dividend-reinvestment plans that offer a cash option. Right now, however, you can build a balanced, diversified portfolio of high-quality stocks that offer dividend-reinvestment plans with a cash option.

Keep Balance in Mind

When you choose stocks for your DRIP investment portfolio, you should pay as close attention to sectoral balance as you do to invest-ment quality. Aim at having some representation in your portfolio from each of the five investment sectors.

Then you need to buy at least one share in each company and get it registered in your name. Companies that have a dividend-reinvestment plan will usually mail information about the plan to you after you regis-ter your shares, and let you know if they offer optional cash investment. (This lets you pay cash for additional shares, within limits, when you reinvest your dividends.)

You can of course speed the process by writing to the company and asking for a dividend reinvestment-plan application form. You can find out if a company offers automatic dividend reinvestment by looking in its annual report (check the inside back cover).

Your Broker May Stall

Sometimes the hardest part of automatic dividend reinvestment is get-ting your broker to register shares you already own in your name, so you can get started. Some investors tell me their brokers have simply ignored repeated requests for share registration and delivery.

Brokers have nothing to gain by co-operating. They stand to lose future brokerage commissions, especially if they register shares in com-panies that offer optional cash investment. What's more, the brokerage firm may have lent your shares to a short seller; in that case, the firm profits from the interest on the proceeds of the short sale. Before it can deliver your shares, it may have to recall them from the short seller.

If the short seller is an active trader, he or she may generate far more commission income than you do.

Obviously the broker has to deliver the shares to you eventually, and most will do so promptly. If you have asked several times without results and with no explanation for the delay, your next step should be to write your broker a letter. State the dates of your prior requests, and make one final request with, say a two-week deadline, for delivery of the certificates registered in your name.

State in the letter that if you don't get the certificates, your next step will be to contact the Securities Exchange Commission, and the action-line columnist in your local newspaper. Send a copy to the broker and his or her branch manager.

This will get some action in virtually all cases. While waiting, you should look for a new broker.

After all, investors who want to join a dividend-reinvestment plan will pester their brokers until they get the certificates. Then they'll take their business elsewhere, meanwhile telling all their friends what shabby treatment they received. You have to question the judgement of a broker who would ignore this simple request.

The broker you want is one who will strive to earn your business in areas where he or she can serve you best, rather than stalling you when you can go elsewhere for a better deal.

Treat Them Like Cash

When you ask for registration and delivery of share certificates, some brokers will simply deliver street certificates to you. These are share certificates that are still in the last owner's name. But the former owner has signed them on the back, which makes them negotiable.

Depending on how you look at it, this is either a money-saver or a nasty trick. The signed-off certificates are almost like cash. If they are lost, stolen or destroyed, you may be able to recover little if any of their value. On the other hand, some brokers now charge $25 to $50 to register shares in your name. However, you can take a signed-off share certificate to a trust company and have it registered in your name for free. (Until you do so, dividends will continue to go to the last registered owner.)

How to Break the News

An investor I know told me a while ago that she wanted to participate in a dividend-reinvestment scheme, but didn't have the heart to tell her broker, who is nearing the end of his career, that she no longer required his services. And she couldn't think of any other reason to ask for her share certificates.

She plans to reinvest several thousand dollars worth of dividends, and add $10,000 to $20,000 to her portfolio every quarter. Doing so through her broker would involve needless expense, especially since he charges top rates.

One way around a situation like this is to ask for the certificates to be registered in your name and delivered to you because you want to leave them with your bank. (You'll want to keep your share certificates in a secure place, such as a safe-deposit box at a bank, even after you've registered them in your name.)

Your broker may assume you need the certificates as loan collateral. He or she may offer to arrange a margin loan for you. Margin lending is of course a brokerage-firm profit centre. In that case you could simply repeat your request, and tell your broker that you've already made other arrangements, and that you have promised to provide the share certificates.

If You Can't Trust the Management...

Recently, a friend asked a question that may trouble many investors. He wondered if dividends reinvested in DRIPs go to buy shares in the market, or if DRIPs are just a corporate device for watering the stock. (That is, issuing new shares faster than the company can grow, so that the value of existing holdings is diluted over time.)

Some companies that offer DRIPs issue new shares. Presumably these companies can put the money to good use in the business, if only to pay down debt and reduce interest costs. Others use DRIP funds to buy shares regularly in the market. Others buy large blocks of shares periodically, when they come available. Some do so to "manage" the stock price—avoid a slump when a block of stock comes up for sale. Note, though, that if the stock yields 4%, and 20% of the total shares are enrolled in the DRIP, this will at most raise the total of shares outstanding by 0.8% a year.

If a company is a worthwhile investment, it's immaterial whether it buys DRIP shares in the market, or issues new ones. You can assume it will act in the shareholders' interests.

If it's not worthwhile investment—if it lacks trustworthy management, or a sound balance sheet, or an established business with a reasonably healthy outlook—then the source of DRIP shares, and the possibility of 0.8% yearly dilution, is the least of its shareholders' worries.

How to Put a DRIP in Your RRSP

One investor I know holds her self-directed RRSP with her broker. She asked her broker if she could enroll her RRSP stocks in a dividend reinvestment plan. He assured her this was impossible.

It's impossible if you hold your RRSP with a broker. After all, the broker doesn't make any money on the $100 or whatever that he charges each year for a self-administered RRSP. Most of that goes to the trust company that actually holds the investments in the RRSP. The broker acts as the trust company's agent, to earn commissions when you buy or sell securities.

The solution here is simple: deal directly with a trust that offers self-directed RRSPs. (This makes the registration and delivery much easier: you fill out an RRSP transfer form for the trust company, and it handles the matter from there.) However, you'll need to stay on top of the fee structure, which may change frequently, and with little notice. You wouldn't want to pay $15 to reinvest a $49 dividend cheque.

DRIPS Are for Long-Termers Only!

Two questions often come up concerning DRIPs: "How do I sell?" and "What do I do with the odd lots I bought while in the plan? Odd-lot commissions will eat up most of my profit."

DRIPs exist to sell shares to you, not to buy them back. When you want to sell, you notify the trust administering the DRIP that you want your holdings (all or part) delivered to your broker. Then you handle sales in the usual way.

In Canada, odd lots are always costlier to sell than round lots (which are 100 shares and multiples thereof, for most stocks). You may not be able to sell fractional shares at all.

If the company's DRIP lets you invest cash along with your dividend, you can invest just enough to top up your DRIP holding to the nearest multiple of 100 shares. Not all DRIPs allow additional cash investment, of course.

The best way around this odd-lot problem is to invest in a company and enroll in its DRIP only if you think you might want to hold its stock indefinitely. That, however, is good advice even if you don't plan on reinvesting your dividends. You'll change your mind in many cases, of course, but the "indefinite hold" is what you should look for.

Notes on Taxes and your DRIPs

• Tax treatment of dividends from eligible Canadian companies is the same, regardless of whether you spend the money or reinvest it through a DRIP. You have to declare your reinvested dividends in the usual, grossed-up fashion, and you receive the dividend tax credit. (If you hold stocks in your RRSP, you defer taxes but lose the dividend-tax credit, regardless of whether you enroll your RRSP holdings in a DRIP. You pay taxes on all RRSP withdrawals as regular income, no matter where the money comes from.)

• Remember that dividends from U.S. companies are ineligible for the dividend-tax credit, and are subject to a 15% withholding tax which is a credit against Canadian taxes.

BARGAINS IN WARRANTS AND OPTIONS

Predictions of rising stock prices can lead some investors to look for high-leverage investments—like warrants or stock options, which give you the right to buy stocks (or some other security) at a fixed price, for a fixed period. Warrants cost less than the stock they give you the right to buy. Yet they can produce the same capital gains as the stock, dollar for dollar. So you can get a much bigger percentage rise.

More often, though, warrants produce a smaller dollar-for-dollar gain than the stock they give you a right to buy. That's because you pay for a warrant's advantages. The price of a warrant includes a premium that reflects its low cost and its high leverage. The premium varies with the time the warrant has left till it expires. As time goes on, the premium shrinks. You might say this is the cost that the warrant-holder has to pay for high leverage.

The size of that premium may reflect exaggerated expectations for gain in the price of the stock. In that case, the warrant trades at a higher price than it deserves compared to the stock, in view of the extra risk involved.

Generally, a warrant is only a better buy than the stock when the stock is getting ready to soar. But as any experienced investor can tell you, deciding when a stock is getting ready to soar is a pitfall-riddled process.

Two Steps to Profit

Choosing between the warrant and the stock should be a two-step process. First, make sure you can accept the warrant's greater risk. After all, it is far more likely than the stock to wind up worthless.

If you can accept that risk, you then have to determine if the premium is so high that it wipes out the warrant's advantage in leverage. After all, the higher the premium, the bigger a rise it takes for the warrant to rise more than the stock.

You can use the "E-value" of a warrant to help you choose between it and the stock. This is the percentage rise in the stock that will produce the same percentage rise in the warrant, assuming the premium goes to zero (and the premium will of course go to zero when the warrant expires). Here's how to calculate that E value:

$$E \text{ (in \%)} = \left[\frac{\text{exercise price of warrant}}{\text{(stock price) minus (warrant price)}} \times 100 \right] -100$$

Here's how it works in the case of BCE Inc. and its warrants. These warrants give you a right to buy one share of BCE for $45.75 until April 28, 1995.

That $45.75 exercise price, as it's called, is above BCE's current share price of $44. It's cheaper to buy the stock in the market than to exercise the warrant, in other words. If BCE shares stay below $45.75 until April 28, 1995, this warrant will expire worthless. This seems unlikely, but it's a risk you take in these or any warrants.

If BCE rises just 4% in that time, from $44 to $45.75, its warrant will drop 100%—it will be worthless when it expires. If BCE shares rise 10%, to $48.40, the warrant's intrinsic value will drop 56%, to $2.65 (that's the difference between $48.40 and $45.75).

Mind you, this BCE warrant may go through a speculative flurry—a temporary expansion in its premium, and rise in its price—before it expires. But that's flimsy support for an investment decision. You do know, after all, that the premium will evaporate by the time this or any warrant expires.

With BCE at $44 and the warrant at $6, its E-value works out like this:

$$E \ (\text{in } \%) =$$

$$\left[\frac{\text{exercise price of warrant (\$45.75)}}{\text{stock price (\$44) minus warrant price (\$6)}} \times 100 \right] - 100$$

$$= \left[\frac{45.75}{38} \times 100 \right] - 100$$

$$= [1.204 \times 100] - 100 = 120.4 - 100 = 20.4$$

So, E = 20.4%.

An E value of 20.4% means a 20.4% rise in the stock between now and expiration will produce an equal rise in the warrant. A 20.4% rise in the stock would take it to $52.97, and a 20.4% rise in the warrants would take them up to $7.22. At expiry, the warrant is worth the stock price minus the exercise price, if we ignore commissions. That's $52.97 minus $45.75, or $7.22. If the stock goes up more than 20.4%, the warrant will rise by a larger percentage.

The E-value calculation tells you that you need to be able to foresee at least a 20.4% rise in the price of BCE shares before you'd even think of buying its warrants. Even then, the stock may be a better buy.

You need to balance the differences in risk when choosing between the stock and the warrants. Hold on to BCE long enough and you are almost certain of getting out with your initial stake, if not a substantial capital gain. Meanwhile, you'll earn an interest-equivalent yield of 7.5%. On the other hand, the warrant has no income and its risk ranges up to a 100% loss.

If you must buy a warrant, BCE's warrant is an attractive choice. But most investors are better off buying the stock.

Two Overlooked Ways to Play Warrants

Many investors look on warrants as a cheap way to profit from a stock price rise. In fact, warrants are often more expensive than they ought to be. But warrants also offer a chance to make a fast but risky 200%, and help in deciding when to buy the underlying stock. Warrants generally come into existence as a sweetener to a new stock issue. You might pay, for instance, $10.50 for a unit made up of one share at $10, plus a warrant that gives you the right to buy one additional share at an exercise price of $10 for perhaps three years.

Many new-issue investors buy with the intention of selling after a few months—sooner, if share prices begin to fall. Some, though, make a practice of holding onto the warrants (especially if the stock is up enough that selling the stock alone gives them back their entire initial outlay). They may do so because they feel the stock will go higher in the long run, and drag the warrant's value up with it. Or they may hold because selling the warrant would scarcely raise enough money to pay the broker's minimum commission (though some brokers will cut their own commissions when a regular customer sells, say, 200 warrants worth $0.50 each). So the warrant enjoys something of an artificial scarcity—a scarcity that has little to do with its value as an investment.

The warrant may also enjoy unduly high demand. It costs less than the stock, so more investors can afford to buy. As a result, warrants often trade at artificially high prices during the first few years of their lives. That is, they trade at prices that leave the buyers little room to profit, as you can see if you run through the E-number calculation.

These factors go into reverse toward the end of a warrant's life—during its last six months or so. Investors who have held since buying the new issue begin to sell while they can still get something for the warrants. Buyers dwindle, because the warrant's short remaining life begins to outweigh its low cost.

Meanwhile, the warrant's dwindling lifespan can depress the price of the stock. Investors recognize that if the stock is even slightly above the exercise price when the warrants expire, holders of the warrants will exercise them, and large numbers of new shares will come into existence. Most former warrant-holders will sell, because owning the stock ties up more capital than owning the warrants.

Long-term investors recognize this and may wait till after the warrants expire to buy the stock. This pent-up demand often begins to push a stock's price up shortly after the warrants expire, if few of those warrants get exercised.

All this suggests two ways that you can "play" warrants. Sell them short during their last six months—or, wait till they expire, then buy the stock.

Selling the warrants short is more complicated, more risky—and more profitable, when it works as you hope. Warrants often lose 100% of their value during the last six months. Since you only put up half the value of a security when you sell it short, you can make 200% on your outlay—400% a year—on a 100% drop. But your broker has to be able to borrow the warrants before you can sell them short. If the owner of the warrants decides he wants them back, and if no other warrants are available for borrowing, you'll have to "buy in"—cover your short sale by buying the warrant in the market. Then too, your broker may call the warrants back and force you to buy in simply because his or her in-house trader or a more favoured customer wants to sell short.

If this happens to several warrant short-sellers at once, it can lead to a classic "short squeeze": You and other forced-to-buy short sellers can wind up bidding against each other, and pushing the price of the warrants to outrageous levels.

Short-term trading—that includes all short sales, but selling warrants short especially—is only for investors with strong nerves and a strong sense of market timing. You have to seek out little-noticed short-selling opportunities. But understanding how warrant expirations influence stock prices can make your long-term investments far more profitable.

Why Options Are Riskier than Warrants

Generally speaking, a warrant is a security that gives you a right to buy shares at a fixed price, for a fixed period. Warrants are generally issued by the company itself, or by another company or investor that owns a block of the shares and wants to sell. Ordinarily, warrants start out with a lifespan of at least a year, and several years in some cases.

Stock options come in two varieties. One of the two—calls—closely resembles warrants. Calls give you a right to buy at a fixed price, for a fixed period. But the period is usually much shorter—in many cases less than nine months (though brokers are now trying to spur interest in long-term calls, called LEAPs, with a lifespan of several years).

The other variety of options—puts—give you a right to sell at a fixed price, for a fixed period. You profit if the stock goes down, rather than up, though only if the stock falls enough to exceed commissions and the premium.

Generally, you'll find that option premiums on puts and calls, on average, are high enough to eliminate your chance of making a profit. On the whole, in fact, it pays to stay out of options. You may have heard that some non-professionals regularly make money in options. This is a financial version of an urban myth, like the mysterious hitch-hiker who disappears out of your back seat when you're on the highway, or the lady who exploded her rain-soaked poodle by drying it off in her microwave. Most options players lose money eventually, sometimes much more than they ever planned to risk. That includes institutional players. Mutual funds that dabble in options mostly wind up losing money, or making less than they would have if they had simply stuck to stocks.

Put Time On Your Side

In the stock market, after all, time works in your favour. That's the difference between stocks and options. If you choose healthy companies, buy shares in them gradually and wait long enough, you're bound to make money.

In options, time works against you. An option's price reflects a reasonable estimate of how the underlying security will perform during the option's short, fixed life. Outsiders rarely earn a high enough return in that short period to wind up with a profit, after paying commissions and the spread (the difference between bid and asked prices, which is the pro traders' profit).

If you must trade options, do it as rarely as possible. Worthwhile opportunities in options turn up around three times per decade.

Optioned stocks often expire "on the nose". One big drawback with options trading is that the traders who deal in options also trade the stocks. This gives them some influence over the prices of the stocks that the options give you a right to buy or sell.

Take, for instance, the calls (options to buy) and puts (options to sell) on BCE at $45. Chances are some large traders have "written" or sold both puts and calls on BCE. These traders have an incentive to do what they can to ensure that BCE closes at $45 on the day those options expire. That way, both the calls and the puts expire worthless. That's a big difference from the outcome at, say, $44 1/2 (at that price the $45 BCE puts would be worth roughly $0.50, or $50 per 100-share option), at $45 1/2 (at that price the $45 calls would be worth $0.50, or $50 per 100-share option).

The big traders can try to make BCE close at $45 on the day the options expire by selling some BCE shares if the stock is just above $45, or buying if it is just below.

Some smaller traders try to profit by selling options when the stock is close to the exercise price, hoping the options expire worthless. This is a risky business. (After all, companies at times come out with market-shaking news just before a series of puts and calls expires.) When that happens, the seller of an option can end up with a loss of several hundred dollars or so per option, rather than a $25 or $50 profit.

Score One for the Bulldozer

You can compare unconventional but high-yielding investments to plucking pennies out of the path of a bulldozer; it seems so easy, until your arm gets caught.

Selling "naked puts" is a good example. When you sell puts, you give the holder the right to sell stock (or some other security or commodity) to you at a fixed price, for a fixed period. When you sell them "naked," it means you aren't bothering to offset your obligation with, for instance, a short sale.

Selling naked puts got to be a popular and, for a while, profitable pastime for some investors in the 1980s. Stock prices kept rising, so most puts were worthless when they expired. So, the price the seller got (minus commissions, of course) was pure profit. Then came the October 1987 stock-price crash; some puts sold for $0.25 a week before the crash, but quickly rose to $10 or $20 when prices fell.

Something similar though less dramatic can happen to investors who put money in commodity-trading funds. They make a series of worthwhile gains, then go through a loss that relieves them of their winnings plus most of their initial stake. If you make 40% yearly for two years, for instance, then lose 50% in the third year, you are losing 2% of your money even before you consider commissions, management fees, tax implications and so on. If you lose 75% instead of 50% in that third year—this is by no means unusual in commodity funds— you are left with less than half your original stake, even before you deduct fees, brokerage commissions and taxes.

Most commodity funds are trend followers: they buy what's going up, and sell what's going down. That can pay off for a time when commodity prices enter a strong trend up or down. Often, however, commodity prices move sideways for long periods. At times like that, trend followers are sure-fire losers. At such times, commodity prices put on a series of false starts—rising enough to suck in buyers, then falling enough to shake out the buyers and lure in some short sellers. Commodity funds can easily lose a third of their capital in, say, four months when that happens.

Remember the Spot-the-Sucker Rule

It all comes down to the spot-the-sucker rule that I talked about a few chapters back. When you sit down to play poker, try to spot the sucker— the outclassed player who spends most of the evening losing. The sucker's losses make it easy for the more highly skilled players to win. If you can't spot the sucker, stop playing, because chances are it's you.

This poker-player's tactic applies even more to options. That's because a friendly game of poker is what a mathematician would call a zero-sum game. The losers' losses equal the winners' profits; add them up and the sum is zero.

Options trading is worse than that. It's a negative-sum game. The winners' profits fall short of the losers' losses, because the house (brokers and floor traders) take their cut off the top, just like in commercial gambling. You can only win by outsmarting the other participants by a big enough margin to overcome the house edge. You can get lucky in just about anything, for short periods. But in the long run, most investors lose money in options, futures, penny mines and other high-risk speculations, because these are all set up to make outsiders into suckers.

SHORT SELLING PAYS OFF

ost investors profit best by investing in a portfolio of high-quality stocks. They buy them gradually, during their working years, and they retire in comfort. They generally resist the urge to invest or speculate in any way that calls for them to outsmart other market participants. If you are going to speculate, however, one of the best ways to do so is as a short seller—that is, a trader who sells borrowed stock in hopes of buying it back after a price drop, and profiting from the difference.

Short sellers found 1991 a painful year. One survey shows the average short-selling partnership lost 25% of its capital in 1991. Some lost 40% to 50%. This compares to a gain of 13% in the Standard & Poor's 500 stock index. Losses continued in 1992, and many prominent "shorts" gave up and turned into buyers.

Quite a comedown! The average short-selling partnership gained 100% from September 1989 to the end of 1990—a time when the Standard & Poor's 500 lost just 6% or so. Since then, though, most short sellers made two big mistakes.

First, like many investors, the shorts overestimated the damage that the Gulf War was apt to do. (They disregarded the minority view we offered at *The Investment Reporter*, that Iraq was a war-weary, spottily developed country whose army was apt to crumple rather than triumph.) Worse, they failed to take into account that the low stock prices of year-end already reflected lasting Persian Gulf problems. The market needed more trouble to stay down. Instead, its troubles began to clear up.

Second, the shorts strayed from what they know best. The shorts' most profitable targets are stocks that suffer from unquestionable but widely ignored drawbacks: huge debt, misleading accounting, technological innovations that don't work and so on. As 1990 wore on, however, most stocks answering that description had already collapsed. So, many shorts moved on to what most investors would agree are respectable stocks—banks in particular.

As 1990 ended, prominent shorts no longer trumpeted glaring faults; instead they began to harp on matters like lagging housing completions and overoptimistic loan write-offs. You might say they started out like the child who proclaimed that the emperor was naked, and wound up like the boy who cried wolf.

This shift came to something of a climax in November 1990. That's when Warren Buffett, known in investment circles as the "Sage of Omaha", bought 9.8% of Wells-Fargo, the eleventh-biggest U.S. bank. (Mr. Buffett is one of those rare self-made billionaires who got rich buying stocks for himself, not selling them to others.) At the same time, the Feshbach brothers' short-selling partnership had begun shorting Wells-Fargo.

I pointed out at the time that the Feshbachs were still in their thirties and had only been in the investment business since 1981. I also pointed out that the Feshbachs, like most successful short sellers, had up till then made money shorting penny-stock promotions with little in the way of earnings or assets. Wells Fargo was unfamiliar territory for them. In contrast, Mr. Buffett made his fortune by buying top-quality stocks at depressed prices. Wells Fargo qualified on both counts. (Within a few months, the price of Wells-Fargo shares more than doubled.)

The Buffett/Feshbach division of opinion was a common one late in 1990. The old-timers saw value, the newcomers foresaw disaster. Short selling became fashionable in 1990, especially among relatively inexperienced investors. But successful shorting takes more work than investing. After all, short sellers don't receive dividends (which can supply, remember, up to a third of your long-term investment return). Quite the opposite—they have to make good on any dividends paid by stocks they've shorted. What's more, time works against them. Thanks to inflation and economic growth, the long-term trend in stocks is upward.

Stock-market weakness like we had in 1990 spurs dumb shorting. One prominent U.S. advisor revealed that year that he was personally shorting Citicorp, the banking concern. He might ultimately have made money, if Citicorp had run into the kind of troubles that afflicted many savings-and-loan associations around that time. But Citicorp was yielding more than 10%, and showed no signs of wanting to cut the dividend. Within 4 months, Citicorp jumped 60%.

Another well-known advisor suggested shorting Procter & Gamble, one of the most successful corporations on this planet. His rationale? Procter & Gamble was selling at 17 times its 1989 earnings, and had a weak chart pattern! Procter & Gamble rose 50% in the next year and a half.

Shares of established, profitable, dividend-paying companies do sometimes go down enough to justify the risk of shorting them. But it happens only rarely. What's more, they are first to rise in a market rebound.

If you plan to sell short, avoid quality at all costs. Stick to stocks you'd never buy, such as most Vancouver Exchange issues. Choose those whose share prices have doubled or quadrupled on flimsy predictions of corporate profit that never seems to come. The Vancouver Exchange is a particularly fruitful place to look for short-sale candidates. You might call Vancouver the "night of the living dead" exchange—all too many stocks trading there are not so much alive, as merely animated by promotional voodoo.

Old-timers refer to these as "greater fool" stocks: the only way you make money buying them is if a greater fool is willing to pay even more than you did. Ultimately many of these stocks wind up worthless. This inherent lack of value works in the short sellers' favour. It can make up for a great many short-selling errors.

Here, as in conservative investing, you need a portfolio approach. Some of your picks are bound to disappoint you, by going on to even more ludicrous prices.

Tell Juniors from Junk

Successful short sellers, like successful speculators, have to develop a knack for distinguishing juniors from junk. A junior is a small business, or a young one that only went into operation a few years ago, that has significant assets per share (even if the shares trade at two or three or more times the value of assets per share). It may never have made any money. The key, however, is that it's in business—it has begun doing the sort of business in which it intends to specialize. That way it at least gets some feedback from its targeted market.

The main business of stocks that deserve to be called "junk" is self-promotion. Some have few if any customers. Yet they may have toll-free phone numbers and full-time staff whose job is to lure investors into buying the stock. You can spot junk stocks by their four-colour, glossy investor-relations materials; reports from multi-billion dollar firms look shabby by comparison.

It takes little more than a glance at the financial statements to tell juniors from junk. Confirmation comes a few years later. Juniors have at least a chance of prospering. Junk almost always winds up worthless. But by then it's too late.

The key to successful short selling is to target companies that are likely to fail to live up to their shareholders' expectations. That's easier to do if you concentrate on companies whose promotional efforts inspired unrealistic expectations in their shareholders. Look for short-selling targets that have a history of high hopes and little or no profits.

Short Selling Has Big Advantages

Selling short has undeniable advantages over other kinds of speculation.

For one thing, you can deposit T-bills as security for your short-selling obligations, and you continue to earn interest on them.

Another point in favour of the shorts is that, on average, stocks fall twice as fast as they rise (though they rise around two-thirds of the time). So short-selling profit can come quickly. Yet many investors lose money as short sellers. They go short in high-quality stocks, simply because prices seem too high or the trend seems to be down. I can't stress the basic principle too much or too often. You should always buy high-quality stocks—those with assets, an established business and so on. Sometimes you have to sit through temporary losses because you bought when prices were too high, or because the stock-price trend was down. But even if your timing is off, their investment quality works in your favour. Coupled with economic growth plus inflation, investment quality makes up for a great many investment errors. In the same way, low investment quality works in a short seller's favour.

The Shorts Have a Bad Image

When stock prices fall, short sellers have always been the favoured scapegoat of government and business. This is nonsense, of course. Short selling is never more than a small part of stock trading. It can only provide a very short-term market depressant. Intelligent short sellers, in fact, act as a moderating influence on long-term stock price cycles. After all, they sell when prices are high. They "cover" or buy back when prices are low.

Many people mistakenly believed short selling brought on the 1929 stock-market crash and contributed to the Depression. Afterwards, short selling came under growing restrictions around the world.

The Nazis banned the practice outright. The U.S. and Canada made short selling difficult, but not impossible. Today, a short seller's broker must first borrow the shares from one of his or her own accounts or from another broker, then sell them on an "uptick", the brokerage term for an upward price change.

Short selling is only for the experienced investor who is in constant touch with an experienced broker. Generally it is more likely to pay off when prices on the whole are weak or falling. Even the most grossly overvalued dog can move higher when the market generally is soaring.

Stock-price trends can change with stunning swiftness, however. Short sellers should protect themselves by scrupulously limiting losses.

Many successful short sellers cover any short that rises more than 10% to 15% above the selling price. Successful short sellers generally restrict their short sales to two groups of stocks—well-known, listed stocks that are volatile, actively traded and under investor suspicion because of weakening industry conditions or a heavy debt load; or, low-quality junk whose moment of glory seems about to fade.

Unlike obscure or thinly traded stocks, shares from either of these groups are easy for your broker to borrow for you. They are also easy to repurchase if they start to rise.

Many investors who are otherwise suited to short selling find the practice philosophically distasteful. They feel that a short sale is a bet on depression and human misery. However, short sellers perform a socially useful function. They make money only by shorting stocks that are headed down anyway. This lowers their prices that much sooner. It means misinformed investors pay less if they make the mistake of buying these stocks. This cuts their potential loss. On the other hand, successful short sellers still have to buy back some day. If they buy back when prices are lower, they will raise the prices received by others who are selling at or close to the bottom.

When you think about short selling, keep it in perspective. Think of the short sellers in the grain market, for instance. If they are buyers, you may condemn them as hoarders who expect a scarcity of food, and hope to profit from it. But grains short sellers are optimists. They are betting on bountiful harvests, low-priced food and full bellies around the globe.

Short Selling Is Risky

Some investors' thoughts always turn to short selling way too early, while stocks generally are still headed up. These investors look on selling short as the reverse of buying. That's arguable, and only up to a point. Beyond that point, the nuances can kill you.

When you sell short, remember, your broker has to borrow the stock. If the original owner sells, you may wind up having to buy it back on short notice. If that happens to you and a number of other shorts all at once, prices can soar, as you and all those other forced-to-cover shorts bid against each other. Buyers run no such risk.

Still, many traders and investors love to sell short, because the action comes quicker. If you join them, it pays to follow what you might call the "old-tiger approach".

You can't short indiscriminately. Instead, look for a low-quality and evidently promotional issue that is running out of steam. The best short sale you can find is a Vancouver penny stock that has gone to several dollars or more per share with the aid of glossy brochures, inflammatory news releases and a lot of unofficial, word-of-mouth touting.

The economics of such a short could hardly be more favourable. You, like the promoter, are selling securities that have little or no intrinsic value, but you do so without sharing in the promoter's expenses. (He pays for the press releases, the touts and so on.)

However, shorting these stocks too soon is going to cost you money. Promotions gain enormous momentum as they go up. Often they hit ludicrously high prices before they begin what may be a stunning collapse. Better to wait till the promotion has lost its vigour. If the stock market as a whole is headed for a setback, so much the better. In that case your potential profit remains enormous, but risk falls drastically.

When stalking a short sale, take as your model the canny tiger who lives to an old age. He knows better than to jump the lead antelope in the herd, and risk getting trampled. Instead he sits in a tree and waits for the herd to pass. Then, at the last minute, he jumps down and feasts on a straggler.

Leveraged Investors, a Natural Target

Short sellers perform a socially useful function. They help to deflate promotional stock issues. When well-established companies are headed for the skids, short sellers sell them short, then try to bring their problems out in the open. As a side effect, this helps steer average investors away from danger, which helps limit their potential for loss. But remember, shorts perform these socially useful services from purely selfish motives. They target stocks that are vulnerable for any reason.

Many brokers set a minimum margin price level. These brokers refuse to lend money to clients who want to buy stocks trading below this level. You can't buy them "on margin", in other words. You have to put up the full purchase price. Stocks that investors have bought on margin and that are close to the minimum margin price level are a natural target for short sellers. If the shorts sell enough of a stock to force it down below the minimum margin level, investors who hold the stock on margin have two choices. They have to put up more money, to pay off their margin loan, or they have to sell. Many choose to sell.

Often a real plunge occurs when a stock breaks below the minimum margin level. Sometimes, though, the minimum margin level proves to be a turning point. In fact, it's a positive sign when a stock briefly breaks below the minimum margin level, then starts to rise. If short sellers get a stock down that far and it fails to bring additional selling into the market, they (and other interested investors) may conclude the stock has gone as low as it is apt to go. Sometimes the shorts and other investors begin buying then.

It pays to remember this and other traders' lore when you decide what stocks to buy or sell short, and when. But keep in mind that all this can give you is a hint of what to expect, not a sure-fire answer.

HOW TO PICK A BROKER

When you select a new broker, my advice is to practise age discrimination. When it comes to brokers, older is better. The first question you should ask a broker who wants your business is, "How long have you been a broker?"

If your prospect tells you how long he or she has been "in the business", ask what part of that was in sales. Some people spend a decade or two in a broker's accounting department or back office, then move into sales to break out of a career or income rut. Some move into sales only because computers have eliminated the job they used to do, and the alternative is unemployment. For all the investment knowledge they acquired before going into sales, however, many might as well have worked at General Motors.

Your worst bet is a young broker who is eager and/or naïve enough to believe everything he hears about investing from his sales manager or any other source. He's like an investor with a comparable lack of experience and scepticism, but lacking as well in one key moderating factor: if something goes sour, it's not his money that disappears, only his client.

New brokers have to start somewhere, of course. So, wish them the best but let them learn the trade by practising on somebody else's account.

Your best bet is the sort of broker that young and eager colleagues in some firms refer to—with a mixture of respect, affection and disdain—as "a senator". This is someone who has been working as a broker for 20 years or more. If he or she has lasted that long, it's probably because of developing a keen interest in avoiding losses by stressing investment quality. This broker rarely wins sales contests (these may confer cash, vacations or the title vice president). He or she sometimes loses clients' money—investing involves some risk, after all. But a senator mainly loses clients when they withdraw from the market. That's because the senator's clients have been through several younger and less experienced brokers, and they know when they are well off.

Is Your Broker Prejudiced?

No, it's not your imagination: brokers' analysts do indeed make a habit of recommending shares in their underwriting clients, even when they don't have a new issue to sell you. This, at least, is the conclusion of a University of Michigan study of analyses from 54 brokers, covering 256 companies, between 1983 and 1986.

The study divided the reports into two piles: those from brokers that act as underwriters to the companies under study, and those that don't.

It turns out that analysts were significantly more optimistic about companies who were underwriting customers of their employers, than of companies that took their underwriting business elsewhere. When they analysed their firm's underwriting clients, they came out with higher earnings forecasts, and more favourable recommendations (buy instead of hold, strong buy instead of buy, and so on).

The analysts were unbiased in one respect: they treated their firms' underwriting clients equally. They looked as favourably on small clients as on large ones, even though the large clients produce bigger underwriting profits.

Possibly this gave the underwriting clients a warm and cosy feeling. But it appears investors were sceptical. The study also found that unbiased forecasts—those from brokers uninvolved with the subject companies—had a much bigger impact on stock prices than reports from brokers who were touting the shares of their own underwriting clients.

Switch, Sue or Go Discount

Rightly or not, many investors feel much of the advice they received from brokers in the 1980s was inappropriate, even without the benefit of hindsight. Many of these investors left the market late in the decade. As they return to it in the 1990s, many plan to switch their business to discount brokers, more to avoid bad advice than to save money on commissions. Before you join them, you should consider whether another full-commission broker would be a better choice.

After all, many investors gave little thought to choosing a broker in the 1980s. Investing seemed too easy to make it worthwhile to shop for a broker. Meanwhile, many inexperienced people became brokers, strictly because they could make a lot of money at it. They didn't especially care for the investment business, so they didn't learn any more about it than they had to.

The too-busy-to-shop investor and the in-it-strictly-for-the-money broker just naturally found each other, often at great expense to the former. Now, however, most brokers who treated their clients shabbily in the 1980s have left the business. The average broker today is more experienced, and better able to look after his or her clients' needs. If you stuck around through a period of low income (a common problem for brokers up till around 1990) it means you enjoy the business. So you are apt to pay more attention to what goes on in it, and do a better job for your clients.

If you shop for a broker today, your efforts are likely to pay off much more than they would have in the mid-1980s. Then too, most brokerage firms have become more flexible in their commission charges. Depending on how much trading you do, switching to a discounter may only save you a few hundred dollars a year. That's a worthwhile saving for some investors. It's a false economy if your experience or time is limited, and if dealing with a discounter would leave you vulnerable to costly mistakes.

From time to time, however, some investors feel they should do more than simply switch. They want to get even—financially and emotionally—through the courts. Suing anybody is a costly, time-consuming and often fruitless process. This is especially so in disputes that come out of dealings like those you have with a broker. These usually come down to one person's word or memory of what happened against another's. Often, though, a reputable brokerage firm will go out of its way to placate any investor who has a legitimate gripe. After all, lawsuits lead to bad publicity.

The brokerage firm will probably begin by stonewalling you. It has to determine that you are serious about your claim. You need to show the firm that you will take the matter further if you don't get the satisfaction you seek. Once you've done that, the firm might offer to refund all or part of the commissions you paid. It may even offer to make good on all or part of your losses.

Much of course depends on the individual case. The investor's sophistication, the suitability of the investments or transactions that the broker recommended, and the broker's record will all make a difference.

In any case, the best thing to do if you have a grievance with your broker is to start by complaining to the branch manager. If you don't get satisfaction there, go on to the national sales manager. If that fails, address your complaint to the president of the company. Meanwhile, ask friends or the provincial law society to recommend lawyers with experience in claims against brokers.

Most lawyers active in this area will listen to your story at little or no cost. They will tell you if they feel your claim is worth pursuing. They'll give you an idea of the costs and so on. However, a letter from a lawyer will sometimes spur a broker to offer a settlement. Meanwhile, look for a new broker. Do so with as much care as you'd put into choosing your largest investment.

When Brokers Say Hold

When attempting to follow your broker's advice, it pays to know the language. Generally speaking, brokers improve on their less-than-complimentary advice by one notch, possibly to avoid offending a potential underwriting client. So, "buy" means buy. But "OK to buy" or "weak buy" probably means hold. A mere "hold" recommendation, on the other hand, probably means take profits or switch. When you get down to "OK to hold" or "weak hold", the analyst means sell. When you get to "swap" or, worse yet, "sell", the analyst is trying to tell you to sell immediately.

I try to make our *Investment Reporter* advice—buy, sell or hold—as straightforward as possible. (In *The Investment Reporter*, by the way, hold is a compliment. It's a recommendation we'd offer on as few as 10% of stocks trading in Canada.) Some investors find it hard to break the reading-between-the-lines habit that they developed during years of following their brokers' advice. Years ago, for instance, I used to alternate the wording on our buy recommendations between "buy" and "purchase", just for the sake of variety. I stopped using "purchase" after hearing from a number of readers who wanted to know which of the two was the stronger recommendation.

Bugging Your Broker

Of the many conflicts of interest that exist between an investor and his or her broker, the most visible is: how much service are you entitled to?

Obviously this depends on the brokerage commission you pay in a typical year. Most firms give their registered representatives 25% to 50% of their gross commissions, depending on the firm's prestige, the broker's position in the firm and the support—in services, promotion and so on—that the firm provides.

If your commissions total $100 a year, your broker may get to keep $25 to $50 before taxes. He or she may feel this entitles you to no more than, say, one 90-second phone call per month for quotes, except when you plan on placing an order. It's hard to cast blame; brokers have to make a living. If your commissions total $1,000 a year, on the other hand, you should expect and get more service.

You're better off to avoid the temptation to call for quotes. Instead, put your share of your broker's time to more productive use, such as getting background information on stocks you own or want to buy.

Many investors who are just starting out expect brokers to woo them early on, so that they'll feel compelled to stay when their portfolios grow large. However, brokers recognize that no matter how well they treat their customers, a certain proportion of them will leave each year. This will happen for a variety of reasons. Some will leave because a friend or relative has gone into the business. Others will die, or move away, or sell their stocks to buy a house or business, or switch because of some real or imagined slight, offence or error.

If you want more attention than your commissions entitle you to, the best way to get it is to become so well informed that your broker seeks your advice as you seek your broker's. This gives him or her a reason to call you. But that's among the smallest benefits of becoming well informed. After all, doing so is also apt to propel you that much sooner into the ranks of sought-after investors with big portfolios who can't help but pay high commissions.

Beware the Glib Broker

A person who's glib doesn't necessarily know what he or she is talking about. This is doubly true of brokers. Nowadays brokers have to be glib just to get hired. Many brokerage firms, especially the bigger ones, now recruit sales people the same way life insurance companies do, then give them rudimentary investment training.

The first hurdle these prospective stockbrokers have to pass may be a stress test—a simulated real-life situation with stock tickers clacking in the background, and repeated phone calls from unhappy and abusive clients. The prospective stockbroker with a calling for investments but a short fuse is going to fail.

So your broker's equanimity while the stocks he or she sold you are falling apart may be due more to genes or upbringing than to a grasp of the situation. If your broker tells you something doesn't matter and you shouldn't worry, it may pay you to ask why, rather than simply accepting this reassurance, however calm and well polished it may be.

When Your Broker Doesn't Want Your Business

Brokers I know tell me that their industry is attempting to freeze out so-called small investors, and get rid of brokers who serve them. At one time, virtually all brokers got to keep 33% or more of all commission dollars they generated. Now the commission-payout schedule or grid is more complicated.

At one brokerage firm, brokers get 20% to 50% of commissions on orders that bring in more than $65—depending on their total commissions for the year, including commissions below and above $65. But they get nothing from commissions below $65 (it's $75 at some firms). In short, a flood of "small tickets" can boost the percentage a broker earns on his or her bigger orders. But a broker who only writes small tickets has zero income.

This leads some brokers to try to spur their clients to trade in larger quantities—regardless of the client's finances or objectives. When investors flocked to BCE's sale of its TransCanada Pipelines holdings a few years ago, for instance, some brokers refused to fill orders for fewer than 500 units. Brokers see this as simple good management—a way to curb losses and make a better return on assets.

You may see this as short-sighted, even insulting. But the fact is that brokers now have less time for anybody but their richest customers. Here are three keys for living with the situation:

• Only call your broker with a buy or sell in mind. Rely on the newspapers and cable-TV for stock quotes. Join or start a discussion group or investment club if you want to discuss the market. If the business you do only entitles you to five minutes of your broker's time each month, save it for when you need it.

• Educate yourself. Learn as much as you can about investing. That way you'll be able to read brokerage research reports critically, rely more on your own judgement and transact your business while taking up as little of your broker's time as possible. (You may of course decide to switch to a discount broker.)

• Find a broker who appreciates your business. As I said earlier, your best bet is an experienced broker—a senator, if you can find one. But if you are just starting out with limited funds, you may have to deal with a broker who is also just starting out and eager for every penny of commission he or she can bring in. After all, small tickets help pay the firm's overhead, even if the broker doesn't make any money. This has obvious disadvantages for you. But an inexperienced broker may be able to provide you with the services you need.

The Cheating Broker

The Association for Investment Management and Research, a U.S. trade group, surveyed 900 U.S. and Canadian investment analysts in 1992 about breaches of ethics in the investment business. It received 400 responses—55% from analysts working at investment institutions, 40% from brokerage analysts.

The results of the survey show something less than an immaculate record. This, though, should be about as surprising as, say, your local newspaper's annual exposé of auto mechanics' overcharges. We've all known from childhood that a strong personal code of ethics is a common human attribute, but by no means a universal one.

The best way to protect yourself from cheating brokers is by following these rules and caveats.

• Start by only accepting advice from, and dealing with, people and organizations you trust. Choose a broker from stock-exchange member firms only. Don't deal with so-called security dealers, who mainly sell penny stocks.

• Before dealing with an individual at the firm you choose, tell him or her about your goals and finances, and judge the response. Use what I call "the encyclopedia-shopper's trick": ask a question about an investment you're familiar with, so you're in a good position to judge the answer.

• Avoid acting on predictions. Investment advice tainted by self-interest often takes the form of predictions. When you choose investments, stress investment quality and diversification. That's good advice in any case; like I keep saying, predictions are the weak link in the investment process. This leads to my final caveat.

• Think long term. Every time you switch investments, you leave yourself open to acting on tainted or self-serving advice. Look for investments that you expect to stick with more or less indefinitely. You still need to follow their progress and get rid of those that fail to meet your requirements, but if you do as little buying and selling as possible, you'll minimize occasions for being taken advantage of. You'll also pay less in commissions and lose less to the bid-asked spread. This, too, is a good idea in any case, regardless of the motives of those you deal with.

PROMOTERS AND PENNY MINES

No investment book published in Canada would be complete without a chapter devoted to penny mines. But the best advice for almost all investors is to stay out of pennies. Instead, confine your investing to companies that are actually in business and have sales, earnings, or better still, a record of paying dividends. If you can't do that, then at least weigh the odds against you. If you still want to play the pennies, then limit your penny-mines investments to funds that you can afford to lose.

As editor of *The Investment Reporter*, I often hear from stock promoters who want me to recommend their penny-mine and penny-industrial stocks. Many start out by wanting to come to our office to make a presentation. Or they offer to take me out to lunch or dinner. I counter by telling them to send a pack of their investor-relations material—quarterly and annual reports, news releases or whatever.

An immense quantity of paper comes into the office this way. Rarely, very rarely, I'll come across something I can recommend in another of our publications that caters to aggressive investors, though it may need several years of seasoning before I do so. Far more often, what I see is a stock that is, at best, at the conceptual stage of its existence.

In other words, the company has a concept. This may be a mineral property, a business plan or an invention. But it isn't in business. It has little in the way of sales, much less earnings. Most concept stocks never progress beyond the concept. The concept is there to attract investors, not to be carried out.

The promoter may try to portray his or her company as the next Xerox. Even if that were true, you could afford to wait until the company went beyond the concept stage, and began making some money. Xerox was a great buy all through the 1950s and much of the 1960s. If I were to stumble across the next Xerox today, chances are it would remain a great buy throughout the 1990s, and possibly into the double-0's as well.

Most of the conceptual stocks I hear of offer about as much quality as Hawk Resources, which I mentioned briefly in Chapter Four. Hawk would have been just another Vancouver Exchange penny mine, and its promoter, Guy LaMarche, just another anonymous voice on the telephone. But it happened that Mr. LaMarche knew a young woman who worked in our office. She described him as her friend and mentor. She asked if he could come in and tell me about Hawk, in the summer of 1986. At that time, I didn't know about Mr. LaMarche's bank-fraud conviction, so I agreed.

Mr. LaMarche was a charming individual, like most successful stock promoters. But the material he gave me on Hawk spoke for itself. The company then had around 1.8 million shares outstanding. It was trading around $4, so the market was putting a value on the company of more than $7 million. (The stock was up from $1 a share in March 1986 when Hawk sold 300,000 shares to the public.)

According to Mr. LaMarche, Hawk's most promising property was the George Martin, a group of 20 claims near Timmins, Ont. This property included a portion—Hawk's material didn't say how much—of another mining property, the Jowsey Denton. Old reports on the Jowsey Denton described it as having "spectacular wire gold in quartz carbonate fissure veins". Wire gold is a prospector's term for thin streaks of gold. Visible gold is always spectacular to the person who finds it. But only rarely is there enough of it in one spot to make money as a mine. Besides, the gold might not have turned up on the part of Jowsey Denton that went into Hawk's George Martin.

The George Martin was promising enough for a Toronto consulting firm to recommend a two-stage exploration program with a total cost of $160,000. (If the first stage came out negative, you wouldn't go on to the second.) Chances were, however, that you could buy an option on a property comparable to the George Martin for, say, $20,000. Hawk also had a property near Cranbrook, B.C. that "covers geologically favorable ground for the occurrence of gold-bearing quartz material", and on which soil sampling had outlined gold and silver anomalies. It had a third property near Hedley, B.C. on which it had turned up "interesting geophysical results", but which "has not been systematically explored".

Both properties were interesting mainly because gold had turned up in the general area. This, however, is true of most Canadian mining claims. You could buy an option on properties comparable to these two for anywhere from a few hundred to a few thousand dollars. In short, Hawk had assets that were worth perhaps $25,000, plus a stock-exchange listing, but it was trading at a price that gave its shares a total value of $7 million.

Mr. LaMarche told me he was promoting Hawk in Europe. Around that time, many institutional investors in Europe had developed a fondness for Canadian penny golds. (Mr. LaMarche was not an officer or director of Hawk—it's best, for public-relations reasons, not to have a convicted swindler on the payroll—and he had no official connection with the company. But he had arranged financing for Hawk, and his sons held substantial numbers of its shares.) I listened to the story and told him that Hawk was not something I'd recommend.

The stock stayed around $4 till the end of 1986, as Hawk issued more shares and acquired more properties. In January and February of 1987, it shot up to $8. Then, at the Prospectors and Developers Convention in Toronto on March 9, 1987, an embittered former colleague of Mr. LaMarche murdered him. Hawk collapsed to below $2 the following week. By the end of 1988, it had worked its way down to $0.11 a share. That's where it is now. It has issued several million more shares since then, and gone up and down several times. But it still hasn't found any mines.

Hawk's performance after the LaMarche murder shows how fragile a stock promotion is. Hawk is another example of a stock with greater fool appeal. Investors who understood what was going on were willing to buy only because they believed some greater fool—in the mid-1980s, the greater fools were mostly European pension funds—would pay a higher price than they did. As a stock promotion, Hawk is unusual; few stock promotions fall apart because of the murder of the promoter. But as a penny-mining company, Hawk is about average. Few pennies get as high at it did in the winter of 1986-87. But that was an extremely buoyant time for the penny market, and Hawk had an extremely capable and experienced promoter.

Few penny-mines players realize how much overlap there is between the worlds of penny-stock promotion, professional swindlers and organized crime. A few penny stocks and their promoters offer investors an honest run for their money. They are the exceptions. But even when the promoter's intentions are honest, most penny-stock investors still wind up losing money.

The Terrible Odds against Penny Mines

Every new mine starts out as what geologists call an anomaly—a geo-chemical or geophysical indication that there is something under the ground other than the usual, worthless stones and dirt. As a highly general rule, one anomaly in 1,000 yields a showing—an actual mineral find. But only one showing in 1,000 turns into a mine.

You get an idea of the odds against you in penny-mine investing when you keep in mind that most pennies have little more than an anomaly to recommend them. In many cases that anomaly is next door to a showing, or down the road from a former producing mine.

You can try to narrow the odds against you by sticking to pennies that have come up with a showing—that have found some valuable mineral on their claims. It helps, too, to confine your penny-mines investing to those that have a geologist as chief executive officer, rather than a promoter.

The funny thing is that this kind of penny rarely costs more than others that have anomalies only, and a fast-talking promoter in charge.

The typical $0.50 mining stock may have 2 million or more shares outstanding, say, so the company as a whole sells for $1 million. Yet its main asset may be a mineral prospect that has a market value of, say, $25,000. To break even, you need a mineral find on the property that improves its value by 40 to 1. The odds are anywhere from 100-to-1 to 1000-to-1, if not far worse, against making that find.

Fewer than 1 penny in 10 has what I'd call geological value: this is a realistic chance, however remote, of having a mineable-at-a-profit deposit on the property. Seasoned investors do sometimes dabble in pennies, of course. But they look on it more as recreation than investment. They limit the funds they devote to pennies to money they can afford to lose.

When Pennies Fail

An investor just starting out might be excused for thinking that "Consolidated" is the name of a famous geologist. After all, so many small mining and oil exploration firms in Canada carry the name. What has actually happened, of course, is that these firms have "cut back" their shares. They've given their shareholders one "new" share for each 5 or 10 "old" shares they held previously. Penny mining exploration companies often do this after issuing 5 million or 10 million or 25 million shares and spending all the money they've raised without finding a mineable mineral deposit (that is, a mineral deposit that can be mined at a profit).

The process leaves them with so many shares outstanding that nobody wants to buy any more. But after a share cutback, these firms can begin issuing new shares, for cash or to acquire property. But the value of an old penny-mine holding always suffers in a cut-back.

After a one-for-five share consolidation or cut-back, your five $0.20 shares won't turn into one $1 share. Instead they may turn into one $0.30 share. That's because investors recognize that penny mines consolidate their shares because they haven't found anything of value.

Many small firms have gone through a series of share consolidations over the years, but on the second cut-back, they drop the "consolidated". So Moose Pasture Mines cuts back one for five, and becomes Consolidated Moose (or, perhaps, simply New Moose); after a second cut-back, 5 or 10 years later, the name might change to, say, Mopast Enterprises.

Consolidations take many forms, but they all mean the same thing: the company has too many shares outstanding; the market is thin because hardly anybody wants to buy, so the promoter can't sell new shares to raise cash. Afterwards the market may be able to absorb more newly issued shares. But the value of current shareholders' holdings will have dropped 25% to 75%.

Contain Your Enthusiasm

Investors often get excited about a penny-mining prospect when it releases news of a rock sample or drill core that assays out at, say, 0.5 or more ounces of gold per ton. However, raw assay results can mislead you, especially where gold is concerned.

Gold often turns up in isolated nuggets. A gold nugget the size of a match head can make an enormous difference in the value of an assay. But it may be the only gold for miles. Here are five rules to keep in mind when you consider assays:

• Pay little attention to "grab" or "chip" samples. These are samples of rock that a prospector or geologist picked up at the property because they looked as if they might contain some gold. They are by no means representative of the property's geology. No matter how rich they assay, they say little about the likelihood of finding a mine.

• Consider depth and thickness. A 20-foot-thick layer of rock with 0.05 ounces of gold per ton, at five feet below ground, may be mineable at a profit. A two-foot layer of 0.8 ounces-per-ton may be worthless at 400 foot below ground, especially if nearby rock is barren.

• Consider location. One of the big advantages of the Hemlo deposit is that it's within sight of the TransCanada Highway. Few undiscovered ore bodies will turn out to be so rich or well located.

• Consider the people. This is essentially a negative pointer. If you have any doubts about the integrity of the people involved, stay out. On the other hand, you need more than an impeccable reputation to make a worthwhile investment. No amount of honesty can make up for a lack of ore in the ground. Success in business takes more than the lack of a criminal record.

• Remember metallurgy. After you find the ore, you have to have an economical way of getting the gold out of it. For instance, a Toronto-listed company, Ican Minerals, found a huge but low-grade gold ore body in Idaho. However, its gold recovery was never high enough to justify the capital cost of putting the property in production. Higher gold prices can of course cure this problem by fattening the company's profit margin.

However, pollutants can present a greater problem, depending on who's downwind. Another penny mine, Pan American Minerals, turned up 3.71 million tons of rock grading 0.17 ounces of gold and 1.72 ounces of silver, plus 2.15% lead and 4.04% zinc, in a property 20 miles north of Revelstoke, B.C. However, the property's assays also show 4.86% arsenic. This is a highly toxic element and one that is expensive to remove.

It takes a series of successful judgement calls to tell a mineable gold deposit from the many unmineable properties than can yield a few rich drill holes. When in doubt, remember that gold is valuable mainly because it's rare. No matter how good a deal you feel you've uncovered, it always pays to diversify, because many things can go wrong.

Beware Superficial Investment Appeal

Gold turns up on many U.S. and Canadian mining claims, but rarely in the quantity you need to make a profitable mine. Yet every year, penny-stock promoters trumpet the presence of gold on their properties. They try to make their gold find seem much more valuable than it really is. Often they do so by confusing these three types of rock sampling:

• Surface samples. Surface-sampling efforts, including grab and chip samples, vary widely in cost and in what they tell you. Some surface-sampling efforts amount to what an amateur prospector might accomplish on his or her day off.

Promoters can report only their richest surface samples, if they choose. Penny-mines players need to keep reminding themselves that you can find gold in many remote parts of this continent, but you'll hardly ever find enough to cover mining costs and leave a profit.

• Diamond drilling. This involves moving a diamond-drilling rig costing many thousands of dollars to the site, and boring two-inch-diameter holes into the earth. This is substantially more expensive than surface sampling. When diamond drilling turns up gold, it's far more significant than gold in a surface sample. Still, many gold-rich diamond-drill samples turn out to be flukes.

• Bulk underground sampling. This involves going underground (through an existing tunnel or shaft, or a newly dug one), and extracting rock samples weighing hundreds or even thousands of pounds. Now you are talking about serious exploration. But you are still a long way from certainty.

As a mining prospect progresses through these three stages, risk falls and the odds of turning the prospect into a mine improve. Stock prices often rise as well, which limits your profit. As a general rule, the odds to the investor improve substantially when a company goes beyond surface sampling.

Even when all indicators say the company has a mineable ore body, production—and profit—is still a long way off

In the midst of the excitement that a few good drill holes can generate, it's easy to overlook the many steps—and pitfalls—that stand between finding a mineral deposit on the one hand, and turning it into a mine.

The transformation from "find" to "mine" is often a circuitous one, and a longer one than investors expect or promoters suggest. After you find the deposit, you have to deal with metallurgical problems (that is, how you'll extract the mineral from the ore). Then you face regulatory problems (getting government approval, often from more than one level or agency of government). Then you have to secure the financing and so on. This can uncover structural or other obstacles that you overlooked at earlier stages.

All through this process, messages from the promoter will overflow with optimism. Most promoters, mining promoters especially, are delighted to spend their investors' money on the development of a project, regardless of its prospects for success. What's important for the promoter is the flow of news that gets his or her stock into the news and into the hands of investors.

Most mining operations, but underground mines especially, need high capital expenditures to go into production. Outlays in the $10 million to $50 million range are not unusual. A mine operator may need to find, say, 15 million tons of ore to justify that great an outlay. If the mine operator only finds 10 million tons, the project could stall indefinitely.

It's for Bankers, not Investors

At times, however, a high-grade core can make the property mineable. This is a section of the ore body that is easily mineable, or has a higher grade or metal content than the rest of the deposit. Finding a high-grade core lowers the threshold level that separates a mine from a mere prospect. It makes it easier to arrange financing.

For instance, suppose a penny mining company finds a deposit with 10 million tons of rock grading 0.12 ounces of gold per ton, at a depth of 400 feet. That may only be marginal, depending on a number of factors, but it may become economical to mine if the company also comes up with a million tons, grading 0.3 ounces, within 50 feet of the surface. In fact, the million tons of 0.3 near surface may make the property feasible to mine even before the operator is certain of 10 million tons at depth.

This high-grade core will pay for the initial capital costs—the access tunnels, mill and so on. Operating costs are a lesser factor, at least as far as lenders are concerned. Mining is always a risky business. Banks and other lenders are only willing to get involved if they see evidence that the operation has a high chance of recovering its capital costs. Once they're in production, some mine operators go on to find substantially more ore than they started out with. However, the company may find it runs into insurmountable problems after it mines the high-grade core.

In fact, many mining projects go through all the stages of exploration and production, doing all the right things all along the way, and still wind up losing money. This can happen because the project runs into unexpected costs or problems, or simply because the ore in the ground turns out to have less gold in it than earlier work suggested.

Heap Leaching a Pile of Stones

Heap leaching is a low-cost chemical process for extracting gold and silver. It can, in some cases, take the place of conventional mining, with its costly grinding, heating and concentrating.

Essentially, a heap-leach operator piles the ore in a heap and pours a cyanide solution over it. The cyanide solution leaches the gold and silver out of the rock. A second chemical reaction separates the cyanide from the metal.

Cyanide is a poisonous compound of nitrogen and carbon. Dead birds tend to litter a heap-leaching site in dry areas, because they have drunk some of the cyanide solution. So heap-leaching projects understandably run into opposition from environmentalist and animal-rights activists. But unlike other mining by-products such as arsenic, cyanide breaks down. With time, air and sunlight, it turns into its constituent carbon and nitrogen, which are both harmless by themselves.

Heap leaching has in some cases made a profitable mine out of surprisingly low-grade gold deposits. One company produced gold with heap-leaching costs of $126 per ounce, from ore grading 0.03 ounces per ton. Underground mines using conventional mining techniques may have to pay $200 or more per ounce to mine gold, even though their ores, at 0.2 and 0.25 ounces per ton, are 7 to 10 times richer.

Heap leaching can work with ore grades as low as 0.01 ounces per ton, when the ore and climate are near ideal. It helps if the ore or "host" rock is soft, porous and interlaced with small fractures, so it needs little crushing. Other favourable factors for heap leaching are a high iron content, and little or no sulphur or carbon. Climate is important too. Cold weather, even when the temperature stays above freezing, can shut down a heap-leaching operation, because cold halts the chemical reaction. Rain can dilute the acid solution so much that it slows or stops the leaching process. Some exceedingly low-grade heap-leach operations have succeeded in the U.S. southwest mainly because there is little rain—only two inches or so annually—so leaching can go on all year.

Time is a factor in heap leaching's success. It can take a heap-leach operation four years to recover 70% of the gold in the ore. Capital costs are low, but interest costs can mount when a project runs behind schedule.

In short, heap leaching makes some low-grade gold deposits mineable at a profit. But heap leaching can't work miracles. Mineable gold is still a rarity in nature. Most "penny golds" won't find any gold, no matter what the promoter says, and even when they find gold, they may still lose money and go broke.

Galactic Mines was among the most successful penny-mine promotions of the mid-1980s. Its shares soared from pennies to nearly $20 each, initially on hopes for its massive Summitville property. However, that property faced a number of drawbacks. For instance, it was at an altitude of 11,000 feet in the Colorado Rockies. So production was only going to be possible six months a year, at best, because of cold and moisture.

Capital costs were much higher than at other heap-leach properties, because the ore needed additional crushing. Clay and fine material were apparent early on, and were likely to lower Galactic's gold-recovery rate at Summitville. Its ore's sulphur content also presented problems. Galactic's promoter felt that he could overcome these difficulties, and his enthusiasm rubbed off on investors and bankers. They provided Galactic with funds to put Summitville in production, and to get Galactic started on similarly grand ventures in the Yukon, the Philippines and elsewhere.

Summitville turned out to be a money loser. Shutting it down in an environmentally acceptable way also cost a lot of money. Early in 1993, Galactic filed for bankruptcy. This is the fate of most penny mines. Even if they go through a period of successful promotion and a rise in share prices, they mostly wind up worthless.

The Promoter's Job

To succeed as a stock promoter, you need boundless enthusiasm and optimism. These qualities are essential if you want to persuade investors to put money in your project. But they may also lead a promoter to put investors' money in projects that are doomed from the start by any realistic assessment. Sometimes promoters keep throwing money at a project long after failure seems almost certain. If they can maintain investor enthusiasm in a doomed project, they can continue to take money out of it by selling their own shares. (Sometimes, almost certain failure does turn into success—especially in the mining business.)

Keep in mind, however, that no government agency will stop a promoter from putting investors' money in a doomed project. All the securities laws insist on is full disclosure of material facts. The probability of success or failure is a matter of opinion.

One of the few encouraging signs you can look for in analysing penny stocks is a degree of understatement in a company's description of its prospects. If the company underplays its positives and is honest about potential negatives, it improves the odds that surprises will be pleasant.

There will, of course, be surprises. This is true of any young company, but especially those that hope to profit from a mineral find. Geology is an inexact science. No matter how much testing you do, the only way to see if a mineral deposit will yield a profit is to put it in production. As you do so, there's a risk that unforeseen costs will make profit impossible.

A promoter's natural inclination is to underplay the negatives, so as not to discourage potential investors. Many promoters make a habit of threatening to sue anybody who tells investors to sell or avoid their stocks. An enthusiastic promoter is an asset to a young company, because he or she can raise the capital it needs. But too much promoter enthusiasm leaves a stock prone to collapse, if investors suddenly realize its prospects are rather less bright than they hoped.

The Problem with Gold Deposits

Some sizeable gold deposits are impossible to mine. It may simply cost too much to get the gold out. Or production may be impossible because it would hurt the local air, water or scenery. You can improve gold recovery by grinding the ore more finely, or running it through the mill a second time. This, though, raises the capital cost of the project and adds to production cost.

Gold recovery may be poor because the gold in the ore is tied up with sulphur. A roasting circuit and further grinding can enhance gold recovery, but it is sure to raise costs. It can also raise opposition from those downwind, unless you take costly pollution-control measures.

Arsenic, a highly poisonous element, can be a far worse problem, sometimes an insurmountable one. Arsenic and gold occur together so often that prospectors sometimes specifically assay for arsenic when looking for gold. But too much arsenic makes the deposit unprofitable (or politically impossible) to mine.

A number of high-grade, arsenic-laced gold deposits in eastern Ontario have gone unmined for years, because of the certainty of political opposition from Ottawa and Kingston. The owners of these deposits hope one day to find a cheap, environmentally acceptable way of dealing with the arsenic. So far, no luck.

Sulphur, a non-poisonous but polluting element, is present in some gold-bearing rock. It raises costs in conventional ore processing; it can halt the leaching-out of precious metals in a heap-leaching process, by changing the pH of the leaching solution.

Sticking with Penny Mines

Often I've heard from investors who hold stocks they bought years ago, for dollars, that now trade rarely and for pennies. They tell me, "With a property like this one has, I know the stock will eventually recover. Should I buy more?"

A penny stock is a device for raising money. Generally stock promoters acquire a property, then arrange to sell stock to raise funds for exploration. At various stages they get money and/or free or cheap stock for their efforts. If they are successful in raising exploration money, they make money even if investors don't. If it turns out they have in fact stumbled across a deposit that can be mined at a profit, and if they carry it through all the way to production, they make a great deal of money, and are themselves promoted by the financial community from "promoter" to "financier". This is a little like rising from ambulance chaser to Supreme Court Judge.

But this of course rarely happens. Geology is an inexact science; it's worse than stock-market forecasting, since true geological finds are so much rarer than money-making stocks. But many marginal deposits exist. You can compare them to poker hands that are only a card or two short of a straight flush. Buying pennies is, in the long run, like trying to fill an inside straight flush—hoping your next card will make your worthless poker hand a winner. This is what you are up against when you buy a penny stock that is in the early stages of the promotional cycle.

However, the penny stock that had such promise 5 or 10 or 15 years ago may no longer have any claim on the property. It has to do work on the property and pay taxes, otherwise the claim reverts to the government. Meanwhile it can get in debt for office rent, printing and mailing of investor brochures and so on.

Many promoters have what you might call a stable of companies. They can and do shift properties around pretty much at will when the stocks are in the hardly-ever-trade stage. They can put the property in a different company, if only to settle a debt.

Your best approach to pennies is to stick with those that are "in play"—that have active exploration programs planned or, better yet, in progress. Deciding whether to sell or hold a dormant penny is like deciding whether a particular lottery ticket is a winner. No one knows for sure, but the odds are against it.

Buy the Company, Not the Promoter

The penny-stock investing public falls in and out of love with stock promoters the way teenagers do with musicians. When a promoter reaches a certain level of popularity, the merest rumour of his or her association with a penny stock can send it soaring. In fact, some investors advise that the track record of the promoter is the most important factor in a penny stock's appeal.

A vivid example of this rule occurred in 1986, when Adnan Khashoggi's involvement spurred a rise from $0.10 to $22 in Tangent Oil & Gas (it was launching a satellite) and from $0.18 to $18 in Skyhigh Resources (it was buying a Khashoggi oil refinery).

Mr. Khashoggi, a Saudi Arabian financier who made a fortune in arms dealing (and who used to turn up in newspapers from time to time not only as the richest man in the world, but also as a dance partner to actress Brooke Shields, and landlord to former Haitian dictator Jean-Claude Duvalier), was rumoured to have plans for additional Vancouver shell companies. Many investors expected Mr. Khashoggi's next take-over would spur a comparable rise. Shares of several other companies rose briefly on false rumours of Khashoggi plans for them.

This sort of Midas touch often ends abruptly. In late 1986, a U.S. federal-court judge issued an order to stop asset sales by Triad American, a Khashoggi holding company. Triad's creditors charge that it quit paying its bills in spring 1986. Tangent (since renamed Pacific Star Communications) and Skyhigh soon collapsed, like most penny stock promotions.

If you must delve into penny stocks, it pays to look into the people behind them. But you should do so mainly to exclude those with doubtful associations or backgrounds.

Mr. Khashoggi's record shows that a world-renowned entrepreneur can fail as spectacularly as any other stock promoter. The ideal promoter is a hard-working business person you never heard of, who has turned to the stock market to raise money for a business he or she believes in, and who has an impeccable reputation in a small circle. Even so, this ideal promoter can wind up costing you money.

Mine finders

Every year some investors lose money in penny stocks that they bought mainly because some "mine finder" was involved with them. (A mine finder is a geologist who has received credit, deserved or otherwise, for finding an ore body that turned out to be economically mineable.) Mining promoters are aware of the appeal that mine finders have for investors. So they seek them out and try to get one to lend his or her name to the stocks they are promoting.

A mine finder may act as consultant to scores of mining prospects. Geologists themselves recognize that finding a mine is 90% luck and 10% knowledge; mineable ore bodies are, after all, rare. In fact, if you looked at the odds instead of the geology, you'd decide against investing in mining prospects that have a mine finder associated with them, since finding more than one mine is so rare.

Then, too, though one or two mine finders get credit for a discovery, many others have a hand in it. These include the exploration manager, the project geologist, the prospector, even the promoter. What can a mine finder's involvement tell you about a mining firm? If he or she is merely associated with it, nothing. On the other hand, if he or she has invested money in it, or taken a full-time role, then it may be worth a look. After all, mine finders have many jobs and investment opportunities to choose from.

Here are more penny-mine pointers:

• Put geologists' opinions in perspective. When using a geologist's opinions on a penny stock to decide if you should buy or sell it, it pays to remember that the best geological advice can only help you assess the odds of finding a mine. But the price of the penny may already reflect its likelihood of finding a mine. In fact, it may overreflect those odds (depending on the promoter's efforts and skills).

Then too, the success of even the biggest finds remains in doubt until production actually starts. Only then can you say for certain that the property can yield a profit as a mine. An opinion from an impartial geologist neither insures that you will get in on the good deals, nor guarantees to keep you out of the bad ones. It simply improves your chances of a profit.

• Consider the source. We all like to believe what we see in print. This simplifies our day. After all, who has time to question everything they read in the morning paper? But you should question everything you read about a penny mine. After all, there's vast scope for misinterpreting and misrepresenting even the most detailed exploration results. And the stock promotion business has vast scope for profit. These vast profits have corrupted many brokers, advisors and journalists over the years.

Often the reporter who covers the story has no background in geology. His or her only source of information is the promoter. That's all the more reason to demand more than a favourable write-up in a newspaper when you're sifting through potential penny-mines purchases.

• Obey the sell-half rule. Sell half of any penny mine you invest in that doubles. That way you get back your initial investment and eliminate the possibility of a loss. You'll be surprised at how this simple rule will help you improve your penny-mine investment results over a few years.

Don't Lend 'em Money!

A while ago a friend asked about an offer he received from a Vancouver mining company that would give him a chance to buy gold bullion at discounts of 17% or more from current prices. He said, "I believe that if an investment sounds too good to be true, it probably is. Or am I missing something?"

He wasn't missing a thing by passing up this offer. You see deals like this from time to time: fund-raising efforts by penny mines that offer you a chance to buy gold at a discount (in this case, a $50 discount per ounce for 10 ounces, or $68 per ounce if you buy 2 kilograms). The catch is that you pay now, and you only get your gold 90 days later. In effect, this is an offer to make an unsecured loan to a penny mine at an effective annual interest rate of 67%.

When you buy a penny-mining stock that trades on the Vancouver stock exchange, you at least have the option of selling it. Not so for this loan to a penny-mining company. All you can do is hope the company is able to pay you back.

In this particular case, a Texas bonding company appeared to be involved, but not in any way that inspired my confidence. Even assuming the principals are well intentioned, you could lose money any number of ways.

The effective annual interest rate of 67% is a danger sign—a giveaway, you might say. If it sounds too good to be true, it almost certainly is.

Watch Out for Penny-Mines Specialists

I never recommend any particular broker to investors, but I do recommend that they deal only through brokers who are members of the

Toronto or New York stock exchanges. You can still lose money on your investments, of course. But this simple precaution will keep you out of reach of many of the market's worst predators.

In particular, investors should avoid dealing with brokers who are not members of major stock exchanges, who try to sell you junior or penny stocks over the phone. Here are some of the sales tactics they use:

• The six-month set-up. The high-pressure pitch used to begin as soon as you picked up the phone. Now, penny-stock hucksters start by telling you there's nothing really great at the moment but promising to stay in touch. A series of brochures, letters and so on follows. Six months later, another sales person calls to tell you "something great" has turned up, but you have to act quickly.

• The penny-stock disavowal. Penny stock telephone operators used to sell stocks that weren't listed on an exchange; they'd keep anywhere from 50% to 90% of the money. Now they more often buy shares in listed but near-worthless stocks, for resale. This eliminates the need for a prospectus, and lets them claim, "We only deal in listed stocks." It's a more liquid kind of junk, but junk just the same.

• The phantom research department. The sales person refers to "research studies we sent to you" and "our analysts". The research studies are the glossy brochures you received during the six-month set-up; the analysts are other sales people. The stocks these people tout are little more than shells. Most have about as much chance of success as a moon rocket powered by cardboard toilet-paper tubes.

My advice, again, is to deal only with brokers whose firms are members of major stock exchanges. Even then, stick mainly to shares of companies that have some history of sales and earnings.

That Busted Penny

What do you do with that penny stock you bought years ago that is now worth a pittance, if anything?

If it's totally worthless and you need a capital loss to offset a capital gain, then ask your broker to write a note to you to confirm that there is no market for the shares. Then, when you fill out your tax return, record the stock as a sale; enter "zero" as your "proceeds of disposition".

If the stock still has some value, but close to or less than your broker's minimum commission, you can have the shares delivered to you. Then sign them off and sell them to a friend or relative for, say, $1, and enter that sum under proceeds of disposition.

Until you need the loss to offset capital-gains taxes, however, your best bet may simply be to leave the shares in your brokerage account. That way you have a reminder in each monthly brokerage statement of what can happen when you depart from a conservative, risk-averse approach to investing.

Fundamentally, penny-mines' pickings are slight indeed—like combing a public beach with a metal detector. You may hope to come up with pieces of eight, but you'll be lucky to find a nickel. All that I've said in this chapter applies just as much to most penny industrials.

Penny-stock promoters sometimes claim that all great companies start out as penny stocks. That simply isn't true. In fact, most great companies make money for a number of years as private companies. They only begin to think about selling shares to the public when they need money to expand. Early on, their managers and insiders are too busy building the business to have time for stock promotion.

SMALL CAPS AND YOUR INVESTMENT PLANS

S ome investors now believe so-called "small-cap" stocks are your best choices for profit these next few years. These are stocks with a market capitalization below some arbitrary figure, such as $150 million. (Market capitalization or market cap is the figure you get when you multiply a company's stock price by the number of shares it has outstanding.)

Maybe so. But it's a mistake to assume any underlying sameness among stocks with market capitalizations below $150 million, or in any market capitalization range. After all, market cap is only one measure of a company, and a crude one at that. Some small-cap stocks are small but debt-free. Others have lots of debt outstanding, so they're much bigger, measured by capital employed in the business, than their market cap suggests. Some are small but fast-growing companies. Others are former big companies whose fortunes and market cap have been waning for years, even decades.

Some dominate their own tiny or newly formed industries. Often, these are the best small-cap choices you can find, but they don't stay small-cap for long. Other small-cap stocks look like flyspecks alongside their major competitors.

Some academic studies suggest that small-cap stocks consistently outperform large-cap stocks. But the above-average gains that small cap stocks have shown may be due to a few enormous gainers, rather than widespread strength. After all, it's mainly among tiny companies that you are going to find gains of 50-to-1, 100-to-1 or whatever.

This points up a common disadvantage of all stock-picking systems: even when they work, they only narrow down the list of possible investments from, say, 10,000 or 20,000 choices to, perhaps, 1,000. No individual, and few mutual funds, can keep track of a 1,000-stock portfolio.

Picking from among the 1,000 can backfire. The 1,000 will include many mediocre performers, plus a few big winners that give the system its advantage over chance. But the 1,000 will also include real losers. When you try to winnow down the 1,000, you may wind up excluding many of the big winners you need to make the system work, while hanging on to too many of the losers. This can leave you with below-average results, if not losses.

A few huge gainers are apt to turn up in any large group of stocks, remember. But you can't assume that even one of the coming crop of small-cap winners will find its way into your portfolio. After all, the big winners often owe their huge gains to the fact that nobody knew about them when they were cheap. Or, they may have been cheap at their lows because they suffered from enormous negative factors that they have somehow, against all odds, managed to overcome.

Rather than divide all stocks into small-cap and large-cap, you might be better off to divide them up this way: think of stocks, on the one hand, that have managed to tap into and profit off and on from the long-term rising trend in the economy, and are apt to keep on doing so; contrast these with stocks that are still scrambling for a foothold. The former will include many large-cap stocks; the latter, many small-caps.

Small-Cap Season

Small cap stocks do often beat other investments during two recogniz-able periods in a typical stock-market cycle: one comes at the start of a market rise, and the other near its end. This, though, is true of all spec-ulative or volatile stocks, not just small caps.

The value of small-cap investments is less certain and harder to measure than the value of better-established or higher-quality stocks. So their prices vary more—that is, they are more volatile. That high volatility expands all the more near market turns, when the investor mood is changing and the economy offers more sur-prises than usual.

Just prior to a market rebound (like the one that started in the fall of 1990, say), many small caps plunge to unrealistic lows. Nervous or over-extended holders of small caps simply dump them for whatever they can fetch. As prices plunge, trading volume dries up.

When confidence returns, there's a surge of buying in all stocks, including small caps. But that buying surge has a particularly strong impact on the prices of small caps that have been beaten down far below any sort of realistic price range. So, prices of these small caps shoot up, in many cases far above realistic price levels.

A few years later, when the market is nearing what will prove to be its peak, a second shift in investor mood may take place. By then, investors generally have lost much of their fear of plunging stock prices, replays of the 1930s and so on. Some feel it's time for a more aggressive approach to their investments. They take up that aggressive approach by buying small caps. The prices of some of these soar far above reason-able levels. This raises the over-all return on small-cap stocks, even if many small caps get left behind.

The Obvious Question

Why not simply buy small-cap stocks at the start of the rising trend in prices, and again at the end?

If you could spot these major turning points ahead of time, buying small caps would be just one way of profiting from them. You'd make even bigger percentage gains in stock options and stock-market futures.

They provide higher leverage—higher profit potential for a given out-lay—though at a cost of higher risk.

Investing in small-cap stocks can pay off immensely, or cost you money, depending on your stock-picking skills, the overall trend in the market, and your luck.

Small Caps, Secondaries and Low-Priced Stocks

There's a great deal of overlap among secondaries, small caps and low-priced stocks, and even some professional money managers use the three terms interchangeably. Wise investors recognize the differences.

• Secondaries are stocks of companies that are substantial by the scale of their industry, but are not industry leaders. This may be because they concentrate on a narrow segment of the market they serve, or because their costs are higher and/or efficiency lower than the majors. Some secondaries will one day join or displace the industry leaders. Others will wind up selling out to a major, or going broke in an industry downtrend. You can't generalize about them, so you need to take special care in investing in them.

• Small-cap stocks are defined by the total value of the shares they have outstanding, rather than their position in their industry. The small-cap label applies if the company's total shares outstanding, times its current share price, falls below some arbitrary figure (a common one, as I've said, is $150 million). Some small caps are leaders in small indus-tries; others are secondaries; still others are junk.

• Low-priced stocks are, quite simply, stocks whose share price hap-pens to be below an arbitrary figure such as $5, $10 or $20. This is the broadest of these three categories. It's the only one largely under the control of the company. It can split its shares to make them low-priced. Or, it can declare a reverse split (exchange each, say, five old shares for one new share), to cut the number of shares it has outstanding, and raise their price.

A great many companies fall within one or more of these three cate-gories. What the three have in common is above-average risk.

Stalking Winners

Investors generally tend to overestimate the chances of success in small-cap and low-priced stocks, and underestimate the risks. As a result, many of these stocks offer below-average value for your money. What's more, low-priced and small-cap stocks include more than their proportional share of stock promotions: companies whose insiders are more interested in boosting the stock price than in building the business. When searching for winners among small-cap and low-priced stocks, you need to keep all this in mind. You need to exercise extra caution and scepticism.

Still, when you find a small-cap winner and stick with it for a few years, the payoff can be enormous.

WHY IT PAYS TO STRESS DIVIDENDS

A while ago a friend said to me, "I'm now in the top marginal income-tax bracket, and I expect to stay in it for the next couple of decades. Shouldn't I invest mainly in stocks that don't pay dividends? After all, most of my dividend income gets eaten up in taxes. On the other hand, I can avoid taxes on my capital gains with the $100,000 capital-gains tax exemption. Presumably you get higher capital gains when a company reinvests its income instead of paying it out in dividends." It's a mistake to let tax considerations weigh too heavily on your investment decisions. It's an especially big mistake to avoid dividends for tax purposes.

After all, as I've already mentioned, most companies that have a big future start paying dividends early in their life. This trumpets their legitimacy and prosperity, and attracts institutional investors. (Institutions can only invest limited funds in non-dividend-paying stocks.) By investing mainly in dividend-paying stocks, you sidestep most of the market's worst investments. For a while you may miss out on a few high-growth opportunities, of course. But on the whole, sticking with dividend payers tilts the odds a little more in your favour.

Doing so ensures that you'll own a higher-quality portfolio—one that's more apt to include some huge successes over a couple of decades. If you object to paying taxes on your dividends, you can offset your dividend income with a like amount of interest expense on money you borrow to invest.

What Dividends Tell You

Here are some investment rules of thumb that can help you understand how dividends fit in your personal investment performance.

• A long string of dividend payments is an asset. A long-standing record of steady or rising dividends confers investment respectability on a company; this makes it easier for the company to raise capital when it needs to. So, companies that have such a record are loath to cut or halt dividends, even when common sense suggests that they should hang on to the money.

• Companies distinguish between regular and special dividends, and you should too. When a company refers to a payout as its regular dividend, it means that it hopes to keep paying it under most circumstances (though it's not obligated to do so), but isn't making any promises. A special dividend doesn't carry that implication, on the other hand, even if the company pays the special every year for decades.

• A dividend cut may occur just as the stock price hits what will prove to be its low. Spotting the bottom in a stock's price after a long slide is of course a tricky business. However, prices sometimes hit a low when bad news hits a crescendo, and a dividend halt qualifies in some instances.

None of these rules can tell you when to buy or sell. But it pays to keep them in mind when you weigh investing in a stock that pays dividends now, or may do so in the future—and that covers most of them.

The value of steady dividends is something that increases with age...your age, that is, not the age of the dividends.

Most investors start out stressing capital gains over dividends. After all, dividends are only worth 5% or so a year, whereas you can make 100% or more yearly from capital gains. But after a series of the bad experiences that come from seeking out 100%-a-year capital gains, most investors eventually learn to respect dividends.

Over 10 or 20 years, dividends may provide up to a third of your investment return. More important, sticking to dividends may help weed out your portfolio. Companies that are headed for financial trouble are cash-starved long before they lose their veneer of prosperity. When you're behind in the rent, you have little spare cash to fritter away on non-essentials like dividends. For instance, National Business Systems rose from $5 in 1984 to $24 in 1987, then collapsed right out of sight. Many Canadian brokers recommended National throughout its glory years. Investors who insist on dividends stayed out of it, however, because National never paid any.

Mind you, investing exclusively in dividend-paying companies will also keep you out of some of the market's biggest winners—Rogers Communications is one good example. (Rogers, another favourite of many brokers, has risen from $1 to nearly $20 in the past 10 years.) Rogers and National Business Systems are both exceptional cases, of course. But investing solely in dividend payers is still an easy way to limit your risk.

Think of Your Portfolio as a Dividend Farm

One long-time investor tells me he buys stocks the way a farmer buys dairy cows. The only difference is that he's looking for dividends instead of milk. Makes perfect sense to me. Capital gains have more appeal for many investors. But capital gains are plentiful in some years, and non-existent in others. Choose your stocks wisely, however, and you'll acquire a stream of dividend income that holds steady in a bad year and rises in a good one.

Just remember, dividends mean more than earnings. That's why many conservative investors pay as much attention to current dividends and dividend history as they do to earnings. A company can pump air into its earnings statements, by failing to write off appropriate sums for depreciation, or by treating maintenance costs as long-term investments. (As soon as the auditing profession bans one way of doing this, another comes along to take its place.) But dividends are cash money. A long-term pattern of maintaining dividends in all but the direst circumstances tells you something about a company's concern for its shareholders.

What's more, a 5-year or 10-year pattern of steady or rising dividends is not something you can whip up in a hurry. Nor is it something you'll throw away lightly. Dividends are less secure than, say, bankaccount interest. But they are far more profitable in the long run.

Mind you, some companies keep on paying dividends long after they should have stopped. This is especially true of companies that use a lot of borrowed money in their operations—Canadian trusts and steel makers are two prime examples. They continued to pay dividends long after their share prices had begun to collapse.

Here again, the dividend record is just one of many factors you have to look at to choose investments profitably. Looking at it in isolation will mislead you. In some cases, looking at it in isolation will cost you plenty of money, but on the whole, it pays to give dividends the respect they deserve.

PROFITING FROM WHAT'S OVERRATED

Some investment concepts get way more attention and respect than they deserve. There's something to them all, of course; their value has simply been blown out of proportion. As a result, most investors experience costly disappointment when they try to apply them. Still, it pays to learn how they earned their reputation. Here are some investment concepts (and techniques, and gimmicks) that are vastly overrated, but it still pays to understand them, and at times you can even profit from them.

New Issues
New stock issues get much more respect than they deserve. Some investors even think that new stock issues are guaranteed sources of profit. A few new issues come out way too cheap in relation to demand; this turns them into hot new issues, and they soar from their first day of trading. That raises the average return on new issues as a whole. The trouble is that brokers reserve their allotments of hot new issues for favoured clients. To become a favoured client, you have to do a lot of trading. Or,

you have to be ready to buy every new issue that comes along—the hot ones and the duds. Many new stock issues come out at share prices that are slightly below the current prices of existing shares. They have to, otherwise nobody would buy. All too many new issues stay at those low prices, however. Or they return there after an initial rise.

Professor Jay Ritter of the University of Illinois analysed the first three years of trading of 1,526 new issues that came out between 1975 and 1984. (The study only covered better-quality new issues, and excluded pennies and other guaranteed losers.)

The average performance of these 1,526 stocks was only slightly better than half that of companies similar in size and industry that were already trading. In other words, buyers of those new issues would have made nearly twice as much money buying old issues rather than new ones.

Existing companies come with hidden assets that cut your risk and enhance your long-term profit. Then too, the average new issue comes out when it's a good time to sell, not buy. What's more, many new issues have hidden faults that only come out in the open months or years later.

To top it off, most hot new issues (those that rise sharply after their first public sale) get sold to institutions and other major customers; the average investor only gets a chance to buy after prices have gone up. Hot new issues are the riskiest new issues, however, because hot areas can cool off unexpectedly.

Regardless of whether you want to invest or speculate, your best bet is to buy shares in old issues, not new ones. That way you're likely to profit from hidden assets, rather than suffer from hidden problems.

Automatic Stock-Picking Systems

Early in our investing careers, most of us dream of finding a stock-picking system that works: one that takes away the indecision and anxiety that go into choosing stocks and succeeding as an investor, and guarantees above-average profit.

From time to time you may see ads or receive direct-mail packages touting stock-market or commodity-futures systems that have consistently produced profits of 50% to 100% or more per year. You may think this is the stock-picking system of your dreams. But the odds are against it. After all, if you could earn 50% a year on your money, you could turn $10,000 into a quarter of a billion in 25 years. Lots of investors had $10,000 to invest 25 years ago; quarter-billionaires are somewhat less numerous today.

It's quite an easy matter for a computer whiz to construct a system (through what's called back-testing) that would have turned $10,000 in 1966 into a quarter-billion today. This, though, is like an archery contest in which you shoot the arrow, then paint the target around it. If you try to do this in so-called real time—real life—you'll find you often have to adjust the rules of your system. What worked in one 25-year or 5-year or 5-month period may fail in another, depending on the approach you take. All that back-testing does is demonstrate what mathematicians call the "bunching of random events". A series of coin tosses may come up heads-heads-tails, heads-heads-tails many times, but it's still a sucker bet that it will keep coming up that way.

Some systems aim at spotting market trends. They buy what's going up and sell what's going down. Systems like these work best at times when trends are long-lived. Sometimes, however, the rules change abruptly. Speculator Jesse Livermore made tens of millions between the turn of the century and the 1920s with a trend-following system that he developed for himself. He lost all his money and that of many backers in the volatile markets of the 1930s. In 1940, he committed suicide. Trend following paid off once again in the fast-rising markets of the 1950s and 1960s. It failed dismally in the late 1970s and early 1980s.

Many of the older systems rely on a "what goes down must come back up" approach. They advise buying more shares when a stock goes down, ignoring the fact that it may keep going down after you run out of money. Some investment systems are home-study courses, others are books, cassettes or computer programs. All come with testimonials, if only from the inventor or promoter. I've spoken to loads of people over the years who have bought one or more of them. I've never heard of one that works.

A while ago I saw a half-hour infomercial for a $295 home-study course on a system for making automatic investment decisions. The ad took the form of a talk-show style interview of the system's inventor. The ad said investors had nothing to lose because they could return the course for a full refund if they weren't satisfied. But it's sometimes hard to collect on a money-back guarantee, especially when the guarantor operates out of a post-office box.

The best system for an individual is to diversify and stick to high quality. You can improve on it by learning to recognize your own strengths and weaknesses as an investor.

Bond-Rating Services

These services are in business to gauge the risk that bond-buyers won't get their money back. However, successful bond raters take a different approach from the one that works best for stock-market investors.

After all, both bonds and stocks expose their holders to the risk of total loss. But, even at the best of times, bonds come with a limit on the return they offer. The most you get back from them on maturity is par value. Stocks, on the other hand, have unlimited potential, at least in theory.

To succeed as a bond rater, you have to take a banker's literal-minded approach to a bond issuer's financial statements. (If you have ever been turned down for a bank loan, you know what I mean.) Bankers and bond raters recognize that surprises are apt to cost them money. So they are keenly interested in cash in hand and less in cheques that may or may not be in tomorrow's mail. A stock-market investor can afford some imagination, on the other hand. The investor, after all, has something to gain when he or she guesses right.

Bond-raters' disease is a healthy, even essential quality in a bond rater. But it's a disease for a stock-market investor, because it guarantees mediocre results or worse. It tempts you to buy at the top, when everybody is reporting high profit. It leads you to sell at the bottom, when losses are common and everything looks relentlessly bleak.

Asset-Allocation Services

These are computerized or formulaic methods for continually adjusting or tinkering with the proportions of stocks, bonds and cash in your portfolio. Promoters of asset allocation claim that it can improve your investment return, or reduce your risk, or both.

This belief is loosely based on a fact, one that has turned into today's most-quoted investment cliché: "The allocation of your assets among stocks, bonds and cash is the key determinant of your investment return." That's another way of saying that it doesn't matter what lottery you play, so long as you pick the winning number. But a large gap separates this commonplace observation from the belief that anybody can come up with a profitable formula for switching among stocks, bonds and cash.

Formulae for determining your optimum asset allocation look for patterns in stock and bond prices and trends, stock and bond yields, or economic data. Their originators start out with a rule or rules for switching, then use a computer to back-test it, or see how it would have worked in the past. But one of investing's most eternal verities is that the market never quite repeats itself.

Asset allocation sounds like a modern version of simple portfolio diversification, because it includes bonds, stocks and cash. But it bears a closer resemblance to old-fashioned trading. The main difference is that instead of selling one stock to buy another, you sell stocks to buy bonds or vice versa, or sell both to hold cash. This costs money. You pay commissions each time you buy or sell; with each transaction, you lose money to the spread (the difference between the highest bid and the lowest offer). These disadvantages are every bit as costly, whether you go from stocks to bonds and back again, or from one stock to another.

Asset-allocation funds and services are particularly popular among funds and institutions that are affiliated with stock brokers, for obvious reasons. Each change in the allocation means more business for the brokers.

Every investor should hold some stocks, bonds and cash. The proportions should depend on your age, financial circumstances and risk tolerance. Some asset-allocation services will pay off for some investors, at least for a while. But on the whole, asset allocation won't add to your return. More likely it will cost you money, in the long run if not in the short.

The Household-Name Board Members

In his book *White Knights and Poison Pills: A Cynic's Dictionary of Business Jargon*, David Olive defines a "financial gigolo" as "...a prominent person recruited to lend prestige to a board of directors while posing no threat to management control." One example he cites is former U.S. president Jerry Ford, who served as a paid consultant to Peter Pocklington's Fidelity Trust. (Fidelity collapsed in 1983—not an uncommon end for companies that stoop to employing financial gigolos.)

Financial gigolos also lend investment credibility. In this respect they are particularly effective—and dangerous. That's because prominent people are often poor judges of investment quality and character, not to mention suckers for flattery. Many serve as financial gigolos without ever realizing it.

A while ago, for instance, I received a mailing from a heavily touted Vancouver penny stock—one that I suspect will eventually wind up worthless. The package included a copy of a five-page letter, signed by a partner in an internationally known and respected accounting firm. The letter confirmed the penny's eligibility for RRSP investment and went on to explain RRSPs in general. (Any stock listed on a Canadian stock exchange is eligible for RRSP investment.)

The letter stated, "This is not an investment recommendation." But some unfortunate investors are bound to assume that if this accounting firm is involved, the stock must be legit.

The promoter probably paid a few hundred dollars for the letter. It will cost some investors a great deal more.

Outside Directors

It's widely believed that outsiders on a company's board of directors (regardless of whether you recognize their names) are there to protect and further the interests of outside investors. In fact, companies are playing to this sentiment by nominating more and more outsiders to their boards. At big U.S. firms, outside directors now outnumber directors from inside the company by three to one, up from two to one 10 years ago. Out-of-work politicians are especially sought after.

As it happens, outside representation on the board does more for corporate public relations than for financial performance. One 1986-1991 study found that companies in the Standard & Poor's 500 index produced average annual total returns of 8.8%. The 60 companies with the greatest share of outside directors—80% and up—produced total annual returns of 5.2%. The 23 companies with the fewest outside directors—under 30%—averaged yearly returns of 17.1%.

Respectable outsiders are unlikely to get involved in an out-and-out scam, of course. But most experienced investors manage to stay out of scams on their own. Experienced investors are more likely to lose money in companies that suffer from overambitious expansion, over-confident managers and an unhealthy reliance on capital gains. But you can't expect outsiders to protect you from these risks. When recruiting outside directors, companies prone to any of these ills will seek out cheerleaders and team players, not Cassandras or killjoys.

Outside directors do have some value for investors, of course, but only in a backwards, mine-canary fashion. Methane and other gases are a danger in a mine. Miners used to bring canaries down into the shafts with them when they went to work. These fragile birds are especially sensitive to bad air. When they started to keel over, the miners knew that they were in danger and that they should drop their tools and get out right away. If a number of the outside directors decide to get out all at once, you should too.

Ground-Floor Opportunities

Theoretically, the earlier you get into a start-up company, the better, assuming it is going to survive and prosper as a business. In reality, it often takes a couple of tries for many businesses to, shall we say, set the profit flywheel spinning. Each time, the interests of outside investors get diluted. You still own 100 shares, but the total of shares outstanding may rise from one million to 10 million to 100 million.

This cycle of near-death and resuscitation is easier on insiders, of course. They get a new bundle of stock options each time it happens, to maintain their motivation. As a rule, you're better off staying out of ground-floor opportunities until they have at least begun making money, or reached respectable levels of per-share sales.

When a stock trades for more than, say, four times its per-share sales, its sales need an extraordinary burst of growth to catch up to its stock price. If it fails to experience that burst of sales, you can lose money, or fail to earn a return to match your risk, even if the company prospers. On the whole, it pays to avoid ground-floor opportunities, at least while they remain on the ground floor. If you stumble onto the next Xerox, it will remain attractive for many, many years. You can afford to wait until the company starts making money, or until its per-share sales reach one quarter of the share price.

Value Investing

This is the practice of buying stocks that are cheap in relation to earnings, assets or both. The trouble is that stocks that are too cheap are, more often now than in the past, dangerous rather than a bargain.

You might say computers ruined things for value investors. It used to take a fair amount of hard work to find stocks trading below per-share book value (what the corporate books say assets are worth per share after you deduct liabilities), or below net-net (short-term assets minus all liabilities, short-term and long). Now all you do is call up a database and key in your specifications. When computers eliminated the hard work, they also exposed all the hitherto undiscovered gems, and eliminated much of the easy money.

Something like that happened decades ago, in antiques. Well-informed antiques enthusiasts used to be able to drive out past the city limits on a Sunday afternoon, and pay poorly informed country folk a pittance for priceless heirlooms. Now the country folk have telephones, satellite-dish receivers and subscriptions to *Antiques Today*. When the country folk come up against the touring antiques enthusiast, it's hard to guess who will take advantage of whom.

In antiques as in obscure stocks, the information explosion and modern communications devices have made the market more efficient, and eliminated what was once a source of easy money.

It pays to know something about value investing. But you have to recognize that it's only a starting point. A key part of the value of many companies is the hold they have on their markets, and the relationship they have with customers. This doesn't appear on the books. It's what you call a hidden asset. In fact, excessive attention to "value" can lead you to load up on stocks of low investment quality, and that's one of the worst mistakes an investor can make.

Inside Information

Corporate insiders are paid to be optimistic—it's part of the job. So you should observe the normal precautions when insiders tell you how swell things are going down at the plant. They may be exaggerating, or they may be ignoring signs of trouble.

What about the celebrated inside traders of the 1980s, who made multimillions but finally wound up in jail? That's a little different. Mostly they profited by betraying confidences, through front-running: profiting from advance knowledge of coming take-overs and other investment decisions made by others, usually their clients.

Legal and ethical questions aside, you could try to profit as they did. Keep in mind, though, that inside traders who made money often paid cash bribes totalling many thousands of dollars. Rumours you get for free may prove less accurate, and less valuable. Then too, take-over rumours are always far more common than actual take-overs—especially now that the great 1980s take-over boom has ended. If you buy every stock you hear touted as a take-over, you may come up with a few big winners, but still wind up losing money.

Insiders can offer valuable insight on their companies. But use it to enrich what you know, and to help you build a balanced, high-quality portfolio. In short, treat it at best as an aid to profit, because it's no guarantee.

Pennies with a Pedigree

Many investors make a point of avoiding penny stocks. But they make exceptions for pennies whose president or founder has, for instance, a record of career accomplishments with a major multinational company. They look on this as a pedigree of sorts; if the company can attract a high-powered executive, it must be more than an ordinary penny.

The problem here is that modern corporate titles are often vague, and penny-stock insiders sometimes take liberties in describing their achievements. The self-described former head of IBM Europe may actually have been a sales trainee. Auditors only vouch for the numbers in a penny-stock prospectus, as a rule. It may be impossible to verify or counterdict an insider's history in any event. Fear of lawsuits makes big companies hesitate to contradict a former employee's story about his or her accomplishments, especially in the U.S.

Your best approach is to consider the résumés of a penny-stock's insiders only if the company's finances inspire your confidence. Accomplished executives are an asset, of course. But the average penny stock comes with deep drawbacks: unlikely corporate profit prospects at best, and far too many shares (and share-purchase options) outstanding to leave much profit for outsiders. It helps to have an IBM dropout to run things, of course. But most pennies need a miracle worker.

Market Cycles

Human nature never changes, but law, culture and technology keep evolving. So permutations on human behaviour are endless. With that in mind, you need to take a sceptical look at so-called market cycles. Often they are little more than market nostalgia, dressed up in computer print-outs.

Take the dividend-interest cycle. Recently, bond yields have been twice as high as dividend yields. A century ago, dividend yields used to exceed bond yields from time to time. Back then, investors justifiably used to feel income from stocks was far more speculative, so stocks should yield more than bonds.

Some investors believe that logic still applies, if only sporadically. So, they think investors should largely stay out of stocks until dividend yields once again beat bond yields. Only then will they assume the market has indeed bottomed out. However, stocks and bonds have both changed in the past century, in ways that seem apt to make bonds yield more and stocks yield less.

Superficially, bonds are the same as they always were. The buyer lends a fixed sum for a fixed term at a fixed rate of interest; if the buyer doesn't get the money back on time, he or she sues. But in the good old days, borrowers lent and got back gold-backed dollars, at interest rates of 3% to 6%. Today, with gold out of the system, there's less certainty about what future dollars will be worth. The odds seem to favour inflation rather than deflation, in the long run if not in the short. That means future dollars will be worth less than current dollars. So, bond yields are apt to be higher on average than they were a century ago.

Stocks have changed too—but for the better, in ways apt to push yields down. Stocks were indeed far more speculative a century ago. Insider trading and other abuses were legal. Accounting standards were primitive. Companies released far less information than they do today; dividends rather than reported earnings were the key to a company's health and value. Dividend yields had to be higher than they are today, to attract investors.

The introduction of the income tax early in this century was also apt to make dividend yields and bond yields diverge. It has no direct impact on bond yields, of course. But it makes companies less inclined to pay dividends, because dividends are subject to double taxation. The company pays tax on earnings before paying dividends; the investor who receives the dividend has to include it in taxable income. (Our Canadian dividend tax credit scheme attempts to lessen this double taxation. However, it does nothing for tax-deferred investors— pension funds, RRSPs and so on. When they own dividend-paying Canadian stocks, their dividend tax credits go to waste.) This double taxation gives companies an incentive to hang on to and reinvest corporate earnings, rather than paying dividends. This leads directly to lower yields on stocks. It also leads to faster growth, which makes lower yields easier to accept.

Yields on stocks are relatively low these days, on the whole. But that's partly because the average dividend yield includes stocks of companies that have chosen to finance themselves with debt. This raises their leverage, and gives them the potential to earn greater long-term profit from capital gains. But it leaves them with little excess cash for paying dividends out of current earnings.

More and more, these companies are attempting to refinance—to pay off old, high-interest-rate debt, either by selling shares, or by selling new debt at today's low interest rates. Either way, getting rid of older, higher-rate debt will make their earnings rise. As that happens, dividends will follow.

Stocks leave you vulnerable to dividend cuts, so you have to diversify. Bonds, on the other hand, are vulnerable to inflation, and no amount of diversification can protect a bond portfolio from that.

The 3% to 6% Shuffle

Some call it an infallible rule of market timing. You buy when the dividend yield in the Standard & Poor's 500 stock index is 6%, and sell when it falls below 3%.

The rule sounds logical and works perfectly, where it applies. The trouble is that it rarely applies. The Standard & Poor's 500 offered a yield above 6% right after World War Two. Little by little, business improved and investors grew more confident, and they were willing to pay more for dividends. Dividend yields gradually fell to less than 3% late in 1961. The rule would have got you out of the market in time to avoid the 1962 crash. But it would have kept you out of the market for the next 18 years. You'd have sat out the market set-backs of 1966, 1970 and 1974...but you'd have missed out on the many profit-making opportunities that also occurred in that period, when the Standard & Poor's 500 yield ranged from 3% to 4%.

The rule would have spurred you to get back in the market in late 1979. That was indeed a good time to buy, but a trifle early. You'd have held on all through the 1982 stock-market set-back. (The Standard & Poor's 500 yield got up as high as 6.4% in 1982.) From 1982, the rule worked superbly for five years; the average stock price tripled before the next yields-under-3% sell signal, which came in mid-1987.

Since then, prices of many top quality stocks have gone well above their mid-1987 levels, particularly in the U.S. Meanwhile, followers of the 3% to 6% shuffle are still waiting for a new buy signal. My guess is that they face a long wait...maybe not till the year 2000 or beyond. Meanwhile, they may miss out on some great investment opportunities.

Market Momentum

Surprisingly large numbers of investors base all or a large part of their investment decision-making on momentum, which you can sum up in eight words: buy what goes up, sell what goes down. You can use a momentum-based approach to study earnings, stock prices or both. It can pay off intensely for short periods, because it leads you to invest strictly in the strongest companies within the strongest groups.

This is a high-risk approach. For one thing, it short-circuits whatever attempts you make to diversify. Even if your momentum-based choices come from a variety of market sectors, most will still plunge in a broad market set-back.

If you want to speculate, you could do worse than to base your buying and selling on momentum, but do so with only part of your investment funds. You should still stick to companies that have an established, profitable business, rather than simply a flashy business concept. Most important of all, stick to companies that trade actively, because the time will come when you want to sell in a hurry. When the momentum approach backfires, it does so on a grand scale.

Stop-Loss Orders

Using stop-loss orders (telling your broker in advance to sell you out if your stock falls to some price level you choose) works best in theory. You limit your losses by selling when a stock you own begins to fall; you hold on to those that rise. In practice, however, many stocks are too volatile to gain from stop-loss orders. In rising from $2 to $10, a stock may frequently settle back by a dollar or two. If you buy at, say, $4 and set your stop-loss at $3, you may wind up selling at $2.95, just before the stock heads for $6.

It may pay to set a limit—20%, say—on how much you are willing to lose in a particular stock. But adhere to it too strictly and you risk acting like Oscar Wilde's definition of a cynic: one who knows the price of everything and the value of nothing. Lots of investors sold on the day of the October 1987 stock-price crash, and since then many share-price indexes have doubled.

You'll understand the drawbacks of stop-loss orders better if you understand a concept that commodity-futures traders refer to as "gunning for stops".

An investor I know was taken aback a few years ago when he came across the following in a report on commodity futures trading: "Wheat briefly got below $3 a bushel this morning, but observers said this was due to selling by locals, who were gunning for stops." He asked what all this meant.

"Locals" are traders who operate on the floor of the futures exchange. They buy and sell for their own or their backers' or employers' accounts. They may go in and out of a commodity many times in the course of a day, as buyers or sellers. When they decide that prices are headed one way or the other, they often do the opposite of what you'd expect—they sell short when they think prices will rise, or buy when they think prices will fall. That way they can "clear out the stops". They refer to this as gunning for stops. Since stops are buy and sell orders that go into effect only under rigid conditions, it stands to reason that locals would try to take advantage of them.

A stop order turns into a market order when the stock, option, commodity or whatever trades at the stop price. Suppose wheat is trading at $3.02, and some locals think it ought to get to $3.05. But suppose only a few wheat futures contracts are available between those two prices. If the locals believe many outside traders hold wheat futures and have entered orders to sell "on stop" at $3, they may sell enough wheat to push the price down to $3. That way, they trigger all those on-stop-at-$3 sell orders. This turns them into market orders. The locals then buy back the wheat they've sold, and more, so they can profit from the rise to $3.05.

This is less diabolical than it sounds. These plots can backfire, if a sudden news flash spurs buying in wheat. Besides, groups of locals often wind up competing against each other.

In commodities and stocks, stops have a way of accumulating at what pro traders look on as obvious levels—round numbers, recent or historical turning points, price targets predicted by widely quoted stock-market gurus and so on. If you buy or sell unthinkingly at these obvious levels, it's apt to cost you money.

Buybacks

When a company announces that it plans to buy back its own shares in the market, its motive may be to take advantage of an investment opportunity, fend off a take-over (at times by squandering a cash hoard that could attract an unwanted suitor), or simply boost the price of shares remaining in public hands. Then too, companies sometimes announce that they plan a buyback, but then fail to carry out the plan.

Whatever the motive, the buyback may have little if any long-term impact on share prices. This seems to be the natural conclusion of a study by a Boston consulting firm of 17 U.S. companies that launched stock buybacks in 1986 and 1987. Each of the companies had a market capitalization (the value of all shares outstanding at current prices) of $1 billion or more prior to the buyback; each of the buybacks retired 8% or more of the company's shares.

One year after the buyback's announcement, only 8 of the 17 stocks had outperformed the Standard & Poor's 500 stock-price index. After two years, only 5 of the 17 were ahead. Pretty much as you'd expect, in other words. A variety of companies buy their shares back, always for their own reasons, and the buybacks say nothing about investment appeal. The rule on buybacks is that there isn't a rule.

Selling Targets

You'll often hear that when you buy a stock, you should also decide on a price at which you'd sell, and make at least a mental note to do so if it gets there. That's good advice from your broker's point of view—it triples his or her income (you pay a commission to buy, another to sell, a third when you buy again). But this tactic will cost you money in the long run.

In many cases, after all, it ensures that you'll wind up selling all your biggest winners far too early. It pays to keep reminding yourself of the happy investor who made a fortune in the market by being, as he described it, "smart enough to buy Canadian Tire shares at $0.50, but too stupid to sell when they hit $2". Having a fixed idea about when to sell can make you disregard new developments that may justify much higher prices.

Far better to try to limit your buying mainly to the kinds of stocks that you're likely to want to hold on to, more or less indefinitely. Ideally, you'll buy them gradually in your working years, then live off sales (if not dividends) in retirement. Along the way, you will of course sell stocks that no longer suit your requirements—because they've changed, or because you have.

Sell targets do make sense if you delve into lower-quality investments, especially penny mines and other highly volatile issues. In these, your best bet is to apply the sell-half rule: sell half of any low-quality investment you own that doubles, so you get back your initial stake. That way, the worst that happens is you break even.

Special Financial Ratios

In my experience, it pays to be wary of investments that come with their own special set of financial ratios. In the cellular-phone business, for instance, you'll hear references to price per POP. The "price" is the total value of a company's shares and its debt, minus its working capital; the "POP" is a measure of population in the area the company serves. One study I saw said Rogers Cantel compared favourably with some U.S. cellular stocks on a price-per-POP basis, so the analyst recommended the stock as a buy. The trouble is that this ratio fails to distinguish between POP in Montana and, say, Manhattan, or between southern Ontario and the Northwest Territories. Some cellular territories are apt to be more profitable than others, depending on business activity and population density.

In biotechnology start-ups, you'll often hear analysts say things such as, "I like Bio-XYZ for its high burn-out (or flame-out) ratio." This ratio is the number you get by dividing a company's cash resources by the rate at which it is running through those resources. Analysts use it on companies that aren't really in business, in the ordinary sense of the phrase. Instead, these companies are "conducting research"—attempting to find or perfect a product or service that can put them in business. A flame-out ratio of 1.2 years means a company can last that long, at its current rate of cash outflow, before it needs to sell new shares, borrow more money or go broke.

Another favourite of biotech analysts is "market cap per Ph.D on staff". This one is especially full of holes. After all, the Ph.D (Doctor of Philosophy) degree varies widely in the achievement it represents. It depends on the university that granted it, the person who received it and the work he or she did to earn it. Besides, many top academic researchers never make a commercial discovery.

You might look on these special ratios as "ratio-oids". They have only a passing resemblance to conventional financial ratios, just as the androids of science fiction have a passing resemblance to genuine human beings. Ratio-oids may help you clarify or organize what little you do know about young or poorly established companies. More often, though, they cost investors money. They lead them to think that simple answers exist when it comes to investing in companies which have not yet established a record of revenues, earnings or dividends.

Having said that, here's my own favourite ratio-oid for culling the losers from your list of junior investment possibilities. I call it the High-Low Auto-Indicator. Stop by a junior company's parking lot several times over the course of several weeks. On each visit, add up the number of Maseratis, Mercedes, Jaguars and so on; do the same with the Chevys, Hondas and so on. If the Maseratis and so on consistently outnumber the Chevys and Hondas, strike the company from your list.

Investment Clubs

Investment clubs seem to be enjoying one of their periodic rediscoveries by the investing public. These clubs can pay off for members, educationally and socially—but they can also cost you money.

Clubs can go off course at the worst possible moment. Psychologists used to recognize a mental condition known as *folie à deux* when two closely associated or related individuals would gradually convince themselves that, say, the CIA was poisoning their municipal tap water, or depriving them of an inheritance that Elvis had promised them in one of his ballads. The related condition of groupthink occurs when a group or committee makes decisions for which no individual member can be held accountable. It's rarely so engulfing as *folie à deux*, but it is sometimes more costly.

Groupthink decisions have a way of veering off into high-risk terri-tory. Groupthink seems to have played a role in the disastrous outcome of the Vietnam War. In the mid-1980s, as stock prices rose, groupthink led some investment clubs to abandon their initially conservative investing principles. One club I know of invested much of its treasury in stock options as prices were peaking—and lost it all. Worse still, many individual members, emboldened by discussions at the club, did the same in their personal accounts, at far greater cost.

Some clubs are actually private businesses. For most of us, the term club conjures up an image of a non-profit, co-operative affair, run by and for the members. But businesses can use the term to describe them-selves; health clubs and book clubs do it all the time. More than once, swindlers have formed or acquired control of clubs, and used them to fleece investors.

Some of these clubs attracted investors by claiming they could arrange to buy gold at a discount, through bulk buying, or pre-paying for gold from a penny mine that wasn't in production, and never would be. Others embezzled funds from the club treasury. One celebrated swindle from the 1980s claimed to be a club that funnelled inside infor-mation and expert advice to its members. The information and advice actually came from the club owner and his stock-promoter associates.

Before you join a club, take a close look at the club agreement and by-laws. You might even ask your lawyer for an opinion. Most mineral finds wind up in court, remember. That's because mining promoters don't really expect to find anything of value, so they put little care into drawing up the property agreements. The same thing can happen in investment clubs. Members may invest only $30 to $50 a month, but that eventually adds up.

In particular, look at how the club will make investment decisions. The club by-laws should spell out diversification requirements. For instance, they should set a limit on the proportion of club funds that can go in a single investment. The by-laws might also limit eligible investments to companies above a certain size (by sales or assets), or to those listed on specified exchanges, and/or with dividend records stretching back some stated number of years.

Above all, the by-laws should say how much time the members need to study material on a new investment before making a decision. Otherwise, the club's best talker may convince those present to invest the club's entire stake in, say, a Vancouver penny mine that he read about in that day's newspaper, while riding the bus to the meeting.

Like a lot of investment topics, the last word on investment clubs comes down to a general caveat: no one, regardless of the purity of his or her intentions, will ever bring as much attention and care to your finances as you will.

THE PSYCHOLOGY OF SUCCESSFUL INVESTING

For most investors, success in investing comes from practising what I've referred to jokingly as that old-time religion—buying high-quality stocks, diversifying and investing with the long term in mind. But many investors depart from the practice of that religion just when it can prove especially costly.

That Special Feeling

The CBC's 6 PM News Hour program ran a special feature a while ago, exposing some of the low-down tactics of some so-called "security dealers" (those brokers I've mentioned, not members of any exchange, who sell speculative stocks over the phone, mostly to inexperienced investors).

As I said earlier, most stocks that security dealers sell wind up worthless. After watching the CBC report, a friend asked, "How can investors be so stupid as to fall for a scam like that?"

Most of us, at some time in our lives, do something we know to be dumb—possibly because we have a feeling that we have entered a special, charmed period in our lives, when the workaday caveats don't apply.

"I know heavy drinkers make bad husbands, but I'm sure Sidney will reform after the wedding."

"I must be crazy to co-sign a loan to a deadbeat like Fred, but he wouldn't dare stiff his own brother-in-law."

"I know you should get three quotes before you buy aluminum siding, but the salesman seemed so straightforward."

The lesson is simple. We all have what we used to refer to as our better judgement. We put ourselves at risk when we fail to heed it, in investments or anything else.

Sound Investing and Fuzzy Logic

When experienced investors read about the fast-rising mathematical discipline of "fuzzy logic", many are struck by how closely it parallels their approach to picking stocks.

Basically, fuzzy logic lets a computer use imprecise standards and measurements when precise ones are unavailable. That way the computer can take a variety of factors into account in making a decision— even when they are all in that fuzzy middle ground between boiling and freezing, fast and slow, light and dark and so on. Fuzzy-logic controls go in most new Japanese home appliances—for instance, in clothes dryers, microwave ovens and rice cookers. These appliances can then decide how much heat to apply, and when to shut themselves off. Panasonic uses fuzzy-logic controls in its video cameras, to keep the image steady when the camera operator's hand shakes. Hitachi uses fuzzy-logic controls in subway-car braking systems; they vary brake pressure depending on car speed, distance to the next car or station, weight of the passengers, angle of the track and so on. This makes most stops imperceptible to the passengers crammed inside. What does that have to do with investing? Well, few investment measures ever give you clear answers; most are a muddle, most of the time. Nobody doubts that a 20% interest rate on T-bills is high, and 2% is low. But most of the time, T-bill rates are some-where in between. That's true of almost every scrap of investment infor-mation that comes to investors, most of the time.

Many investors try to deal with the imprecision of investment infor-mation by looking at only a narrow spectrum of it. But investment decision-making is a complex task. The more information you look at, and the more experience and judgement you bring to it, the better your chances of success.

Terror, Exhilaration and Boredom

From time to time, investors find they are bored with their portfolios. This leads many of them to take drastic action—getting out of stocks entirely, or switching to more exciting choices that they later regret. But you have to get used to boredom to succeed as an investor.

The market really only operates in three modes: terrifying, exhilarat-ing and boring. Terrifying markets are those that are plunging enough to make you wonder if you are in for a replay of 1929. By the time they reach that stage, however, much of the drop is usually behind us.

Most investors prefer exhilarating markets, when stocks soar and profits come effortlessly. In truly exhilarating markets, many investors give at least casual thought to quitting their jobs and taking up stock trading full time. In these markets you find the greatest risk. However, boring markets offer the best balance of low risk and high potential.

Does it pay to get out of the stock market when it becomes boring, and return when things liven up? Well, the market's action has a way of arriving in clusters. One study ranked month-by-month performance of the Standard & Poor's 500 index for the 62 years (744 months) from 1926 through 1987. If you eliminated the best 50 of those months—the top 6.7%—you eliminated the entire gain. If you were out of the market in those 50 top months, in other words, you wound up with the same number of dollars after 62 years, and a huge loss of purchasing power to inflation.

In short, there's a risk at any time in being in the market. But, bor-ing or no, there's a greater risk in getting out entirely.

The Fruitless Investments of Mr. D

Staying out of penny stocks and other speculations can help you avoid deep losses in your portfolio. However, it's no guarantee of profit, as one investor, Mr. D, has shown in three decades of fruitless investing. The most frustrating part of investing is the uncertainty of it—the constant, seemingly random (but, ultimately, controllable) risk. Some of your favourite and most apparently desirable investments are bound to go sour on you. But you won't know which ones will do so until it happens, months or years in the future. This is true no matter how strongly these stocks appeal to you, and no matter what broker, advisor or newspaper article recommends them to you.

On the other hand, some of your biggest winners may inexplicably dip in price before their rise begins. This may lead you to sell at the worst possible moment. Widespread and uniformly mistaken predictions of disaster may also spur you to sell when you should buy.

In short, you can avoid all the obvious investment errors—gambling on low-quality stocks, or in warrants or options, investing on margin, allowing fear or greed to overwhelm your decisions—and still lose money, or earn a poor return. All you need to do is suspend your common sense, cultivate a high level of suggestibility and fail to learn from your experience. Consider the case of Mr. D.

Mr. D started out investing in stocks, despite a lack of respect for them. He refers to the stock market now, as he did three decades ago when he first entered it, as "a mug's game at best". He sees it as little different from a game of chance. This is a loser's attitude. It stops you from profiting from experience. If the outcome is random anyway, why pay attention to the nuances?

When Mr. D makes money, he credits his own shrewdness at overcoming the odds. He never looks any further to see what, specifically, he did right. When he loses, he blames poor advice, insider trading or conspiracies against the small investor. This approach has, needless to say, failed to pay off. Even Mr. D is unsure of the exact outcome of his investing over the past three decades, because of messy record keeping. But it appears he has done little better than break even.

Over the years, friends often suggested to Mr. D that he educate himself about investing, that he try to figure out where he was going wrong, that he try to adhere to sound investment fundamentals—all the usual investor caveats that we offer each week at *The Investment Reporter*. Mr. D agrees that this would be a wise thing to do...but even now, decades later, he has yet to get around to it.

Friends ask why he persists in investing in common stocks. "Lots of reasons," he replies. "They give you a hedge against inflation, plus a tax break from the $100,000 capital-gains tax exemption and the dividend tax credit. But most of all, they're convenient—they leave me with lots of time for my work and my home life."

In fact, stocks are so convenient that Mr. D puts little effort into choosing them, and sometimes ignores his portfolio for a year or two at a time. His holdings include dozens of issues, mostly of reasonably good quality—no pennies, warrants or options. So he can afford to leave them untouched for long periods, without incurring large losses. But large profits have proven equally scarce.

He's a sucker for what I'd call a "best-of-both-worlds" sales pitch. So he has a particular fondness for convertible securities.

Personal finance writers often describe convertibles as offering more income than common stocks and more appreciation potential than bonds. But it's equally true that they offer less income than bonds, and less appreciation than stocks. You need to weigh the advantages against the disadvantages, as you would before making any sort of purchase.

When investing in convertibles, however, it's particularly crucial to assess the premium—the extra cost of buying the convertible instead of the underlying security into which you can convert. Failing to do that guarantees mediocre results, and these are what Mr. D has achieved.

Mr. D has always tried to avoid risk, so he stayed out of penny stocks, and only bought shares in companies with an established business. But he also bought a lot of "stories", and wound up with a great many "story stocks" in his portfolio. These are stocks whose appeal can be summed up in 30 seconds or less. (An example: "Buy Bombardier because it makes subway trains, and subways are the wave of the future for urban transportation.") The story always makes superficial sense. It may, however, rely on faulty reasoning, or false or incomplete information. It may also overlook glaring drawbacks inside or outside the company.

Stories can come from anywhere—brokers, clients, friends, newspaper articles. They can appear in any sort of investment. No wonder, then, that Mr. D's portfolio includes virtually any sort of investment you can name: income stocks, growth stocks, cyclicals, special situations. Some of his choices are not widely followed now, but all were in the investment limelight when he bought them.

During his investment career, Mr. D has repeated the same pattern over and over: a series of small gains interrupted by (and, in many years, more than offset by) an occasional huge loss. He has increased his likelihood of random results by being utterly inconsistent in the sums he invests in each stock he buys. The amount in each case depends almost entirely on how much cash he has on hand when he hears the story.

Avoiding the Standard Errors

Mr. D avoided all the standard errors, at least all the blatant ones. He stayed out of the clutches of the telephone penny-stock sellers who are responsible for so many tales of investment woe. He avoided overtrading (in fact, he hardly traded at all). He even diversified his holdings, but without any concern for pursuing well-thought-out investment objectives, or for seeking balance among the investments he chose.

His lack of a plan was what saved him from far worse results. He never got carried away with any particular sort of investment. He never averaged down (that is, never bought more of a stock because its price had fallen, simply to lower his average cost, an all-too-common error). On the other hand, he also refrained from averaging up—buying more of a stock as its price rises. (This can be a wise or foolish move, depending on your reason for buying more.) By the time a stock he owned had begun to rise or fall, Mr. D's attention had gone on to something else.

Most investors will see a little of themselves in Mr. D. Most of us, however, will eventually wake up, realize what's wrong and make the necessary changes. If not? Well, chances are your investment results will look a lot like Mr. D's.

Clichéed Investment Thinking

Years ago, a psychological study asked college students to judge the IQ of a number of subjects, based on brief conversations with them. The students were able to divide the subjects into high-IQ and low-IQ groups, but they weren't sure how they were doing it. Close analysis of tapes of those brief conversations revealed that subjects in the low-IQ group were simply using more clichés—"pretty as a picture", "flat as a pancake" and so on.

You can apply the same test to an investment opinion. The more an investment opinion relies on investment clichés, the less faith you should have in it. Take the term "bottom line". It started out as business/investor slang for a company's profit (which of course appears on the bottom line of its income statement, after deductions for expenses, depreciation, taxes and so on). Little by little, the term has crept into everyday English. In so doing, it turned into a cliché. Its meaning became muddled, and it lost some of its usefulness. Now, the bottom line can be, for instance, the speaker's view of the key fundamental point about a company, rather than its profit. This broadening of the term's meaning seems to promote misleading oversimplifications.

For instance, an investor I know recently said, "The bottom line on Alcan is that it can't compete with the Russians." Many of those within earshot nodded in agreement. The pithiness of the remark gave it authority, as did its core of truth—Russian aluminum dumping is hurting Alcan's profits. As investment opinions go, however, this is an incomplete one. After all, Alcan's future also depends on growth in aluminum demand, which is apt to rise along with economic recovery. It also depends on how long it takes for Russian aluminum demand to get back to earlier peaks.

Now, the term "top line" (business/investor slang for a company's revenues or sales, a figure that appears at the top of its income statement) seems headed for a similar transformation. Nowadays you hear brokers and promoters talk about "focusing on top-line growth"—that is, attempting to make sales grow, even at the expense of current profit. This too can lead to oversimplification. Many a company can grow faster than its competitors, measured by sales, if it is relieved of the need to make money. But you need to assure yourself that the company is building its top line in a way that builds long-term profit potential.

Keep Your Distance

A while ago, an *Investment Reporter* reader wrote to say, "I bought some shares in a Vancouver development company a year ago, and now I've been invited to visit the mine at company expense, and see how things are going for myself before I invest any more money. Certainly that's the best way to cut risk, don't you think?"

This is a widely held view. But it's at odds with the experience of many investors. In fact, some of the most expensive trips investors ever take are paid for by development companies that want them to invest money.

An investor I know accepted a flight to Costa Rica some years ago, to inspect operations at a company that claimed to have developed a way to extract gold from the black sand that is common on some beaches in the area. Scores of Spanish-speaking locals were shovelling sand onto a conveyor belt that carried it into an impressive-looking machine the size of a small car. The promoter explained that this single machine was running 24 hours a day, and making a big profit. He needed capital to build more machines. This would make a fortune for investors and, incidentally, create employment for nearby villagers. "Do well for yourself, and your fellow man," the promoter said. My friend was ready to take out his cheque-book. Luckily for him, he stayed behind to practise his high-school Spanish when the group moved on.

"Is there much unemployment here?" my friend asked one of the men wielding a shovel. "*Sí, señor,*" the labourer said, "even us, we are lucky to get two hours' work every month, when the gringos come to visit."

This is an extreme case, of course. But it makes a point worth remembering: if ordinary investors could cut risk simply by visiting a company's operations, then think of the advantage a tour would bestow on people in the business, who presumably know what to look for— who can ferret out the truth without stumbling onto it. Yet professionals within an industry don't exhibit any great success when they invest in their specialty. Often, the reverse is true.

Nor, for that matter, does the proverbial tour-of-the-plant do much for the results of investment analysts. That's as true at top-quality multinationals as at Costa Rican gold-from-sand swindles. Public relations people and corporate executives are hired for their ability to inspire enthusiasm in others about what they do, and bring them around to the company point of view. Most won't lie to you. They don't need to. They just need to infect you with their optimism. That way you'll accept the sort of morale-boosting assumption that's bound to lead to errant forecasts.

It helps to learn as much as you can about your investments, but no matter how close you get to them, there's still an element of risk. Along with a healthy dose of scepticism, you also need humility. You have to recognize you can indeed be fooled, especially in unfamiliar surroundings. To cut risk, cultivate a sense of detachment about your investments, so you can sell without feeling short-sighted or disloyal if things start to go wrong. Keep your distance, in other words, rather than getting intimately involved. The best way to cut the risk is simply to diversify and balance your portfolio.

Four Investors—Which Is You?

• The omen-seeker. Always on the lookout for ominous historical parallels. Some of these investors feared the 1932 suicide/bankruptcy of Swedish match king Ivar Kreuger would replay itself in the 1991 death of Robert Maxwell, so they assumed we were headed for a 1930s-style depression.

• The visionary. Lasers are the wave of the future, this investor will assure you, so you can't go wrong buying stocks with laser in their names.

• The weather vane. A convert to the optimism (or pessimism), and a believer in the possibilities (or doubts), expressed in the last newspaper article he or she read.

• The sceptic. Being human, he or she is alert to possible omens, open to visions (good or bad) of the future, and willing to listen to the views of others. Unlike these other three investors, however, the sceptic tempers his or her fears and enthusiasms with common sense. He or she recognizes that opinions range more widely than reality, that no one can foresee the future, and that progress comes in spurts.

This naturally leads the sceptic to conclude that the investment quality, balance and diversification in your portfolio, not the precision of your forecasts nor the strength of your views, is what leads you to investment success.

The Odd Ailments of Wall Street

Many pastimes and businesses afflict their participants with specialized ailments—tennis elbow, surfer's knee, hatter's dementia, to name just a few. New York money manager Ray DeVoe talks about some specialized stock-market afflictions:

One-way hearing/vision: the inability, when a bull market is underway, to hear or see anything bad about the stock market or economy. Usually combined with a tendency to magnify anything positive. (The reverse condition applies in bear markets, when everything looks and sounds terrible.)

Goldbug-induced heebie-jeebies: nausea, hives and a crawly-skin sensation brought on by listening to goldbugs describe the economic outlook. (Remedy: internal administration of alcohol.)

Bull market mental expansion: realization that you are a Stock Market Genius Who Will Never Again Make a Mistake. A growing problem whenever the Dow rises 10% in any six-month period.

Midnight aspirin syndrome: headaches and insomnia due to mentally adding up the value of your portfolio every night while trying to fall asleep.

MEGO. Acronym for "My Eyes Glaze Over". Afflicts those who should be reading prospectuses but who are instead daydreaming about new cars, a bigger house, world travel, fancy restaurant meals and so on. Nature's way of ensuring your daydreams stay just that.

Avoiding the No-Win Portfolio

We all have our favourite investment situation—due to past successes, say, or to our psychological make-up. Overindulging in them can cost money. See if you can spot yourself in any of these investor niches.

• The turnaround specialist. Some investors shop for new investments on the list of stocks making new highs; the turnaround specialist
prefers to buy stocks that have made new lows. There's something to
both approaches, but looking for buys among stocks that are making
new lows is more demanding. When you buy stocks that are making
new highs, you are betting that an existing trend will continue.
Momentum works in your favour. When you choose among those hitting new lows, on the other hand, you are betting on a change in the
trend.

Trend changes, when they occur, can of course be extraordinarily
profitable. Chrysler bottomed out at $2 in late 1981 and, 18 months
later, got to $24. A decade later, Magna International, a Chrysler parts
supplier, did even better. It bottomed out at $2 late in 1990, and got as
high as $43 by early 1993. But comebacks like Chrysler's and Magna's
are unusual to say the least. They are the proverbial exceptions whose
rarity proves the rule.

Big, established companies have indisputable advantages that help
to keep them out of trouble. But the rule is that when a big, established
company gets in serious trouble, that trouble has a way of feeding on
itself. When a company like this gets into serious trouble, it is more
likely to go through a long, wrenching decline, to zero or close to it—as
Dome Petroleum did a decade ago, and as Royal Trustco did more
recently. False recoveries always interrupt these declines, of course, and
lure in a new cohort of turnaround specialists, but the improvement
soon fades.

I suspect these long, wrenching declines will become even more
common as the decade wears on. Chronic money-losers will find it even
harder to deal with their addled finances, and meanwhile cope with the
increasingly fast changes that we can expect in the scalding 1990s. Now
more than ever, turnaround candidates should make up at most a small
part of your portfolio, if you invest in them at all.

• The true believer lets belief get in the way of profit. Profits in
investing go most readily to those who base investment decisions on the
way things are, rather than the way they feel they ought to be. Some

investors overindulge in golds and other inflation-hedge stocks simply because they feel inflation's return is inevitable, and the world really should go back on the gold standard. Other investors buy pollution-control stocks indiscriminately, without regard to sales or earnings prospects, because they expect the rest of the world to react as emotionally to pollution as they do. Investors like these do make money from time to time. But they rarely hang on to it. For long-term investment success, you have to base investment decisions on external reality, not on your own quirks.

• The "I-hate-to-lose" club. Deciding when to sell is the most troublesome part of investing—it's far more difficult than deciding when or what to buy. But you make it even more complicated when you let your own gain or loss weigh too heavily in deciding whether you should sell. Keep in mind that the really big profits go to investors like my friend (the one you're sick of hearing about by now) who credits his success to the fact that he "bought Canadian Tire at $0.50 and didn't have brains enough to sell when it got to $2". On the other hand, the odds are against any single company doing as well in the next, say, 20 years as Canadian Tire did in the 1950s and 1960s.

One fault that costs many aggressive investors dearly is to turn a short-term buy into a long-term hold, simply because it went down, and they hate to sell at a loss. This sort of long-term hold can slowly strangle a portfolio, the way weeds strangle a lawn.

Conservative and Aggressive Investments

If you lose money in aggressive investments, you probably make the kind of mistakes that would also cost you money in conservative investments. In aggressive investments you simply lose more money, more quickly. You're more likely to profit in any investment if you follow these three rules.

• Insist on value. Anybody can hire a public-relations firm to turn out a glossy, four-colour brochure to tout his or her company's goals. But the big, long-term gains go to investors who stick mainly with stocks that are taking concrete steps toward fulfilling their goals and have accomplished something other than printing up brochures and prospectuses.

• Consider what can go wrong. What would a recession do to your financial situation? A new bout of high inflation? A return to the interest rates of the early 1980s? You can't protect yourself from everything, of course. But you should have an idea of what each of these calamities could cost you.

• Cut your losses. Aggressive investments are more volatile than conservative ones, so it's hard to put a strict limit on the maximum loss you should accept before selling. But when you decide it's time to sell, do it right away. Don't wait for a 5% recovery that may only come after a further 50% loss.

The Second Time Around

Few investors can truthfully claim they never sneak a peek at the current prices of stocks they held long ago (regardless of whether they made money or lost when they sold). Chances are you at least keep haphazard tabs on stocks you used to own. For instance, hearing a song that was popular when you held the stock may lead you to check its price: perhaps you'll ask brokers and other investors if they have any news of the stock. If you make money, you may check every now and then to see if the stock has returned to what you consider an attractive buying range. Even if you lost money, you are apt to feel curious about the way things turned out after you sold.

The way to profit from this wistfulness is to investigate the stock as coldly and unemotionally as possible. Then, welcome it back into your portfolio if you feel it deserves a place there. Without realizing it, you may find that keeping an eye on the stock over the years has helped you develop a feel for when to buy or sell it. Your results the second time around may prove far more enjoyable than the first.

Books on Investing

The best books on investing have something in common with the best books on fishing. Both tell you how to tie a lure and cast a line. But they say little about where the fish are biting, because the authors know this will change by the time you read the book.

Two of the best recent books on investing are Peter Lynch's *One Up*

188 · RIDING THE BULL

on Wall St. and *Beating the Street.* John Train also has published some great books on investing. If you plan to read about investing, start with these two authors.

If you want to read about stock trading, get a copy of *Reminiscences of a Stock Operator*, the pseudonymous biography of Jesse Livermore. As I've already said, Livermore was a near-legendary stock trader who made millions in the market several times, and went broke several times, starting around the turn of the century, and continuing into the 1920s. Edwin LeFevre wrote the book in 1926. Yet it still has a great deal to teach anybody who wants to trade stocks. For one thing, note the degree of single-mindedness. Livermore's life was stock and commodity trading. You get the impression that marriage and fatherhood were barely worth mentioning. Readers should also keep in mind that Livermore eventually lost his stock-trading ability and supported himself by advising others and living off annuities he had bought in better days. He shot himself in 1940.

One of the best 1980s books on the psychological side of investing is *The Tao-Jones Averages: A Guide to Whole-Brained Investing.* It looks at scientific findings about the division of activity inside the brain and applies them to the stock market. The left side of the brain (it controls the right side of the body) looks at parts of things, describes them in words or numbers, and is rational, intellectual, deductive and so on. The right side (which controls the left side of the body) is non-verbal and more emotional and intuitive. The right side looks at the whole, rather than the parts. Bennett W. Goodspeed, the book's author, says most Wall Street analysts are left-brained, and mystics and artists are right-brained. Successful investors and traders, however, use both sides.

Most successful investors and advisors seem to have gone through a phase in their lives when they read everything they could get their hands on about the subject. The key to profiting from investment books is to remember that virtually all have some good ideas, and some bad—bad for you, at any rate. You have to read lots of them to recognize what's good in them—in other words, what will work for you.

When Stock Prices Fall

When a stock's price falls, investors often remark to themselves, "If I liked it at $7, I really ought to love it at $4.50!"

Well, not exactly. As we've seen many times in recent years, investors generally have access only to limited amounts of information. They sometimes learn about changes in the facts some time after they occur.

If a stock goes down, it means somebody is selling. Maybe they are selling for personal or poorly thought out reasons. But if the sellers are insiders or associated with the company in some way (as suppliers, competitors or lenders, say), they may know something you don't.

Investors have to recognize the obstacles they face. An unusual rise or fall in a stock's price is simply one more tidbit of information that you need to assess. You need to keep reminding yourself that a stock that looks too good to be true can sometimes turn out to be just that. You need to weigh and allow for that possibility before you buy or sell.

When Timing Stinks

Few investors improve their investment results by "timing" the market, or trying to buy at the bottom and sell at the top. But bad personal timing—making financial commitments in the midst of personal turmoil—is almost certain to cost you money. For instance:

• Death in the family. Real-estate and stock brokers, insurance agents and auto dealers sometimes comb the obituaries for names of survivors. Often they pretend that it's coincidental that they are calling when you may be in the market for the goods and services they offer. At such times, you may feel tempted to do exactly what they recommend, without thinking about it or weighing alternatives.

Keep in mind that even the most reputable and honest brokers and sales people work on commission. Their income depends on what they sell, and when. This can warp their judgement, if not their ethics. At the same time, the shock of a death in the family can impair your natural scepticism. Your best bet when you are in mourning is to limit your transactions to those that improve your liquidity and investment quality—in other words, sell the junk, then hold on to the cash. Above all, don't enter into any irrevocable major transactions in insurance, real estate, limited partnerships, mutual funds, tax shelters or anything else.

• Loss of a job. These days many people find themselves suddenly out of work, but with a large severance payment in hand. At such times you may feel an urge to do something bold and decisive. Far better to stay liquid. Things will seem clearer when your emotions settle down, and meanwhile you may need the cash.

• Birth of a child. It pays to start investing early. But the best investment choices may not be those recommended by the first sales person you hear from the day after your child or grandchild comes into the world. In fact, some investments aimed at parents and grandparents of newborns—zero-coupon bonds, registered education savings plans— labour under high commissions, limited flexibility and other drawbacks. You'll find better deals if you seek them out yourself.

Make Notes

Every investor can improve his or her chances of investment success by applying a few all-important basics. To get the most out of them, write them down rather than trusting your memory.

• First, identify your goals. You have to decide what you want your investment program to do for you. For instance, your main goal may be to earn dividend income, along with reasonable protection of your purchasing power. Or you may aim for long-term growth and place little emphasis on current income. If you're like most investors, however, your objectives are apt to include safety as well as long-term growth.

Once you have decided on your objectives, write them down. Many successful investors report that they did so early in their investing careers. It helps you avoid veering off in fashionable but ultimately unprofitable directions that are poorly suited to your goals or temperament.

• Fill out a check-list before you buy an investment. Ask yourself some basic questions about it and write down your answers. How much are you thinking of investing in this company? Do you plan to buy all at once, or gradually? What do you hope to gain—income, capital appreciation or both? How great is the risk? What new developments might change your opinion of your new investment?

When you make yourself explain (if only to yourself) why you are buying, it will help you overcome the urge to act on impulse, or in response to tips or rumours. Mind you, some rumours turn out to be true. Some tipsters have good information and the best of intentions. But over the years, most investors find they've lost money, on the whole, by acting on rumours and tips. Writing things down will clarify your reasons for buying the stock. It will force you to reconsider your investment decision, if the company disappoints you. It will help you avoid the temptation to substitute new reasons for holding a stock when it fails to live up to your original expectations. After all, too many investors have had the experience of buying a stock as a "short-term trade", then seeing it turn into a "long-term hold", and from there into a "total write-off".

GOLD, INFLATION AND THE BEER-TICKETS THEORY

nflation has been waning, off and on, since the early 1980s. It got down to the 2% to 4% range these past few years. But it refused to go away entirely. It's a little like an economic herpes infection. Inflation can go dormant for lengthy periods, for so long that we almost forget about it. But there's always a risk that it will spring back to life when the system is under stress. That's apt to happen at the least convenient time for those who have failed to prepare for it.

My guess is that we'll have some inflation, in Canada and the U.S., almost every year, for the foreseeable future. Much higher rates of inflation may appear intermittently in the 1990s.

Inflation is built into our monetary system. When I was in grade school, our school-books used to refer disparagingly to "fiat money". ("Fiat" is Latin for "so be it"—it refers to government fiats or edicts, and has nothing to do with the Italian carmaker.) Fiat money was paper money, issued by dictators and backward countries, according to our school-books. They contrasted it to the gold-backed money we had in the English-speaking countries and parts of Europe. Fiat money only had value because the government forced you to accept it. Gold-backed money had intrinsic value, on the other hand, because you had the right to swap it for gold.

Since then, we've eliminated gold from our monetary system. Central banks still own gold, of course, and they buy and sell when they get the urge. But gold has at best a public-relations connection with the value of our paper money and bank accounts. (Central banks also own foreign currency, which they buy and sell as needed.) We have, in effect, converted our gold-backed money into a fiat money system. But it's a little more complicated than fiat money, as my old school-books explained it. There's more to it than government edicts. Confidence, plus the fact that you can earn interest on your savings, is what supports our monetary system.

Now, instead of gold, our money supply consists of paper money and funds on deposit with banks. Let's skip over the customary explanation of the money supply and its main components, such as M-1 (it's mostly cash in circulation, plus bank accounts with cheque-writing privileges), and M-2 (the broader measure of money supply, which includes everything that's counted in M-1, plus money-like assets such as money-market funds and certificates of deposit). You can find out more about them and other technical details in any economics text.

What most investors need to know more about is the monetary base. This is a measure of money that banks have on deposit with the Federal Reserve (plus currency in circulation). The monetary base is the raw material of money-supply growth, and of inflation. (For simplicity's sake, let's concentrate on the U.S. central bank, the Federal Reserve. The basic idea is the same in all countries.)

The Federal Reserve tries to make sure that the U.S. has relatively low inflation, reasonable interest rates, plus acceptable economic growth. One of its main tools for accomplishing all this is the buying and selling of government bonds. On the whole, in the long term, so long as the federal government spends more money than it takes in from taxes, the Federal Reserve is apt to be a net buyer of bonds. It buys them by simply issuing a cheque.

The monetary base rises when the Federal Reserve tries to lower interest rates, by buying U.S. government bonds. (The Federal Reserve's bond-buying pushes bond prices up. A bond, remember, is simply a loan that can be bought and sold. The interest you earn on a bond is always the same, regardless of what you pay for the bond. When bond prices rise, bond yields—the interest you earn by investing in bonds, divided by the price of the bond—automatically go down. This tends to push down other interest rates.) Like I say, the Federal Reserve pays for its bond purchases by simply issuing a cheque. This is the first step in the money-creation process, which creates money "out of thin air". These cheques represent a deposit with the Federal Reserve. Banks can exchange these deposits for currency—paper money. Or, the banks can use them as reserves for additional lending.

The point to keep in mind is that the Federal Reserve has unlimited capacity for writing cheques to buy bonds. But all that its bond buying does is take government bonds off the market, push down bond yields and add reserves (that is, deposits with the Federal Reserve) to the banking system. The money supply only expands when banks use these added reserves to lend money—to create new bank deposits, by granting credit to borrowers.

The terminology can quickly get confusing when you try to explain money-supply creation. When you take money out of one bank and put it in another, you're simply shifting money around—one bank gains a deposit, another loses one. The banking system hasn't gained or lost any deposits or reserves. No new money has been created.

When a bank makes a loan, on the other hand, it creates a new deposit—out of thin air, you might say. That's because banks can lend out more money than they have in their reserves. (Their reserves consist of cash in the vault, plus funds on deposit with the central bank.) When the banks make loans from these new reserves (that is, deposits with the Federal Reserve), you might say they are converting monetary base into M-1.

If the Federal Reserve went on a real bond-buying spree, more paper money would of course get printed. That's because some of those newly created Federal Reserve deposits would get turned in for U.S. currency. But the money supply only expands in a hurry when banks use their added reserves to lend more money. When they make new loans, remember, they multiply the impact of growth in the monetary base. That's because they can make loans that are a multiple of their reserves.

But back to M-1. Economists used to assume that the rate of growth in M-1 was equal, very roughly, to the inflation rate, plus economic growth (that is, the growth rate of gross national product). That relationship—known as the St. Louis Equation, after the branch of the Federal Reserve that brought it to economists' attention—held sway from the early 1940s till 1982. Since then, M-1 on the one hand and inflation/GNP growth on the other seem to have less to do with each other.

That was especially so in 1992. Inflation and economic growth were relatively weak, but M-1 kept growing. So did the monetary base. On the other hand, growth in M-2 was weak. That was at least partly because investors were shifting out of M-2 components such as money-market funds, and into the stock market.

Some economists blame financial innovations—interest-paying chequing accounts and money-market funds—for the downfall of the St. Louis Equation. They feel these new investments muddled the distinctions between M-1 and M-2. Another, perhaps more direct way to look at it is that the change is due in part to a drop in the velocity of money: how frequently the money turns over, or changes hands. You might say there's more M-1 around than there used to be, but its owners don't move it around as much.

High velocity, fast economic growth, fast money-supply growth, and inflation all seem to occur together, in varying amounts. But it's hard to separate causes from effects.

In the early 1990s, banks were hesitant to lend money, for a variety of reasons. For one, bank examiners were looking more sceptically at the quality of each bank's loans. Besides, banks were able to earn attractive returns in no-risk government bonds. (Government bonds are of course plentiful these days, because of high federal budget deficits.) Borrowers were hesitant to borrow anyway, because of fears about the economy. This made them want to pay off debt, rather than borrow more.

The monetary base continues to grow, though its rate of growth is erratic. In the first couple of months of 1993, for instance, the monetary base grew at an annual rate of more than 13%. Growth in the monetary base provides the potential for, but not the certainty of, a revival in inflation. It is merely the fuel of inflation, after all. It takes a stimulus of some sort—a spark or trigger—to convert that fuel into a faster rise in inflation. In the past, the trigger of inflation has come from war, from business expansion, from failed grain harvests and from OPEC's raising of the price of oil. There's no telling where it might come from next. But the potential is there. Today's commodity surpluses are acting as a cap on the inflationary volcano, but one day it's apt to blow.

Right now, in early 1993, the economy seems to be gaining momentum. But inflation is still relatively low. Eventually, though, you can bet that a new trigger will come along and spark a rise in inflation.

Letting Out the Leash

When the Federal Reserve pushes interest rates down and the economy responds as sluggishly as it did in 1992, economists say the Federal Reserve is "pushing on a string". They question whether the Federal Reserve has any real influence over interest rates and economic growth. I think that's crazy. The pushing on a string analogy is misleading. Better to think of the monetary base as a leash, not a string. When the Federal Reserve balloons the monetary base, it is letting out the leash.

At the other end of the leash is a curious economic animal—a cross, you might say, between Lassie and a pit bull. It's that bastardized mongrel of inflation on the one hand, and faster economic growth on the other.

Remember, it's always troublesome to say where growth leaves off and inflation begins. In fact, when government statisticians measure the economy, they start by doing so in current dollars. Then they make an estimate of inflation; then they cut the current-dollar figure down, to allow for inflation. (In the early 1970s, economists accused the government of underestimating inflation, and thus overestimating economic growth. In 1992, government statisticians may have made the opposite mistake: overestimating inflation, and thus underestimating growth.)

Lately, despite the slack in the monetary leash, this curious economic cross-breed continues to cower around the Federal Reserve's ankles. Ideas differ as to what it needs to bring out the Lassie side of its nature, and make it trot a little faster—that is, what the U.S. needs to turn that extra monetary base into faster economic growth. The risk is that the animal's inflationary, pit-bull genes may make it unpredictably take up the slack and lunge at a passer-by.

Inflation: the Beer-Tickets Theory

Mind you, maybe all this talk of M's, the monetary base and so on makes things needlessly complicated. The point of it all is that predicting future inflation is just as trouble-prone as predicting the stock market, because confidence and crowd behaviour matter so much to both. Think of the beer tickets that a college fraternity sells at a beer blast. Those in attendance simply assume that a connection exists between the number of tickets on sale at the front door, and the amount of beer sitting behind the bar. They assume one ticket will always be exchangeable for one beer. This belief leads attendees to buy a handful of tickets and use them as needed, rather than stand in line to buy one more ticket every time they finish a beer. You might say they have confidence in the system and will continue to have confidence in it, so long as the beer flows freely, and the frat brothers behind the bar honour the tickets they have sold. But if rumours come along suggesting that the fraternity is running out of beer, ticket holders may rush to cash in their tickets— exchange them for beer—sooner than they otherwise would. Worse yet, beer-ticket holders will stampede and trample each other to cash in their tickets if the beer taps begin to spout foam.

Hyperinflation (what we used to call South American-style inflation) is a little like a beer blast that runs out of beer. People lose confidence that they'll get anything for their money—just like those beer-ticket holders. In both cases, the crowd can abruptly turn mean and erratic, when it dawns on them that they may have been deceived.

One key difference between hyper-inflation and North American-style inflation is that most of the time, we have reasonably high interest rates to compensate us for holding on to money while its buying power falls. However, you never know just what the rate of inflation is. Prices go up and down every which way, rather than rising like a group of people in an elevator. Technology masks inflation by reducing costs, even when raw materials get more expensive. But a crop failure, an oil embargo or any number of factors can spark a sudden burst of inflation, so long as the monetary base provides leeway for the money supply to expand.

One thing we know for certain is that inflation is a built-in risk in a fiat money system, and it can spring back to life quickly. So the last thing you want to do is invest all your money in investments that are at the mercy of inflation, such as long-term bonds or annuities.

Inflation and Gold

A link exists between gold and inflation, but investors overestimate its strength. That's because gold and inflation both reached extraordinary heights from the early 1970s through to the early 1980s. Investors assumed that gold was soaring in the 1970s because inflation was soaring in the 1970s. This, though, is only partly true.

The U.S. fixed the price of gold at $35 an ounce from 1933 through the late 1960s. Then it began to let the price of gold creep upward. In 1971, the U.S. gave up on trying to control the price of gold. Soon after, the U.S. legalized gold ownership for U.S. citizens (that had been a crime since the early 1930s). Inflation was lower in the era of gold-price controls than during the 1970s and 1980s. Still, gold had a lot of catching up to do. Gold soared in the 1970s to make up for 1970s inflation, but also to make up for inflation from the 1930s, the 1940s, the 1950s and the 1960s.

The best investor rules of thumb help you absorb and profit from observations and analyses that experienced investors have made over the course of their lifetimes. The worst investor rules of thumb (and they are far more common than the best) fail to profit from life-long analyses and observations. The worst investor rules of thumb make superficial sense.

These glib but shallow rules—you might call them myths of thumb—
are based on a narrow sampling of experience. Like any poorly thought
out approach to investing, they are apt to cost you money.

Take the one that says, "Gold is a store of value, and gold prices go
up during times of inflation." That so? We've had some inflation in
each of the past dozen years. But gold prices are down more than 50%
from the 1980 peak.

One national magazine incorporated this myth of thumb into a cover
story a while ago. The story said a portfolio made up of gold and zero-
coupon bonds would protect you against inflation and recession. The
gold, you see, goes up in times of inflation...while the zero-coupon
bonds go up in a recession. But this story based its hopes for gold on the
metal's performance during the once-in-a-lifetime events of the 1970s.

Gold enthusiasts like to think gold rose because of the inflation of
the 1970s. But it makes more sense to give the credit to the unleashing
of the pent-up demand for gold, during all those years when it was illegal for Americans to own it. Gold had a lot of catching up to do.

Then too, inflation and recession are just two of many economic
conditions we may encounter over the next few years. What about
stagflation (weak economic growth coupled with high inflation)? Or,
more likely, what about prosperity? In either case, a portfolio of gold
plus zero-coupon bonds sounds like a mediocre performer.

Your best way to profit in inflation, recession, stagflation or prosperity is to buy a balanced portfolio of top-quality stocks. Choose those
that are reasonably priced in relation to asset values and earnings possibilities. As always, try to include some representatives of each of the five
main industry groups.

The top stocks in each field offer some dividend income, plus the
likelihood that they'll grow faster than the economy. You can safely
leave golds out of your portfolio. Better to choose shares of major diversified resource companies, such as Noranda. It produces gold, along
with other materials—base metals, forest products and so on—with
more down-to-earth uses than gold has.

Rules of thumb concerning gold are particularly apt to be myths of
thumb, because U.S. government manipulation of gold prices in this

century has muddled all historical comparisons. Copper was a better inflation hedge than gold in the 1980s. But stocks, bonds and T-bills came out way ahead of either metal. However, gold may put on a better performance in the 1990s than it did in the 1980s (it could hardly do worse). All resource prices may be stronger in this decade than in the last one, as newly prosperous citizens of newly liberalized countries join in the bidding.

More Gold Myths

Gold brings out the mystic in investors, and leads them to accept fallacious reasoning that they would otherwise dismiss out of hand. You see it all the time in ratios that compare prices of gold to something else and supposedly tell you which way one or the other is headed.

The old granddad of the bunch is the gold/silver ratio. In the late 1970s, a number of analysts claimed to have uncovered a longstanding 16-to-1 relationship between prices of the two metals, going back to the time of the pharaohs. The idea was that you'd profit if you sold gold and bought silver when the ratio was above 16 to 1, and did the reverse the rest of the time.

Before acting on any sort of investor ratio or rule of thumb, you should first look for its economic underpinnings. If you can't find any that make any sense, you need to consider if the ratio is due simply to long-term coincidence. Or, ask yourself if it's due to a self-fulfilling prophecy. Investors get in ruts, just like everybody else. Something along those lines seems to explain the gold/silver ratio (assuming the ratio goes back as far as its backers claim, and that's a generous concession).

Gold and silver prices diverged early in the 1980s, right around the time the gold-silver ratio got well known. Now the prices of gold and silver often diverge by 100 to 1.

Other ratios with dubious economic rationales, and profitability to match, are the gold/platinum ratio and the gold/crude oil ratio. Gold, silver and platinum all go into jewellery, of course. They are all electrical conductors. But they are hardly interchangeable. And what do gold and crude oil have in common? Well, both trade in U.S. dollars, and are owned by rich Arabs and Texans.

Latest in the line is the ratio of gold to the Dow Jones Industrial Index. It has sunk to an all-time low. To some investors, this means gold is a buy, but all it says is that stocks have gone up but gold hasn't.

You need to contrast these ratios with those that do work, up to a point. These include, for instance, the ratio of soybean prices to the combined value of soybean oil and soybean meal—the two materials you get when you mill soybeans.

One rule on gold that goes back hundreds of years and does seem to work, after a fashion, is the "man's suit rule". It says gold is over-priced when an ounce of the metal is worth more than a top-quality man's suit; it's underpriced when the suit is worth more. Maybe this rule works because a top-quality suit needs lots of hand-tailoring, and its cost rises with the general cost of labour, as gold is supposed to do. (Note that this rule doesn't say when to buy or sell. It only tells you when the price is out of line.)

Gold's 1980 peak of $850 U.S. an ounce—$988 Canadian, at 1980 rates—was too high. Today's gold price—$365 U.S. in mid-1993—looks cheap compared to top-quality tailored suits. They start around $700, and range up to $3,000 or more.

Gold itself probably has limited risk at today's prices. It will rise if inflation speeds up. This may tempt you to buy gold stocks. However, gold-stock prices already reflect a coming rise in inflation, and the rise in gold prices (and gold miners' earnings) that it would bring. Gold stocks need a rise in gold prices to justify their prices today, let alone go higher. My advice is that golds should make up at most a minor part of your portfolio.

Gold As the Answer to Inflation

A while ago I spoke to an investor who voiced a common though by no means unanimous sentiment: "Everything started going to hell after we went off the gold-exchange standard in about 1971. What are the chances that we'll bring gold back into the financial system, to stop the excessive debt creation we have today, and stop inflation dead?"

I shudder at the prospect. Never mind debt creation; what about existing debt? Debt is one of many modern statistics that keep setting new records. But borrowers and lenders agreed that they would deal in fiat money—paper money with no gold backing. Both assume paper money will continually lose value, through inflation. If we switched to a gold standard, borrowers would have to repay their loans in something different: gold-backed or gold-exchangeable money, which is apt to hold on to its value. Many borrowers would simply be unable to do so.

In short, a return to the gold standard would enrich lenders, and impoverish everybody else. Inflation is only one of many things that would stop dead in a return to the gold standard.

Gold might play a growing but still parallel role in the system, of course. Gold miners often finance mine development with "gold loans". They borrow ounces of gold instead of dollars, at interest rates of 2% to 3% a year. They then sell the gold and use the proceeds to finance the mine. After production starts, they repay the principal and interest on the loan in ounces of gold they have mined themselves, regardless of whether the price went up or down.

The rigidity of the old gold-based system probably played a role in turning the 1929 recession into the depression of the 1930s. My guess is that gold would only make an official comeback in the world monetary system in the event of world-wide hyperinflation. You might argue that our gold-free system is failing us. Perfect it isn't, but it seems to work better than anything else we've tried.

Gold is still near the low end of its 12-year price range. It will probably move up in the 1990s, as widening prosperity leads to a revival of inflation. But gold receives more veneration than it deserves. As a result, gold-mining stocks almost always trade far above prices they'd command if they were involved in something more mundane. Before investing in gold stocks, weigh the drawbacks.

When investors weigh the appeal of gold stocks, they often let their financial guard down. Instead of looking at today's earnings and dividends, they dwell on, and often overestimate, what will happen to gold miners' earnings and dividends if gold goes up. This leads them to pay too much for most gold stocks.

Gold stocks and the gold-mining industry went through a heyday in the mid-1980s that is unlikely to recur for many decades. Gold soared from under $40 U.S. per ounce at the start of the 1970s, to $100 (U.S.) an ounce in 1976, to a peak above $800 early in 1980. Since then, gold has stayed in a $300 to $525 trading range. This may seem cheap if you bought gold near the high above $800. On the other hand, this $300 to $525 range is an all-time high, if you exclude the unusual period of late 1979 through early 1981. This new and higher price plateau opened up vast areas to gold explorers. After all, the higher the price, the more likely you are to make money from a given gold deposit.

The 1980s stock-market boom, plus the widespread belief that gold was poised for a return to its highs, led investors to finance a great deal of gold exploration. An entire industry of "hard money advisors" sprang up, devoted to spurring investors to buy gold stocks despite their low or non-existent earnings and dividends. The government of Canada helped too, by creating "flow-through" shares. These conferred tax benefits on mining exploration, no matter how dubious its chances of success.

After the 1987 stock-market crash, the price of gold peaked around $500 an ounce. Since then, most gold stocks have dropped 50% to 90% or more from their 1980s peaks. Yet even now, many are still expensive in relation to current earnings and dividends.

Gold seems likely to creep upward these next few years, as economic recovery spurs inflation. But the funny thing is that many gold stocks won't gain much profit from a rise in gold, at least initially. That's because they've already sold their gold production for the next year or more, at fixed prices that are above current cash or spot prices.

Gold-Mine Earnings

Another widely overlooked drawback to gold stocks is that conventional accounting methods are sure to overstate a mine's earnings. The richer the mine, the worse the overstatement.

After all, a mine's earnings come after a deduction for depreciation and depletion. This deduction is supposed to reflect the cost of replacing the mine, in theory. What it actually reflects is the cost of finding the mine. That's an accurate way to account for the cost of, say, replacing a gravel pit. The gravel is simply the raw material; the profit in that business comes out of processing and transporting the gravel. Not so in gold mining. The profit comes out of gold's scarcity. But that's simply another way of saying that gold deposits are rare, and hard to find. Let's say you spend $10 million and find a mine worth $100 million. Chances are you won't find a second $100 million mine, the next time you spend $10 million. In fact, the next time you spend $10 million on gold exploration, you may not turn up anything of value.

The sole gold on our *Investment Reporter's* Key Stocks list is Placer Dome. Better choices for the resources sector of your portfolio are oil and gas stocks, major miners like Alcan, Inco or Noranda, or forest-products stocks. Companies in these industries would gain with a rise in inflation. However, they are much closer than most golds are to making substantial profits and paying dividends. Inflation or no, profits and dividends are the underlying reasons for buying stocks.

20

WHEN TO SELL

nowing when to sell is the most pitfall-riddled aspect of investing. It's a skill that nobody ever masters. However, real-estate investors have an old and valuable adage: you make your profit when you buy. You can say something like that about investing in stocks, because sound portfolio planning can overcome a lack of selling skill.

Many investors mistakenly believe that knowing when to sell is the key to investment success. For instance, one investor I know has had miserable investment results in the past six years. He blames this on his failure to sell when he should have. But his portfolio suffers from other, more easily corrected problems.

For one thing, he does most of his buying at times when he feels highly confident about the market's prospects, and everybody he talks to agrees with him. These, though, are often times of highest risk.

He also depends way too heavily on stock-price changes as a guide to when to buy and sell. He hates to sell at a loss. He bought most of the stocks he owns today back in 1987, at far higher prices. All these stocks went down after he bought. Some were worth holding on to. But he couldn't bear to sell any of them at a loss, even those with deteriorating fundamentals. He decided to hold on in every case, at least until he broke even.

He told me, "Of course, I have made some small gains in other stocks over the years, but nothing to cover my losses." In other words, he sold his stocks that went up for small profits, and he held on to those that went down, for big losses.

Filtering Out Your Profit

You are sure to make deep and costly errors if you base investment decisions purely or even mainly on price changes. If you sell what goes up, you'll never have a big winner—and you need a few big winners, to cover your inevitable losses.

The key to success for most investors is to build a balanced, diversified portfolio of high-quality investments. Then, rely as little as possible on market timing and predictions of market trends. Instead, pick out a list of high-quality stocks that are right for you—stocks that fit your investments goals and your temperament. Then, buy them gradually, over a period of years.

Bunching your buys can of course pay off, if you happen to buy at a market low. But you are more likely to do so at a market high. With the aid of hindsight, it's always easy to see which stocks should have been sold, and when. But needless to say, nobody has a buy-sell record that measures up to hindsight.

You might look at it this way: selling is your second-most important decision (after you decide what to buy) and it's two-fold: what and when. To learn this skill, start by recognizing when and what *not* to sell. Selling stocks merely because you have a profit available is generally a poor idea. First off, every sale involves costs—brokerage fees, possibly capital-gains taxes as well. That leaves you with something to make up for right from the start.

Second, every sale is in fact a switch. If you don't reinvest the proceeds right away, you have switched from a security to cash. Cash (in the form of T-bills or short-term deposits) earned unusually high returns from an historical point of view during the 1980s. In those years, many investors got into a habit of switching to cash and leaving their money in cash for lengthy periods, where it earned high short-term returns. But short-term interest rates are much lower now, closer to the historical norm. Over the past several decades, inflation has made cash a poor investment. Perhaps things are simply going back to normal.

Yet many investors feel they can overcome the costs of frequent switching, and find something better to invest in, rather than stick with what they've got. So they are quick to take a profit when they get the chance. My advice is to forget the old saw that says you can't go broke taking a profit. You can indeed go broke taking profits, if those profits and associated costs fall short of your losses.

Sell Your Losers

Selling losers—eliminating stocks from your portfolio that fail to live up to your expectations—is usually a better strategy. Selling involves difficult choices at the best of times. So you should keep it to a minimum. Sell only after you've given the transaction considerable thought, rather than on the spur of the moment or in response to a friend or broker's suggestion, or an isolated news event. Mind you, you can only follow this advice on high-quality stocks that you wouldn't mind holding on to indefinitely. These kinds of stocks—the BCE's, Motorola's, McDonalds's and so on—have special appeal that seems to stretch beyond most attempts at foreseeing or forecasting the future.

Artificial Sells

Investors sell stocks for all sorts of reasons. But it pays to distinguish between "artificial" and "portfolio" sells. It pays to try to do less of the former and more of the latter.

The reasoning behind artificial sales has little connection with the securities themselves. You may want to sell to establish a tax-deductible loss, to reduce or eliminate margin debt or to raise money for an unrelated purpose.

All too often, investors sell for tax purposes late in the year, when everybody else is doing so. That almost guarantees you'll receive extra-low prices that aggravate your loss. Stocks that are subject to heavy tax selling late in the year often bounce back early in the new year—the buyers often make more from this bounce-back than the sellers saved on taxes. In fact, tax-loss selling candidates of one year often include the best buys for the following year, because they start out at artificially depressed prices.

Your worst sell signal is a margin call. That happens when the stocks that serve as collateral for your margin loan have fallen in price. Your broker then insists that you put up more money, or sell enough stock to reduce the loan. In fact, the costliest sales you ever make may be those that you are forced to make, because you've received a margin call. That's because sales due to margin calls have a way of clustering. They are most apt to occur at the end of a steep slide in prices. So you and other undermargined sellers compete against each other when you sell, and this drives prices still lower.

To avoid margin calls, use margin loans sparingly if at all. It pays to reduce or eliminate your margin debt as stock prices rise, no matter how confident you are that they'll keep on rising. This of course means that as prices rise, you'll automatically take some profits.

The Portfolio Sell

You may want to sell to improve the balance or diversification in your portfolio, to reduce (or increase) risk according to changes in your objectives or to get rid of small positions that have minimal impact.

Sales like these are easy to make. They let you disregard guesswork, emotions and irrelevant factors. You base them strictly on the facts. As a result, they often turn out to include the shrewdest sales of an investor's career.

Some selling is desirable. If you see a good reason to sell, don't hesitate. Even the most successful investors find that around one out of three of their most carefully chosen investments disappoints them eventually. But many investors do too much selling rather than too little. This overtrading (or churning) saps your investment profits, and leaves you with unsatisfactory results even in the strongest markets. If you are careful about what you buy, your sales rarely need to exceed 35% of your portfolio's total value in any single year.

In short, you can go broke taking a profit. But you're apt to make money in the end if you sell the junk and keep the good stuff.

Remember the Quicksand Factor

From time to time I hear from an investor who owns a stock now worth $0.50, for which he paid $5. "Should I sell now," he asks, "or wait for a rebound?"

Holding for a rebound raises another question: a rebound to $0.60? To $0.75? To $1? (Mind you, most investors ask the same question all the way down, at $4, $3, and so on.) This all-too-human indecision is a little like the urge to bull your way through a shallow pool of quicksand.

When you find yourself in quicksand, the smart thing to do is get out right away and go around. If your $0.50-down-from-$5 stock fails to meet your investment objectives, your best approach is to sell right away. A rebound to $0.75 (or even $5) may occur after you sell, of course. But with no underlying value, the stock is more likely to keep on falling—to $0.05, if not zero.

Resist the Urge to Average Down

What do you do when you own a stock that is down 75% to 90% or more from its high? You may feel an urge to buy more, simply to "average down", or reduce your per-share cost. Wise investors dismiss this temptation out of hand; it amounts to putting up more money, rather than considering whether you made a mistake. Unless you see a change in the fundamental outlook, your practical choices are to hold or sell.

One rationale for holding is that when a stock dives from, say, $50 to $5, a 30% rebound to $6.50 is a mere fluctuation for it. It can rebound that much in a few days or weeks. A more stable and prosperous company may take years to gain 30%. The trouble is that the next 30% rebound may only come after your $5-down-from-$50 stock hits $3.

Also, consider your portfolio. If it's full of stocks that used to trade at $50 and are now down to $5, you are likely to wind up with unsatisfactory results at best. You can probably afford to hold one or two, up to possibly 5% of total value. Beyond that, get rid of them.

Which Stocks to Sell

When you have to sell stocks because you need the money, here are some guidelines to keep in mind:

• Sell stocks with p/e's (the ratio of a stock's price to its per-share earnings) that are significantly above the p/e of the market as a whole, or above the p/e of the industry the company is in.

• Sell poorer performers first, because stronger performers have momentum on their side.

• Sell stocks with erratic dividend records.

• Sell stocks with obvious disadvantages. Sell foreign stocks (it's harder to stay informed on their activities, and they are ineligible for the dividend-tax credit). Sell stocks with limited share trading, a high level of debt or a cyclical business (in resources or manufacturing, say). All these factors make them vulnerable to unforeseeable downturns.

• Sell companies with high debt, particularly if they are losing money.

• Sell shares of companies whose chief executive has turned into a celebrity. Some executives do manage to combine a high public profile and continued business success, but the odds are against it.

In short, when you have to sell, do so in a way that strengthens rather than undermines your portfolio. Start by selling what you ought to sell anyway.

Think about the Economic Cycle

Market timing—trying to sell at the top and buy at the bottom as Bernard Baruch described it—backfires for most investors. If you sell a high-quality investment to avoid a short-term set-back, it may not go down enough to justify the costs of selling it and buying it back again. You may never get back in again. While market timing often backfires, you still need an idea of where you are in the economic cycle. Risk is greatest after several years of economic growth, when interest rates are high and rising. Another danger sign occurs when short-term interest rates rise above long-term rates. That's why *The Investment Reporter* came up with only a few Best Buys each month in 1989 and 1990. I felt the best of the boom years were over, and the next major economic change would be downward. Risk was graver for some companies than others, of course. I regularly pointed out our top sale candidates in those years—Campeau, Cineplex, Unicorp and so on—particularly in our periodic Forecast issues.

However, matters never reached a point when it made sense to sell everything, including all your high-quality stocks. Far better to retain some balance in your portfolio. Mind you, the day may come—possibly toward the end of this decade—when stock prices get so high that it pays to sell all your stocks and switch entirely to fixed-return investments.

When to Apply the Sell-Half Rule

You should be quicker to sell when you dabble in low-quality stocks—penny mines or industrials in particular. You may want to set a limit ahead of time on how much you are prepared to lose. Selling when you lose 10% to 20% may be about right. Anything less and you risk getting "shaken out" on a mere fluctuation.

If you buy a low-quality stock and it suddenly doubles, it pays to apply the sell-half rule: sell half your holding and get back your initial stake.

Four Special Kinds of Sells

The best way to deal with deciding when to sell is also the easy way: you simply stick with high-quality stocks that you want to hold on to more or less indefinitely. Here, however, are some special sell situations.

• The "glad-to-oblige" or "take profits" sell. Sometimes, high-quality stocks get way too costly, and are inevitably headed for a fall. This may happen because of a take-over bid, or a short squeeze (when short sellers panic, and rush to buy back shares they've borrowed and sold). When a take-over bid or short squeeze is underway, you should plan to sell early rather than late. Another name for this situation is the "take the money and run" sell.

• The "get out, get out" sell. If you come across any reason to doubt the honesty or integrity of a company's management, sell immediately. Don't wait for an explanation, or a rebound in the price of the stock—

just sell. If your suspicions are even partly correct, the situation can unravel quickly.

• The "it's my fault, not yours" sell. When your investment objectives change due to aging, job changes or whatever, you sometimes need to sell high-quality stocks for reasons that have nothing to do with, and may run counter to, investment fundamentals. Your best bet here is to try to foresee your need to make these forced sales, and carry them out gradually, over a period of months or years. That way you avoid the risk of selling at a market low.

• The "asking for trouble" sell. Another reason to sell is a decision by a successful company to diversify into a field with which it has little familiarity or connection. When a maker of, say, wooden pallets decides now is a good time to branch out into feature-film production, it may have more to do with the president's divorce and mid-life crisis than with genuine profit opportunities. If the stock price rises on the news of the shift in direction, you may want to hold on for a time. But when any company, successful or not, sets out on a whole new line of business, it pays to sell at the first sign of trouble.

Buy Gradually, Sell Abruptly

The author of the phrase "buy in haste, repent at leisure" may well have been thinking about the stock market. After all, when investors spot a stock that looks as if it will make money for them, they are apt to pounce. They want to buy immediately and all at once, before prices rise.

When the time comes to sell, on the other hand, many investors hesitate—regardless of whether they are making or losing money. You're especially likely to hesitate when you are selling to improve your portfolio quality, diversification or balance. After all, you have no specific reason to get out. You'll feel like a chump if prices shoot up after you sell.

With time and experience, however, investors come to reverse these habits. They buy gradually; that way, they buy more shares when prices are low, and fewer when they are high. But when the time comes for successful investors to sell for any reason, most will simply get out. They reason that short-term fluctuations are largely random, and are as likely to cost you money as to make money for you—on average. But risk is greater, at least for you, in stocks that are inappropriate for your portfolio. So, if you must sell, sell now rather than later.

Profit from Panic

In short, it pays to put a lot of thought into a decision to sell. But when you've made that decision, just do it.

On the other hand, many investors do just the opposite. They sell impulsively, rather than deliberately. This is a good way to wind up selling at the bottom. Consider, for instance, those investors who sold on the outbreak of the Gulf War. The market was "supposed" to go down when war broke out, according to a lot of published commentary prior to the start of the war, in late 1990. Instead, it shot up (I'm glad to say that *The Investment Reporter* spent the final weeks of 1990 pointing out what I called, at that time, "the earmarks of a bottom in prices".)

A perennial investor bugbear is the coming Great California Earthquake, or "the Big One", as Californians refer to it. Some seismologists now think the Big One is due some time in the next, oh, 30 years; up till recently, they thought it might only come in the next 100 years. All acknowledge, though, that it could also come tomorrow.

When the Big One comes, the U.S., Canadian and, indeed, world stock markets are bound to suffer. Chances are, though, that the damage will be temporary—comparable, perhaps, to the set-back that followed the 1963 Kennedy assassination (the market was back to pre-assassination levels within weeks), or for that matter the 1906 San Francisco earthquake and fire (back to pre-quake levels within months). Nowadays, though, news travels faster than it used to. By the time you hear about the Big One and get your broker on the phone, it may well be too late to sell. The damage may already be done, at least in the stock market.

Economic damage from the Big One will depend on its strength, and on whether it is centred in a city, or out in the countryside or desert. Keep in mind, though, that a winter storm that shuts down the northeast for a few days does as much economic damage as most quakes. A tropical storm like Hurricane Andrew does even more. Then too, California businesses have quake insurance, which is reinsured with insurance companies all around the world. It's wrong to think of the Big One as leaving a meteor crater in the California economy. Instead, the damage will ripple outward.

The best way to hedge against this or any unforeseeable disaster is simply to practise sound portfolio planning. Diversify geographically— avoid holding too many California-based investments (just as you'd avoid too many Ontario-, Quebec- or New York State-based investments). And, if news of a California quake drives the market down some day, resist the urge to join in the panic selling. Chances are that the Big One will instead present you before long with an attractive buying opportunity.

WHERE TO GET ADVICE

Investment advice is inescapable these days. You get it in newsletters, from your broker, but also from newspapers, magazines, TV and radio, banks and trusts, as well as from accountants, financial planners, lawyers, and elevators and barber shops. Some investors seem to do well without investment advice. They simply focus on a few high-quality stocks, and gradually, possibly over a lifetime, accumulate major positions in them. Most investors prefer a little help. But because help is so readily available, the problem becomes one of picking and choosing. Not all advice is well intentioned or impartial; some in fact is self-serving, even dishonest.

All Advisors Have Limitations

No one can guarantee above-average (or even average) investment performance. But good advice can help you avoid investment disasters and help put you on a path of steady growth. It can help you profit despite the many roadblocks and frustrations of an investment career, which include commissions, taxes, your own anxiety and second guessing, cash-flow limitations and so on. From time to time, readers ask me to recommend individual stock brokers, or investment counsellors who serve individuals. But it's impossible to follow up on a recommended advisor or broker, the way you can on a publicly traded stock. Besides, trusting your savings to an advisor is a serious matter, and one where it pays to get personally involved.

Here are a number of signs to look for when you judge the professionalism and commitment of an advisor or broker:

• Don't settle for the proverbial smooth talker. One way or another, an advisor should come with some good reason for you to value his or her judgement. This may include a record of past recommendations, testimonials from satisfied customers, experience or education, or a qualified research department. All too often, however, advice from a brokerage firm's research department is simply a string of buy and sell recommendations. (The buys are unmistakeable. Often the sells are merely hinted at—okay to hold, a weak hold and so on.) The broker you choose to deal with should offer a sense of direction and purpose, and a point of view, if he or she is going to help you profit from the firm's research.

• The best advisors will warn against complacency about the risks of investing. Ideally, advisors draw to your attention dangers lurking in areas that you don't worry about or don't think much about, or that you unwisely dismiss. Sometimes the worst mistakes and errors take a long time to make themselves apparent. All investments have a "downside" of some sort as well as an "upside". A good advisor can explain both.

The best advisors also see all forms of profit—interest, dividends or capital gains—as equally worthy of pursuing. They take note of the tax differences, risks that exist at the company level, and risks that are peculiar to the type of security you are buying—a bond, stock, preferred share, limited partnership, mutual fund or whatever.

• The best advisors hone a keen appreciation of individual differences. They know the needs of a retiree and a 20-year-old are apt to differ widely. Similarly, the multimillionaire has different priorities than the investor of average means. The advisor should sense even more subtle individual differences, including risk tolerance (the sleep-at-night factor), saving and budgeting desires and needs, work and income variables and family responsibilities.

The best advisors also recognize that some investors have developed personalized approaches to their investments that seem to work for them. Before advising a wholesale switch in methods, they'll find out how successful and how satisfying a client's own approach has been. Beware the broker whose first recommendation is "Let's clean out this account and start over."

• The best advisors have humility. They recognize that they are dealing in probabilities and are bound to be wrong at times. They recognize that all they have to offer is common sense and judgement, honed by years of learning and experience.

• The best advisors don't make sure-thing predictions. They pay lots of attention to your overall holdings, and to how a new holding would clash or fit in. They are also willing to give credit where it's due, even if it comes from a source that operates contrary to their own philosophy or outlook.

• The best advisors stress facts over opinion. Brokers can make a great deal of information available to their clients, or they can simply relay buy and sell advice. Some investors merely want the advice, and that's all some brokers offer. This simplifies the task, but doesn't necessarily help results.

How to Steer Clear of Bad Advice

The investment business, dealing as it does with intangibles, has more than its share of undesirable characters. Here are several signs that you may have encountered one:

• Recklessly disregarding your investment objectives. Few stocks are right for every investor. A good advisor or broker will want to know something about you before he or she advises a specific investment.

• Glossing over negatives. If a company has negative net worth, say, or has been losing money for the past several years, your advisor or broker ought to tell you.

• Hinting at "inside information". Apart from the legal and moral aspects, supposedly inside information may already be reflected in the stock's price. Or, it may be blown all out of proportion. For that matter, it may be inaccurate or non-existent.

• Asking for unjustified trust. No one worthy of your trust will stoop to asking for it until they have earned it and you are ready to give it freely. If some near-total stranger says, "trust me", you are better off doing just the opposite.

• Insisting on a snap decision. A good investment today is apt to be a good investment next week or next month, even if it has already begun its rise. Even for hopeless procrastinators, being rushed (which stops you from weighing all the facts) is anything but a service.

Questions to Ask

Recently some brokers have begun offering a service that tries to match investors and investment advisors. They provide lists of acceptable advisors to investors; you pick one, then give him or her power of attorney over your account with the broker. You pay a fixed rate of perhaps 2% a year, but that includes brokerage commissions.

Before you get involved, here are some precautions I'd advise:

• Ask to see sample portfolios. Then, look for investment quality, balance and diversification. If the sample portfolio includes, say, a high proportion of junior oils or golds, then you know you are letting yourself in for substantial risk.

• Ask about the clientele. Ideally, you want an advisor who specializes in your kind of portfolio, based on size and risk tolerance. You should hesitate to sign up with an advisor who makes most of his or her fee income by serving big institutional clients. In a situation like that, there's a risk that the small clients will turn into garbage dumps for thin-trading or low-quality stocks that the big clients don't want, and can't sell elsewhere.

• Ask where else the advisor gets new clients. If they come mainly from brokerage referrals, you need to ask yourself who your advisor is really working for—you or your broker.

You should be extremely cautious and sceptical before handing over control of your money, or any part of it, to anybody—no matter who vouches for them. Remember, no one will ever work as hard protecting your interests as you will.

The Electronic Elevator

Soon after the invention of the automatic elevator, Canadian stock promoters began hiring two-man shill teams to spend their days riding up and down in these newfangled contraptions. This gave the shills a captive audience for a stage-whispered exchange of "inside information" about spectacular drilling results soon to come from the promoters' companies. In the uranium stock boom of the 1950s, it got so that if you rode in enough elevators, you could often chance upon the same tip more than once.

The narrow lesson here: beware of acting on stock tips you overhear, in elevators or anywhere else. The broader lesson is this: the enormous profit potential of the stock-promotion business is a great spur to human ingenuity.

One new invention that seems tailor-made to stock promoters' needs is the electronic bulletin board. This is a computer that can receive electronic messages by phone and make them available to computer users who dial in. The operator may be a business, an interest group or an individual. It's an anonymous, open-to-all arrangement, a bit like an elevator.

One investor I know told me a while ago that he was getting great tips on biotechnology stocks from a U.S. electronic bulletin board devoted to the stock market. In fact, he said he was ready to act blindly on his next tip from this source, whose record up till then was unbeatable. The trouble is that dishonest sources may supply a variety of assortments of stock tips, under a variety of pseudonyms, to a variety of bulletin boards. They're sure to hit occasional hot streaks. When they do, they may quickly build a following. They can exploit the situation by advising their followers to buy stocks they own, or that a promoter has paid them to tout.

No doubt some honest, well-informed investors are delighted to share their knowledge with total strangers, through electronic bulletin boards, but you have no way of telling them from the crooks. Your best approach is to treat stock recommendations from electronic bulletin boards much as you'd treat, say, a wedding-hall recommendation that you received over a CB radio. It may be worth looking into, of course. But act on it only after you've done your own investigating.

REAL ESTATE IN
THE 1990s

The post-war real-estate boom created many real-estate millionaires. But this is partly due to the leverage that real estate offers, and use of leverage can backfire. Before getting involved in any real-estate investment that stretches your finances, consider what all this would do to your personal balance sheet, and to your expense-to-income ratios. You might also consider a visit to New York City, where decades of rent controls and pro-tenant legislation have left apartments scarce and expensive.

Take the boat cruise that circles Manhattan island. It gives you a secure vantage point for viewing the boarded-up apartment towers of the South Bronx. Their owners have abandoned them, even though they are in sight of New York's skyscrapers. Canadian cities don't have New York's drug or crime problems, and rent controls here are far more straightforward, but the view helps put real estate's risk in perspective.

The Summer Cottage As an Investment
When it comes to real estate, these days everybody seems to agree:

office buildings and retail space are dead for a decade, if not a generation. Yet those same people think cottages and second homes outside of
big cities are sure-fire winners in the 1990s. Partly this comes out of the
view that computers, modems and fax machines make it easier to work
from home, and to live out of town. Demographic arguments enter
into it too. The baby boomers are headed into middle age, when cottage buying generally hits a peak.

The so-called greying (rising numbers of older people) of the population adds to potential cottage demand. Retirees often want to sell a
city home and move to a lower-priced home in the country. All this
adds up to higher demand for cottages and country homes. But you
have to look at the supply side of the question as well.

There's an artificial shortage of country property because of political
opposition. That may also change in the 1990s. The widely accepted
notion is that you should "buy real estate, because they aren't making
any more of it". They are, however, cutting it up into smaller parcels.

Many baby boomers will inherit cottages that stand on 2 to 10 or
more times as much land as they truly need. Some will apply for a severance (permission to lop off and sell excess land). Cash-starved rural
municipalities may look on these and all subdivision and development
applications more favourably than they have in the past. More building
lots mean more taxpayers. Extra taxes can pay for more police to investigate vandalism by snowmobile-riding locals, and hit-and-run visits
from city burglars.

Then too, some people of prime cottage-buying age will opt instead
for more travel. Changes going on around the world give travel more
appeal than it had just a few years ago. That's especially true of countries in the former Soviet sphere and elsewhere that have newly opened
themselves up to mass tourism. They can now begin to offer Hiltons,
McDonald's and so on.

Another point to remember is that as of February 1992, real estate
no longer qualifies for the $100,000 capital-gains tax exemption. Some
cottage owners bought their properties or put off selling them because
any profits they earned were tax-free. The longer they wait to sell, the
larger a proportion of their profit will be taxable—even if all the gain

occurred before the change in the law. This by itself will divert many dollars out of cottage country, and into the stock and bond markets.

Taxes and happy memories aside, a cottage is inherently speculative, because of its lack of income. Few cottages can produce enough rent to pay the taxes, upkeep and insurance, much less leave the owner with a profit. Then too, the value of a cottage is highly dependent on the economic health of nearby areas, zoning changes and so on. The weather obviously matters too; a wet, rainy summer like 1992's reduces city air pollution and stifles the cottage-buying impulse.

You should look on owning a cottage the same way you look on collecting stamps, coins or art. It's a consumer item—self-indulgence, not investment. Treat any profit as a happy coincidence.

At least once a year, consider how much time you spend at the cottage, and its cost. Include in that cost the income you could have earned with the money you have invested in it. Then, weigh that against the cost of renting. Owning costs more, and you need to decide if it's worth the difference.

Population Growth and Leverage

Real-estate investments gain from population growth and from leverage. But both these factors can work against you.

Leverage is the key to the huge profits you can make in real estate. But it also works in reverse, so it magnifies your losses when you make a mistake. The traditional entry-level real-estate investment is the family home. From there, some investors think of buying a second home to rent out as one, two or three units. Some do so with the intention of letting rents pay the mortgage and, 20 or so years later, winding up with a paid-up rental property that can generate a healthy income.

Others hope to "flip" the property, as real-estate brokers and investors say. They hope to buy now and resell at a profit in a few months or years, either because they got a bargain or because prices generally will rise. This, however, works best when people are moving into an area and buyers are coming into the real-estate market. It works in reverse when people are moving out.

Cash Flow Matters

Ever hear the old cliché about the three most important factors in real estate being location, location, location? For most investors, it simply isn't true. In fact, the three most important factors in real-estate investment are cash flow, cash flow and cash flow.

Location has a lot to do with how quickly you can sell a property. It determines whether you'll have to take the first offer that comes along if you sell in a hurry, or if you'll be able to hold an auction among several buyers. Location is also the key to getting rich overnight in real estate. If you own the one parcel that the developer needs to complete a land assembly for a new mall, he or she just might pay the $1 million you want, even if you paid $100,000 three years ago. (In real estate, three years is "overnight".)

When investors lose money or go broke in real estate, bad location may have something to do with it, but the direct cause is negative cash flow. The property didn't generate enough cash flow to pay the mortgage and other expenses. The investor got fed up with paying the difference. Eventually he or she turned into what real estate guru Robert Allen calls a "don't wanter"—a disgruntled real-estate investor who simply wants to sell and be done with it, even at a loss. (If the investor misses a mortgage payment or two, the mortgage lender will of course take care of the sale.)

Location is paramount in the case of, say, the proverbial country gas station (of 1950s film and off-Broadway fame) that gets bypassed by the new highway. But country real-estate investment has problems all its own. Besides, most North American highways are already built.

If you want to invest in raw land, the time-honoured rule is to figure out in which direction a city is growing. Then, drive along a highway that runs in that direction and buy land where it begins selling by the acre, rather than by the lot or by footage. But keep in mind that until you sell, you'll have to pay taxes and other expenses (local improvements, weed control—you'd be surprised at the costs involved in owning raw land). Your property earns no income in the meantime, and you can wind up losing money when you sell if growth slows, or if the local zoning law changes in ways that limit what you can do with your land, or that expand what neighbouring owners can do with theirs.

Many real estate fortunes begin with the little-money-down purchase of a rental property in a stable or improving residential area. The
price should be low enough, and the rent high enough, that the property pays for itself. Meanwhile, inflation pushes up property values and
rents. If you can do that at a good location, so much the better.

Taxes Matter Too

Real-estate taxation is complicated by what Ottawa calls the capital-
cost allowance, a deduction you can take against rental income, which
reflects depreciation on the property. This allowance is based only on
the building and furniture, not on the value of the land. You have to
come up with some reasonable breakdown between the value of the
building and furniture on the one hand and the land on the other
when you buy, and again when you sell. If the building and furniture
value falls by less than the capital-cost allowance you've claimed, you
face "recapture". That is, you'll have to pay taxes on the difference.
There are various ways of minimizing recapture or avoiding it altogether. Any accountant can explain them to you. By the time recapture gets to be a problem, however, you'll have capital gains to ease the
pain.

The key to real estate's tax appeal is that you can deduct out-of-
pocket expenses from ordinary income. When the property begins to
produce positive cash flow (because rents have gone up, or because
you've paid down the mortgage), capital cost allowance cuts current
taxes on the rental income. When you sell, chances are you'll pay a
reduced rate of tax on your capital gains.

Real-estate investment has earned a terrible reputation these past
few years, as one real-estate developer after another has gone broke.
Virtually all these developers made the classic mistake of ignoring cash
flow and banking on capital gains. But if you buy in an area where population is steady or rising, and the price is low enough in relation to
rents that you start out with positive cash flow, then you stand an excel-
lent chance of making money in the long run.

Some jurisdictions control residential rents, of course. But if you
start with positive cash flow, this is less of a problem. What's more,

there are ways around rent controls, In some areas, for instance, you can set the rent as high as you want if you renovate a dwelling unit. You have to invest time and money to profit from real estate. You may invest less money than it takes in other investments, but far more time (to get acquainted with the local market, find tenants, collect rents and so on). If you're well informed and careful and go in with the long term in mind, real estate offers great potential profit and little risk.

Getting Your First Real-Estate Loan

If you plan on borrowing to invest in real estate, here's one iron-clad rule that will save you a lot of time and disappointment. When you apply for a real-estate loan, insist on talking to a loan officer who has real-estate experience. Real-estate loans are beyond the capability of most secretaries and clerks, who may be perfectly able to take down the details on a car-loan application.

One investor I know applied a few years ago for a second mortgage on his home to finance the down payment on a Toronto rental property. The lending officers were busy, so a secretary volunteered to take his application. She turned him down on the spot, for two reasons:

• She felt she couldn't consider income from the property because it had no tenants. It didn't matter that it was owner-occupied and was supposed to stay that way till the purchase closed, so my friend could choose his own tenants. It didn't matter to her that Toronto's apartment vacancy rate at that time was less than 1%.

• She felt my friend should have had some of "his money" in it, as is the requirement with car loans (his money, needless to say, would be put to better use paying off loans on which interest is non-deductible, such as his home mortgage).

My friend went to another institution next door and got his second mortgage. This can happen anywhere, of course, even at major firms that should know better. If you want to borrow to buy real estate, talk to a lending officer who knows something about it. It's best to do so before you buy the property. Or, make your purchase conditional on obtaining financing, so you can show the lender the agreement of purchase and sale.

Land Is the Key

When you invest in real estate, remember this: it's the land that appreciates. A new building depreciates as surely as a new Ford. (The Ford simply depreciates faster, because it has more moving parts and because style changes make its age more apparent.) You can find seeming exceptions to this rule in restored Victorian houses and restored model A's. For that matter, sometimes two- and three-year-old homes in a new subdivision rise in price when the subdivision is completely built. This is because some people won't buy when construction is still underway and because sellers of existing homes in the subdivision no longer face competition from new homes. But the rule still holds.

When you shop for investment real estate, ignore the new drywall and broadloom, the unspoiled wood panelling and so on. By the time you sell, these features may all have worn out anyway, perhaps with some assistance from your tenants. Instead, try to figure out what the property is or would be worth if no building stood on it.

Is it large enough to build a new structure under current by-laws? (Better yet, large enough to subdivide into two or more lots?) Is future commercial or industrial use a possibility? Eventually it will no longer make economic sense to keep the current structure standing. When that day comes, you want to be able to make some money.

TAX-WISE INVESTING IN CANADA

I t's a mistake to let tax considerations weigh too heavily on your investment decisions. Doing so can lead you into investments that you'd be smart to stay out of, regardless of tax questions. For instance, lots of Canadians got involved in real-estate tax shelters in the 1980s purely to cut taxes. They wound up paying so much in fees that they were almost assured of a loss, even before real-estate prices began falling late in the decade.

On the other hand, knowing something about Canada's taxes can help you pay less in tax without harming your investment results—in fact, it may even help.

What to Put in Your RRSP
Investors should think of their Registered Retirement Savings Plan, or RRSP, as part of their overall portfolios. You should arrange your investments in and out of your RRSP so that you make the most efficient and profitable use of the dividend-tax credit, the $100,000 capital-gains tax exemption, and the reduced tax rate on taxable capital

gains.

• Start by holding all your interest-paying investments in your RRSP. Interest payments don't receive any tax advantages, so you have nothing to lose by putting them in your RRSP, where their predictable interest income can compound free of tax.

• Your next best RRSP choice is high-quality U.S. stocks, up to the foreign content limit (20% in 1994). Your RRSP can't use dividend-tax credits. But dividends from U.S. and other foreign companies don't qualify for the credit; these dividends get treated like interest income. Capital gains on foreign stocks still qualify for the $100,000 exemption, but that could change one day. Ottawa has already disqualified real-estate gains for the exemption. (Of course, there's always a risk that Ottawa will get rid of the $100,000 exemption altogether.)

• Next come high-quality Canadian stocks. Note, however, that you lose the dividend tax credit on your dividends when you put the stocks in your RRSP. This tax credit is worth 27% of dividend yield—that is, it makes a dividend the same, after tax, as interest income 27% higher. You also lose the advantage of the lower tax rate on capital gains, not to mention the $100,000 capital-gains tax exemption.

• The worst RRSP investments are low-quality speculations. That's especially true of stock options and penny stocks. They have a way of producing capital losses for most investors. Outside your RRSP, capital losses can at least offset taxable capital gains. Inside your RRSP, all they do is reduce your capital.

Always keep that basic rule in mind: as much as possible, hold the fixed-return investments in your RRSP, and the stocks in your personal, taxable account.

RRSPs and Job Insecurity

While we are on the subject, RRSP rules let you carry forward this year's RRSP contribution for up to seven years. But you should keep in mind that by making your RRSP contribution as early as possible, you can shift income from a year when you make a lot of money and are in a high tax bracket, to a later year when you make less and are in a lower bracket.

If you are worried about losing your job, it makes sense to make the maximum RRSP contribution before the end of February. After all, any serious bout of unemployment is going to cut your income, and your marginal income-tax rate. Before the end of the year, you can simply take your previous year's contribution out of your RRSP and bring it into the current year's income. (Be sure to keep your RRSP deposit in a liquid form, like a savings account or money-market fund.)

Here's how it worked in 1992 in Ontario, for example. If your marginal tax rate (combined federal and provincial) fell to 26.9% (taxable income in Ontario of $28,784 or less) from 41% (taxable income between $28,784 and $57,568), you made (or got to keep) 14.1% after-tax on the money you shifted from the high-income year to the low-income year. This was in addition to whatever income your funds earned while in the RRSP. (The difference is greater now, following Ontario's 1993 tax increases.)

On withdrawals of $5,000 or less, the withholding rate is 10%—the RRSP institution withholds that much, and you get to use it as a tax credit on your next income-tax return. (The withholding rate is 20% between $5,001 and $15,000. So you should open two or more separate plans of less than $5,000.) Most major institutions have now imposed a $25 fee on all RRSP withdrawals. But the smaller banks and trusts, and most life-insurance companies, still offer no-fee versions.

Tax-Exempt Capital Gains

As I've said, the $100,000 capital-gains tax exemption may disappear one day. So it pays to nail down tax-free capital gains while you can. Before you sell any high-quality stocks merely to nail down some tax-free capital gains, however, you should make a few quick calculations. You have to consider how much selling and buying you will have to do to produce the tax-free capital gain you seek, while maintaining a desirable portfolio. You need to know the cost of this buying and selling. That cost includes brokerage commissions—selling one stock and buying another—and so-called slippage (buying at the "offer" price and selling at the "bid" price). You can try to avoid slippage by holding out for a better price. But in that case, you may never get a "fill"—the stock you want to buy may keep going up, and the one you want to sell may keep going down.

Compare those transaction costs to the taxes you stand to save. Suppose the federal government eliminated the capital-gains tax exemption entirely. In that case, how much tax would you have to pay on your gain at your current tax rate? How about if it merely cut the benefit of the exemption in half? You also need to consider whether your tax rate is likely to rise in the next few years, or go down.

Two Tax Limitations

You also need to consider how these two tax limitations might affect results:

• The alternative minimum tax. Ottawa created the alternative minimum tax to limit your use of tax shelters—not just the capital-gains tax exemption, but also RRSPs and a multitude of tax credits and deductions. In essence, the federal government wants you to pay a minimum of 17% federal tax (plus provincial tax, of course) on all your earnings over $40,000, tax-sheltered or not. If you overuse tax shelters, you can wind up paying the alternative minimum tax.

Payments you've made for the alternative minimum tax will usually reduce your ordinary taxes in future years when you make less use of shelters. Meanwhile, though, you don't get any interest on funds you've paid as alternative minimum tax. Another drawback to the alternative minimum tax is that you can only use it to offset taxes you owe.

The alternative minimum tax doesn't apply in the year you die, and payments you've made under it can offset your final year's taxes. But remember, alternative minimum tax payments aren't refundable. If you can't use them up on your terminal tax return, they die with you.

• Cumulative net investment losses, often referred to as CNIL (pronounced "senile"). This is a running total of the extent to which your investment-related deductions have exceeded your investment income since 1988. (If you earned more income from investments than you took in investment-related deductions, you have no CNIL.)

You can only use the $100,000 capital-gains exemption each year on otherwise taxable capital gains that exceed that year's CNIL. In other words, your CNIL reduces your use of the capital-gains tax exemption over and over again, until you offset it with net investment income (this is investment income, not counting capital gains, that exceeds investment deductions).

Note that if you have $15,000 in CNIL, you'll have to pay taxes (at capital-gains rates, of course) on your first $20,000 of stock-market profit each year. That's because one dollar of CNIL offsets one dollar of taxable capital gains, which are only 75% of actual capital gains.

Your best all-around strategy is to avoid building up CNIL until you've used up your $100,000 capital-gains tax exemption. To do that, aim initially at keeping your investment deductions equal to or less than your investment income. But in any single year, you should limit your use of the capital-gains exemption and other shelters, to avoid getting hit with the alternative minimum tax.

Cut Taxes, Hold Winners

One way to secure a tax-free gain in a stock you own, but continue to invest your family fortune in it, is to sell it to your spouse. Or, deposit it in your RRSP; Revenue Canada treats that as a sale if the stock has gone up since you bought it. (If it has gone down, by the way, you can't use a transfer to an RRSP to create a capital loss. In that case you simply lose the capital loss, which you could have used to offset taxable capital gains.)

Note that if you want to buy back a stock after you've sold, you should wait 30 days—all the more so if you are selling mainly to secure a tax-exempt gain. If you buy the stock back any sooner, or if you bought more of the shares within 30 days before your sale, Revenue Canada may call the sale a superficial transaction. In that case it can disregard it for tax purposes.

Double-dip and Pay Less Tax

Just as nature abhors a vacuum, the tax department abhors double dip—that is, tax manoeuvres that carry a double benefit, such as a tax deduction on the one hand, plus a tax credit or tax-free income on the other. That's why Ottawa thought up CNIL.

One double-dip tactic that still works is to buy dividend-paying stocks on margin. You can deduct the interest on your margin loan from ordinary income; you still get the dividend-tax credit.

Some conservative investors in high-tax brackets achieve double dip by using margin investing regularly but sparingly. They try to balance their margin-interest deductions on the one hand with taxable, grossed-up dividend income on the other. That way they avoid paying taxes on their dividends. But they still get the dividend-tax credit. And they also avoid building up CNIL, which would block their use of the lifetime $100,000 capital-gains exemption. They hope to sell for tax-free capital gains. Even if the capital-gains exemption disappears, capital gains may still enjoy some tax preference.

In any event, it generally pays to defer taxes and keep your funds working for you, especially if you expect your income will one day drop into a lower tax bracket.

Making the Most of Your Dividends

Many investors fail to appreciate the role that dividends play in long-term investment success—they can supply up to a third of your lifelong return. But you can enhance the value of dividends all the more by carefully timing your purchases to minimize your tax bill.

Every dividend comes with three important dates: the payment date, the record date, and the ex-dividend date. Understanding the differences can help you save on taxes.

The payment date is the day when the company parts with the money. If you have registered your shares with your name and address, your dividend cheque should arrive a day or two ahead of time, but dated with the payment date. If you hold the shares in a brokerage account, your account should be credited with the dividend on the payment date.

The record date determines who gets the dividend. The dividend goes to whoever appears as the owner of the shares of record (that is, on the books of the company's registrar) on the record date.

The ex-dividend date, usually a few days before the record date, is the day when the stock starts trading without the dividend. The dividend goes to whoever owned the stock the day before, when it was trading "cum" dividend (*cum* is Latin for "with").

Generally, a stock falls by the amount of its dividend on the day when it begins trading ex-dividend. If you buy when the stock is still cum-dividend, you'll receive that dividend, and include it in the current year's income. If you buy after it goes "ex", you'll pay a little less for the stock, and you won't have a dividend to report on that year's tax return. However, you will have a slightly higher capital gain (or smaller loss) when you sell.

Cum- or Ex-

Other factors could make the stock go up or down on the morning that it goes ex. In the long term, these average out. After all, some income-seeking investors routinely hold on for a final dividend before making a sale. This seems to offset the market's natural long-term rising tendency.

Suppose you follow what I've referred to as that old-time investment religion—choosing a portfolio of mostly high-quality stocks, and gradually buying more of them over your working years. You might want to dollar-cost average—invest a fixed sum in your choices on a regular basis. That way you buy more shares when prices are low, and fewer when they're high.

Suppose you decide to buy four times a year. You could pick buy dates when your choices are always cum-dividend; or, you could push each buy date forward, and buy only after your choices go ex.

How do you choose? Well, if you have use of your $100,000 capital-gains tax exemption, your capital gains are tax-free. So they are a better choice than dividends. So you'd buy after the stock goes ex (though in doing so you run the risk that Ottawa will one day get rid of the $100,000 exemption).

On the other hand, if your $100,000 exemption is gone, or if you have too much CNIL to make use of it, you pay higher taxes on capital gains than on dividends. But capital gains have the advantage of flexibility. You only pay taxes on them after you sell (assuming you still have capital gains by then), and the timing of your sale is up to you. This lets you put off or defer paying taxes, and retain use of your money.

Deferring taxes is a particularly good idea if you are headed into a lower tax bracket—because you are retiring, taking a sabbatical, starting a business or simply facing a stretch of unemployment. In that case you may be better off buying after that first dividend. That way you'll pay less tax in the current year. You'll pay tax on a higher capital gain when you sell, though possibly at a lower rate. But even if you stay in the middle and top tax brackets, deferring taxes can improve your results, if you buy top-quality investments and hold them for lengthy periods. An Ontario resident in the under-$29,590 taxable income bracket paid a 1992 tax of 7.3% on dividends, 20.4% on (non-exempt) capital gains, and 27.1% on interest. With taxable income between $29,591 and $59,180, the rates were 25.1%, 31% and 41.4%; above $59,181, the rates were 33.7% on dividends, 37.4% on capital gains and 49.8% on interest.

Pay 7.3%, not 20.4%

If you are in the bottom income bracket, and you've used up or don't have access to your $100,000 exemption, you're probably better off buying stocks cum-dividend, and paying tax on the dividend that year at 7.3%. If you wait and buy ex-dividend, your eventual tax bite nearly triples, to 20.4%. If your stock goes up 10% a year, it would take nearly 11 years before the tax deferral made up for the fact that you'll eventually pay tax of $0.204 per $1 on that first dividend, instead of $0.073 per $1. (Note: I'm talking here only about that first dividend that you do or don't receive, depending on when you buy. Buying cum- or ex-dividend has no effect on subsequent dividends or capital gains.)

In the middle bracket, the wait is shorter. You pay tax of 25.1% on dividends and 31% on capital gains. If your stock goes up 10% a year, it would take only about two years for the capital-gains tax deferral to offset the higher tax.

In the top bracket, the wait is halved. If your stock goes up 10% a year, it would take only around one year for the deferral to equal the added tax.

If you're in the top bracket, you should ordinarily buy stocks (outside your RRSP, that is) after the payment of dividends, rather than before. After all, if you don't plan to hold for at least a year, and make 10% annually, then you probably shouldn't buy to begin with.

How It Works with Big Dividends

In the normal course of your investing career, buying stocks ex- or cum-dividend will make only a modest difference to your results. Still, better that this modest difference goes in your pocket than in the government's. Besides, modest differences have a way of adding up to major profits.

The situation is different with big, one-time dividends—like the $3 dividend that Gennum Corp. paid in the summer of 1991, when it was under $10. With payments like these, you can't necessarily assume the stock will ever get back to the cum-dividend price. In these cases, you may receive and pay tax on a dividend which is, for practical purposes, a partial return of your purchase price—a tax on your capital!

If you own and want to hang on to a stock that plans a big dividend, consider putting it in your RRSP. This neutralizes the dividend, from a taxation standpoint; regardless of what happens within your RRSP, you only pay tax when you take the money out. Note that if you have a gain on the stock when it goes in your RRSP, you'll have to declare that gain on the current year's tax return. (This gain qualifies for the $100,000 exemption.) If you have a loss, on the other hand, you can't use it to off-set capital gains, as you could if you simply sold.

ONE LAST WORD

*Projected average annual growth rate for the U.S. economy
during the 1990s, according to Merrill Lynch: +2.2%
Average annual growth rate of the U.S. economy during the 1930s: +2.1%.*
HARPER'S MAGAZINE, DECEMBER 1991

How better to sum up the economic consensus of the early part of this decade: a major broker thought the 1990s would outdo the Depression-wracked 1930s by one-tenth of 1% per year. This mirrors the thinking of an investor I know who grew up in the Depression. "We borrowed our way to prosperity in the 1980s," he says. "It's got to end sometime."

No doubt about it—high debt is always a risk factor. But high debt only becomes a problem when you can't make the payments. We've seen some celebrated bankruptcies these past few years. Nowadays, though, most debtors can make their payments, and even reduce their principal. But suppose you concentrate on politics. This leads you to a different view.

Civilization hit an unimaginable low around 1940, when the area from France to Japan was under what you might call concentration-camp government. World War Two liberated half the camp, and spurred the 25-year post-war economic boom. World growth slowed after 1970, as civilization backtracked and concentration-camp politics spread in Africa, Latin America and Southeast Asia. Events since 1989 have changed all that—you might say these events resumed the liberation that started in 1945. They ended the Cold War and gave the rest of the world at least a chance at a North American/Western European/Japanese standard of living.

Today, politicians in almost all countries at least claim to be in favour of some semblance of free enterprise, liberty and democracy. Where dictators are still in charge, they realize they'll have far more wealth at their disposal—a far larger economy to dictate to—if they allow some semblance of free enterprise to take shape.

Sooner or later, a semblance of free enterprise, liberty and democracy always seems to bring prosperity. To me, this is the key to the direction of the stock market in the 1990s. Other factors I've barely touched on here will work to enrich this decade too. One is the maturing of the baby boomers. This means that a big part of the population is now in the most productive time of life. Most baby boomers have acquired an education, and the experience they need to put it to work. Meanwhile, advances in communications and other technology multiply the product of everyone's effort.

Worldwide liberalization will revive the resources business, and that's just what Canada needs. The Canadian stock market lagged behind the U.S. market from 1988 through 1992. This was mainly because of weakness in the resources business, which carries much more weight here than in the U.S. By mid-1993, however, the Canadian market had begun to catch up.

Ultimately, worldwide economic liberalization is apt to make the resource business boom. When people around the world improve their standard of living, they'll need more resources. Meanwhile, the worldwide environmental movement makes it harder to set up new mines and other resource-processing facilities. Initially, of course, liberalization brought resource surpluses, but those surpluses won't last forever.

As always, a glance back over the past few decades gives you a better understanding of where resources fit into the economy today. In the early 1970s, an international organization called the Club of Rome published a book entitled *The Limits to Growth*. It predicted an era of commodity shortages. This seemed prophetic throughout the 1970s, as inflation ballooned and commodity prices soared. But *The Limits to Growth* overlooked the fact that rising prices give commodity producers an incentive to raise their output. At the same time, rising prices give commodity users an incentive to use less and waste less of a commodity.

High prices also spur the search for and use of alternative materials. They make recycling more worthwhile. These factors work to push prices down, and replace shortages with surpluses.

The era of shortages lasted until 1980 or so. Afterwards we entered what has turned out to be an era of surpluses, and you don't hear much about the Club of Rome anymore.

This era of resource surpluses deserves much of the credit for the fact that the Canadian stock market has lagged behind the U.S. market since 1980. The resource bust seemed to be on the verge of ending by the late 1980s, but right about then, a large part of the world economy began to move away from central planning. This leads to more efficient use of resources, which holds down resource prices.

The Russians, for instance, have shut down many antiquated factories. (Many of these had a knack for taking four cents' worth of raw materials, adding two cents' worth of energy and labour, and turning out goods with a value of three cents.) Meanwhile, until they modernize their manufacturing, the Russians are selling their nickel, aluminum and other materials on world markets—dumping it, according to domestic producers.

Russian commodity dumping won't go on forever. Then too, the recession has ended and the economy seems to be gaining momentum. Interest rates are low, and auto and home sales are picking up. The switch from surplus to shortage could occur abruptly, if resource consumers decide it's time to hedge against a rise in prices by building inventories.

Back in the late 1980s, when it seemed we were heading into a recession, I advised *Investment Reporter* readers to lower their exposure to the resource sector. You should still avoid heavy commitments to this highly volatile sector, but now, most investors should include some resource issues in their portfolios.

You'll still have to sit through deep market setbacks, like those of 1987 and 1990. The next one could come as early as the first half of 1994. But the setbacks could prove to be surprisingly shallow. They may end abruptly, if this decade's positive factors are as powerful as I think they are.

Mind you, I wasn't exaggerating when I called the decade the Scalding 1990s. Lots of companies will fail spectacularly in this decade. Newly liberalized economies around the world are going to upset many long-standing trade patterns, for one thing. Continued technological advances will undermine companies that fall behind in their research, but if you diversify and stick to companies that are making money, paying dividends, avoiding excess debt and generally advancing along with or ahead of their industry, chances are you'll come out far ahead. The gains you make on your winners will vastly outweigh your losses.

My advice is to avoid the temptation to try to pinpoint the right time to buy and sell. The outlook for this decade is favourable. The time to buy is during your working years, if you confine your investing to high-quality stocks. The time to sell depends mostly on when you plan to retire.

INDEX